PORTRAIT OF PATTON

THE HARDHITTING, HARD-TO-PUT-DOWN STORY OF THE MOST LOVED, MOST HATED, MOST CONTROVERSIAL COMBAT GENERAL OF WORLD WAR II.

"A sympathetic biography of one of America's greatest battle leaders, a hard-riding, flamboyant, profane, religious man who fought as he played —to win. Fine reading."

—Journal of the Society of American Military Engineers

"Patton was known to his soldiers as a flashy, hell-for-leather cavalryman whose personal courage and initiative made him feared by his enemies and loved by those who served under him. . . . His life story is an inspiration to America's future generals and should be required reading for the nation's officer training schools . . ."

—Daily Oklahoman

"THE FULL SIZE PICTURE OF A FORCEFUL, COMPLEX MAN. IT BELONGS IN ANYONE'S COLLECTION OF BIOGRAPHIES."

—Birmingham News

PORTRAIT OF PATTON

By Harry H. Semmes

PAPERBACK LIBRARY ®

A KINNEY SERVICE COMPANY
NEW YORK

PAPERBACK LIBRARY EDITION

First Printing: *November, 1964*
Second Printing: *January, 1970*
Third Printing: *August, 1970*
Fourth Printing: *November, 1970*
Fifth Printing: *May, 1971*
Sixth Printing: *July, 1971*

To J.H.S. collaborator always

Library of Congress Catalog Card Number: 55-9434

This Paperback Library Edition is published by arrangement with Appleton-Century-Crofts, Inc.

Paperback Library is a division of Coronet Communications, Inc. Its trademark, consisting of the words "Paperback Library" accompanied by an open book, is registered in the United States Patent Office. *Coronet Communications, Inc., 315 Park Avenue South, New York, N.Y. 10010.*

FOREWORD

THIS afternoon I sat in the grandstand, facing The Plain, and watched the President of the United States review the Corps of Cadets on their graduation parade. Beside him were the other "old grads," from the classes of 1954 to 1881. And among them I could almost see those other Academy men, who had fared forth from just such a ceremony, their hearts as high and their hopes as soaring, to hold this country's frontiers and to support her justice and her ideals with their own lives and deaths. Through the trees I saw my father's statue, larger than life, as he used to seem to be, in so many ways, and I thought then how he must love to be there, his own burdens laid down, his faults and mistakes nullified by his final payment of man's debt, the best of him remaining to inspire and to encourage the young men who are what he once was. And I thought that he would be so glad to know that one of his own officers—whom he described to his children as "one of the bravest men that I have ever known"—had written down the story of their more than thirty years of friendship throughout two wars and in the peace between them.

I know no kinder tribute to my father, George Smith Patton, Jr., than that of the man who knew him so long and so well, and who has written of his life with judgment and friendship and understanding. I think of this book as a memorial of inestimable worth to his family, as well as to his profession and to history.

Ruth Ellen Patton Totten

June 7, 1955
West Point, N. Y.

PREFACE

THIS book originally was intended solely to paint an informal portrait, by the written word, of General George S. Patton, Jr. By the standards of many, both in and out of the military, he was considered the greatest combat general of modern times. His career reached its culmination with his leadership of the Third Army during 1944 and 1945.

In writing this story I find myself interjecting my own thoughts and experiences, for I had the honor, as a commander of tank units, of serving under this fiery leader in two World Wars, and was his friend and hunting companion between wars.

This story is not a history, though there is some history in it. Above all, it is the story of a human being, hot-tempered and profane, but, at the same time, humble before God, sentimental and deeply profound in his way of life, whose leadership permeated armored and mobile warfare, and all those he commanded.

A deep understanding of leadership and its execution, especially in battle, was George S. Patton, Jr.'s lifetime ambition. From childhood he aimed his entire life towards achieving his goal to be a great battlefield commander. To say he fulfilled his ambition is a mild understatement.

In writing this story I have had access to his diary, his personal letters, memoranda and speeches. Excerpts from these have been made to show the high spots of his thinking and illustrate the motives and the circumstances that molded his life. Also I have endeavored to show the impact of his character on battle actions under his command and on those who fought with him.

This book could not have been written without the help of Beatrice Ayer Patton, who died in the hunting field before it was finished.

I wish to acknowledge the generous and welcome assistance of Lieutenant General Geoffrey Keyes; Major Generals Charles D. Herron, Guy V. Henry, Hobart R. Gay, Ernest N. Harmon, Paul D. Harkins, Walter J. Muller; Brigadier Generals P. M. Robinett, Oscar W. Koch; Colonels Redding F. Perry, Percy G. Black, Leonard H. Nason, Herbert H. Frost, Charles R. Codman, Charles H. Reed, Wendell Blanchard, Hugh M. Cole, Wilfred M. Blunt; Lieutenant Colonel William H. Zierdt, Jr.; Major Leonard O. Friesz; Sergeants George Meeks, Herman Jacubiec; Anne Wilson Patton, Sally Flint, Ruth Ellen Totten, Aaron Davis, Gordon C. Prince, Charles D. Drayton, Mark S. Watson, General Jean Houdemon of the French Army, and many others.

H. H. S.

Great Elm Farm, Maryland

TABLE OF CONTENTS

1. Incidents Tell the Man

How poor, how rich, how abject, how august, how com-
plicate, how wonderful is man! distinguished link in being's
endless chain! midway from nothing to the Deity! dim
miniature of greatness absolute! an heir of glory! a frail
child of dust! helpless immortal! insect infinite! a worm!
a God!—Young

"WHAT manner of man is this?" What traits go to make
up the complex character of this great World War II battlefield commander? Truly a great tactical leader—yet he
is one of the most controversial international figures of the
twentieth century.

After successfully completing a campaign he invariably
gave the credit to his subordinates and personally thanked
God for guiding him. Again, he was capable of a complete
reversal of character at any time. He could deliver a tem-
pestuous tirade—either to a group or an individual—or he
could praise this same audience, making them feel that
they were the most important persons on earth.

From early childhood he had one ambition—to lead
troops in combat.

Much of what Patton did seemed outrageous by ordinary
standards, but often was a studied attempt to work on the
youthful imagination and curiosity of soldiers. An important part of this was his apparent contempt of cold, dis-
comfort, mines, and shellfire.

Many of his characteristics are shown through a chron-
ological pattern of incidents and stories as they occurred
throughout his lifetime. A few, naturally, do not apply to
a particular period. In fact they tend to leave the reader
more inquisitive, and it is hoped, will spur him in the later
chapters to seek the answers to the whys and wherefores
of this proud but humble, stern but likable, religious but
profane, courageous but fearful, coarse but poetic character.

"Blood and Guts" versus Georgie

The various nicknames attached to him in themselves

differ greatly. On one hand, by many he was called "Blood and Guts." By those close to him he was not George but "Georgie."

At the time Patton reported to the 2d Armored Division, he already had a reputation as a hell-for-leather riding cavalryman. He was an expert swordsman and had designed the heavy cavalry saber. And with his flair for the sanguinary he had had deep blood-lets put on either side of the saber.

He lived up to his reputation in many ways. He had brought along his polo ponies and in his own individualistic way he rode his horse out to supervise those early, crude tank training periods. When the monotony of small training bored him, and it often did, he took off in his plane to solo over the wide reservation to learn every bit of terrain for future training. Also, on these flights he would test his nerve by cutting off the engine and then wait to see if it would cut back on as he spiraled down over the wooded reservation. He loved to face this self-imposed danger. His talks to the troops were as vividly profane as they had hoped to hear.

With all this he was in character, but to many he was disappointing. With his flashy showmanship and talent for the unusual, there was an amazing sense of his groping for something. He was not the positive, dynamic leader that some had envisioned. One began to hear, "Is this the great Patton?" Probably no one ever gave a perfect performance in his first major role, even though he had studied his lines for years. Here was a man with his long-desired armored command, and yet he seemed to be grasping, almost violently, for his part.

As the Division went all out in its daily grind to make itself, there were still the nights left for lectures and lessons. Once or twice a week all officers were assembled to have tactics and techniques of armor expounded to them. The late General Charles L. Scott, that fantastically forceful pioneer of armor, had his full say of pithy observations. Then the second in command, the new Brigadier General Patton, would speak on his ideas and experiences with armor. His talks were direct and forceful, but had the pedantic earmarks of a memorized speech.

The following story shows how the name "Blood and Guts" originated. One sultry summer's night the weekly assembly of officers sat listening to General Patton talk on what the great adventure of war, lying just ahead of them, would be like. He left his prepared observations and theories; he seemed to be just himself as he paused to feel out the words to express how the battle would be won. He seemed to burst into his own vivid self as he blurted out, "War will be won by Blood and Guts alone." It had an electric effect on his listeners. Here was the real man they had heard so much about, and wanted to know, and to follow.

This phrase went the rounds of the Division and carried on through the world to be the expressive nickname of Georgie Patton. Some able, but forgotten, artist caught the spirit of it in a gay crayon sketch. Resplendent in his then famous green dragon costume, Patton, excelsiorlike, dragged forward into battle a rearing, frantic horse, which merged centaurlike into a tank. In his other hand was a shot-torn guidon with his battle cry of "Blood and Guts" sewn on it. The spirit of his men was sketched in a lone figure of a wounded tanker being carried off on a stretcher as he madly fired his revolver at the enemy. It embodied the idea of George Patton in the eyes of the officers of the Division.

This one instance seemed to be the turning point of a colorful character becoming great. He grew in stature immeasurably. From that time, he was positive, dynamic, forceful, and always the great leader.

Childhood

Even as a boy George Patton had wanted to be a general and lead troops in battle. His prepossession with the military is understandable because his Virginia grandfather and seven great-uncles had been Confederate officers. His grandfather, a V.M.I. graduate, was killed at Cedar Creek. There was much discussion of Civil War battles and there were albums of photographs of these military kinsmen, three of whom, including his grandfather, had been killed in battle leading their troops. He was raised in an atmosphere of adulation for those in the family who had fallen in the War Between the States, with strong overtones of pride in their Virginian ancestry.

His family said that, as a young boy, he used to go around the house with a wooden sword saying, "Lieutenant

General George S. Patton, Junior." Never, from his earliest childhood, did he wish to be anything else. All that he did throughout his life was aimed at becoming a combat general. Most youngsters change their aims as they grow older, but not young George. He knew what he wanted, and he never switched.

George Patton was born in California. His father was District Attorney of Los Angeles, a rancher, an able lawyer, and a successful businessman.

His father's theory of education consisted almost entirely of the child's being read to by his elders. It was founded on the belief that the youthful mind should be led along a path that parallels the development of the mind of the race. The books should be read aloud to the child until his early teens, because his ability to absorb by ear is far greater than his ability to read, and the rhythm and beauty of sound adds a great deal to the pleasure.

Under this theory of education, the child would find his proper channel, his true interest. At the youngest age, nursery rhymes and jingles are read; these give way to witches, animals that speak, and goblins; in turn these are replaced by legends and epics, leading into heroics. When adolescence is reached the reading out loud is replaced by the youngster's reading to himself. The fare at this period is romance and history. As people approach middle age and pass into old age, the favorite reading is memoirs and biographies, often of people the reader has known. Nearly always in old age, the Bible is a favorite.

Young George never cared greatly for any of this program except the legends, epics, heroics, and the Bible. He found there his true interest. At the age of seven, he could repeat whole pages of Pope's translation of *The Iliad*. The earliest recollection of a game that his sister can remember is playing the horse that dragged the body of Hector (a dead sparrow) around the walls of Troy. She was then about five, and George was seven.

He and his sister had to make their own games; and they were fashioned on the interesting books, all good literature and often the classics, that were read to them by their mother, and sometimes by their father and their aunt. Always they acted out these stories. This habit of dramatizing scenes and actions of the past left its mark on his study and training, and even his recreation, throughout his entire life. After he was married, his wife and children

14

would often picnic on the battlefields of nearby Virginia when he was stationed at Fort Myer. Each individual would be assigned a part, such as an Army or Corps Commander in some Civil War battle on that field.

One day George and Charley Nordhoff, who lived nearby, planned to go on a long trip and live like prospectors. They loaded a donkey with sacks of standard prospector's food: flour, coffee, dried beans, and bacon. About two miles from home, in a nearby canyon where they considered it wild enough, they pitched camp for the night. There was no success at cooking supper with the dry food they brought, for they had only a dim notion of how to cook a meal. They spread their blankets under the stars, very hungry by this time, and then the coyotes started to howl. By midnight the two hardened desert rats had come back home to George's house and silently crept into bed. There was no comment the next day by the family, but the life of a prospector had lost its charm. Incidentally, this was the same Nordhoff who later collaborated with James Norman Hall on *Mutiny on the Bounty*.

True to his lifetime aim, young George devised training routines to harden and toughen his spirit, but they were of doubtful efficacy. On one occasion to insure that he would not become tenderhearted in battle, he gazed fixedly at a dead frog, fairly well along in decay, while nonchalantly eating an orange.

He did not go to school until he was twelve years old. He could write but had yet to learn to read print, and he was consequently always a bad speller. His first day at school he wrote a composition on Johnson's *Rasselas* with which he was quite familiar, because it had been read to him many times.

Religion

From his adolescence, he had always read the Bible, particularly the life of Christ and the wars of the Old Testament. He knew by heart the order of morning prayer of the Episcopal Church. His thoughts, as demonstrated daily to those close to him, repeatedly indicated that his life was dominated by a feeling of dependence on God. Unless this is borne in mind, it might seem that Patton had the *Gott mit uns* complex of the German Kaiser of World War I.

15

This was not true, for he turned to God for comfort in adversity and to give thanks in success.

General Patton was an unusual mixture of a profane and highly religious man. At one time in Europe, a dozen clergymen visited his Third Army Headquarters. They were surprised, because of his reputation as a rough-speaking soldier, to be treated in a dignified and decorous manner, and as the visit was nearing an end, it could be sensed that they felt something was lacking. Just before they left, one of the clergymen saw a Bible on Patton's desk. He said, "General, do you read the Bible?" "Goddammit," George Patton replied, "I read it every day!"

The Pattons had a cook during one of his tours of duty at Fort Myer, Virginia, when, as a colonel, he commanded the famous 3d Cavalry Regiment. He had to leave on one occasion for several weeks on maneuvers. On his return, the cook said, "It sure is nice to have the Colonel goddamming around the house again."

Some distant relative died and the Patton family was sadly discussing it. The General heard the family talking and came in and said, "What is so strange or unusual about dying? You just walk back out the same door you came in. When you came in, you had no complaints about where you'd come from."

Discipline

It happened during the spring of 1941 at Fort Benning, Georgia. The 2d Armored Division was training there, and in midmorning a jeep was traveling on a company street of the Division encampment. At the hood of the jeep flew the two flags that showed a major general was a passenger.

The jeep passed a sergeant with his back to the street and a lieutenant facing the street. The sergeant and the lieutenant were busily talking. The car passed and proceeded about twenty-five yards when Patton, who then commanded the 2d Armored Division, yelled, "Back up this goddam car." The driver threw on the brakes. The car backed to the lieutenant and the sergeant. "What do you mean by not saluting this car when it goes down a street of this command?" shouted Patton. "You know what these two flags mean. I'm not talking to you, Sergeant, you had your back turned. I'm talking to you, Lieutenant. Never let that happen again."

The lieutenant and the sergeant were left practically in a state of collapse. He turned to me, the civilian who was riding in the jeep with him, and said, "Sounds cruel, doesn't it? But it saves lives—that'll spread." Such was the Patton philosophy.

It is noteworthy that in two World Wars, the soldiers and the officers who served under Patton always bragged about the "bawlings out" that they had received from him. They took pride in having been "eaten out" so wholeheartedly—with such enthusiasm and energy. Instead of resentment, there were many tales about how tough the reprimand was that the particular storyteller received. It was part of Patton's personality to put his heart and soul into any disciplinary action. His reprimands were never halfhearted. His high carrying voice could be heard over great distances. He knew that time in both World Wars was short, that many of the soldiers and officers under him were untrained and undisciplined, and that in the little time available they must be molded into first-class fighting men.

In discussion with young officers Patton has explained saluting as a sign that those who exchange the salute belong to the brotherhood of the army. The salute says, "You are mine and I am yours." His salutes to subordinates were never sloppy.

Patton was a great stickler for discipline in uniform and in saluting because he knew that in these small things he would develop a hold on the men and officers working under him. He was always strict in these matters. He often said, "If you can't get them to salute when they should salute, and wear the clothes you tell them to wear, how are you going to get them to die for their country? Often you will order them to carry out a dangerous task that may mean their lives. Be sure you have your hand on them in all things and they will be dependable when the heat is on."

These matters of discipline are definite holds that a commanding officer has on his men, and if he enforces them strictly, he has a closely knit outfit, an outfit that will immediately respond to his orders, whether they are in accord or not, simply because he gives the order. Patton knew these fundamental facts; realized the paramount importance of strict discipline; and he ran a very tight outfit in both wars. He demanded and received prompt and willing obedience.

It is human to resent being told what to wear and how

17

to wear it. Insistence on strict compliance with uniform regulations breaks down the barrier of resentment to discipline, possibly more than anything else. If men strictly obey the regulations about wearing the uniform, they can be held truly disciplined men. Discipline is the background of all military operations. With it the task is half done and the soldier or officer can add his individual initiative and his imagination to the task.

Loyalty

His hold on the men and officers under him was not only that of strict discipline; a large factor was admiration for the man himself. He was always unstinting in efforts to improve his unit, and to look out for those who worked under him.

Those close to him have often heard him say that it is as culpable not to praise a man when he does well as not to discipline him when he does poorly. In a short time those who worked with him came to understand that he drove himself with the same furious energy that he drove others, and as a result, in both World Wars his commands always did 50 per cent better than expected.

It has been said that two divisions under him were equivalent to three divisions under almost anyone else. The Germans recognized this, and feared him.

George Patton attracted and held men who recognized his inspiration. Their devoted contributions in combat increased his stature, so that rarely in history has a country been blessed in times of peril with such dedicated officers and enlisted men as those who served under him in both wars.

History

Patton was a keen student of military history and particularly of the biographies of the great rulers and wartime leaders, and had a large military library. All his life he wrote well, colorfully, and with imagination for the military journals. From the time he was a lieutenant until intensive training started for World War II, many of his articles appeared in the *Cavalry Journal*, now *Armor*. Often he wrote for himself alone, in order to clear up, classify, and fix in his memory what he had read, and to indelibly

18

impress on his own mind the conclusions that he had reached from his study. He particularly studied the great cavalry leaders of our Civil War. Many of his armored break-throughs were based on similar cavalry tactics under the leadership of Jeb Stuart and the other greats of cavalry when cavalry was in its prime.

West Point gave him a general education, but he studied all his life in the fields that particularly interested him. Any history pertaining to wars and tactics was at his finger tips. He referred to old Roman and Grecian campaigns, giving dates, generals, and the troop dispositions. Once on the Moselle a German attack at night was headed by a cow with a lantern on her horn. This unusual procedure amazed everyone but Patton. He quoted an instance of its being employed in an early Roman campaign.

In Africa and Sicily he was an avid student of the old forts and ruins and could easily identify their era. He was thoroughly versed in the principles of Grecian architecture and at the Temple of Segesta could point out the small things that gave it such symmetry and beauty. Through France and Germany he knew each river and land mass, and why they had played such important parts in continental wars.

Paradoxically, once he was vague when the Third Army captured Jena and he had to ask the details of the former battle there. What makes this slip the more glaring was the fact that he had fully studied all of Napoleon's campaigns and learned French just to read Baron Marbot in the original.

Chivalry

The Patton's first child, a daughter, Beatrice Ayer Patton, was born at Fort Sheridan on March 19, 1911. A soldier's daughter, she gave her first cry as the last few notes of "The Star-Spangled Banner" rang out at "Retreat." Before she was born her mother was worrying about whether her husband felt very stongly about having a son, and she said, "Oh Georgie, what if it is a girl." He grinned and said, "I married one, didn't I?"

Patton had a flair for speaking. His toast to "The Ladies" at the West Point Dinner in Kansas City, April 5, 1924, shows a skillful change of pace:

19

"Good water is the greatest gift to set before a King,
But who am I, that I should have the best of everything?
Let monarchs gather round the pump and pass the dipper free!
Gin, whiskey, wine and even beer are good enough for
me."

In quoting the above I refer simply to the feeling of
unworthiness expressed and not in the horrid idea of
excessive potations, for in toasting The Ladies, similar
feelings of unworthiness oppress me.

Had I been called upon to toast Horseflesh, or Profanity, or some other subject on which I may possess
erudition, I would have been less abashed. As it is, the
timorous modesty of my nature and my well-known
celibate instincts are compounded. I am at a loss.

I might raise my glass to those generous-spirited ladies
of the Paris boulevards; but abstain out of regard for
the feelings of some, and from the knowledge that there
are others here better qualified to sing their praises
than I.

And so, in lighter vein, I might review many women,
(ladies, if you will) brown, mauve or painted; dressed
or "au nature"; but should I do so it were a sacrilege to
later offer you the toast I shall propose.

In the chapel at Leavenworth, on the monument at
Riley, on the walls of Cullum Hall, are names: names
of officers dead on the field of honor; bits of marble,
slate or bronze commemorating the fact that Lieutenant
Willie Jones made the choice and without ostentation or
hope of reward, did his duty even unto death. The little
plaques tell the story and fame, such as it is, and high
honor from us who know, are accorded Willie. But
where is Mrs. Willie's tablet?

Such were the women who year on harrowing year
made homes for officers in these bleak western posts;
such the women who today uncomplainingly share the
luxury of cantonment quarters.

Think of the horror of the slow torture of suspense
between the night of Wounded Knee or Chateau Thierry,
and the morning at the cemetery. Think of it and thank
God for the quick mercy of the bullet.

Gentlemen, I reverently pledge you: The Ladies who

have shared our lives from the Equator to the Arctic; the Ladies who have condoned our reverses, and inspired, but to applaud, our successes.

May we live to make them happy, or, and the Great Day come, so die as to make them proud.

The Army Women: God Bless Them!

For such a complex figure he was naïve and wholly idealistic about women. While he might bluster some wild observations, at heart he was Sir Galahad. He was ideally married and no other woman ever entered his life. He was charmingly courteous and gay in mixed company, even if his observations were a bit rough at times. Any association that was off-color was repulsive to him. Once a battalion gave a stag party and imported entertainers from a nearby vice-ridden city. General Patton was the guest of honor. When a nude woman came to dance before them, he became furious and hurriedly left without his cap and gloves —a sure sign of his anger. The next day the commanders were told in scorching terms how his officers should deport themselves.

Years later a Red Cross girl in France came to him through his chief of staff for help. She needed money to have her baby, place it in an orphanage, and, if possible, go back home to try for a new life.

When his chief of staff presented this appeal to him, his only questions were, "Do I know this girl? Is there any possibility that I may be implicated in this case?"

Being assured that he had no association or knowledge of this case, he simply handed over $800 in currency to look after her needs. Probably not half a dozen people in the Army ever knew of this offhand compassionate act. Nor was any thoughtful act too small for him to do for his officers' families. He wrote a prodigious number of letters home to his officers' wives, praising their husbands and giving them words of comfort. Nothing could have meant more to those lonesome women back home. On the few flying trips he made back to the States he always found time to call up the families of his staff and principal commanders.

Flamboyance, Luck and Other Stories

Like facets of an intricately cut diamond which flash

with different lights in varying positions, so did Patton's character change, at times unpredictably.

Around his headquarters he lived in splendid isolation with his chief of staff and his aides.

He always dressed immaculately and expensively. His combination riding breeches and jodhpurs, with a specially made English combat boot, were distinctive. His famous glistening helmet liner was the result of literally dozens of coats of varnish by ordnance personnel. Around this shining halo were the insignias of all his former commands, like a garish chaplet. When he traveled he carried an arsenal of guns and an extensive wardrobe in several traveling bags, packed by his loyal Negro orderly, Sergeant George Meeks.

Of all his amazing costumes, none approached the green dragon outfit that he designed and wore for a while. It was his glorified idea of what a proud unit like his 2d Armored Division should wear. Basically it was along practical lines because it fitted snug for tank use and was made of lasting material. But when he had added his own sartorial whims, it became a sight to behold.

A short cadet jacket of soft green leather was resplendent with two long rows of gold buttons, slanting downward towards his golden belt buckle. Tight jodhpur breeches carried this green ensemble on down to his short, soft boots. His heavy pearl-handled revolver was carried in a shoulder holster under his left arm.

To crown this already amazing uniform, he had obtained from the Washington professional football team an almost-luminous, plastic helmet in a golden color.

Soldiers stopped short in amazement when they saw him. The fame of this startling getup spread throughout the Army and was featured in the press. All of this publicity Patton thoroughly enjoyed.

Once as the division was maneuvering around Fort Benning a visiting staff from Washington went down to the C.P. to observe. An eager staff officer offered to outline the maneuver and situation on the map. "No, don't bother about that," said the visiting general. "We just came down to have a look at Georgie's uniform."

But this splendid uniform was discarded as the division training went on. One last remembrance of it was in the first Carolina maneuver. It was in the late fall and the dust from the country roads was blinding. As day was breaking, two tank columns converged on a dusty cross-road. The traffic snarl was being handled by a tired tank captain, with bloodshot eyes glaring from his dirt-grey face. Tempers were short everywhere as idling tanks backed up, and the night had been long and rough.

Out early to lead his troops, General Patton came onto this scene of temporary confusion. He was in his full green dragon uniform, complete with golden helmet. His scout car, with his own special gabriel horn on it, pulled up to the crossroad. This horn was another specialty of his, listed as "a steamboat trombone, that can be heard eight miles on a clear day." With the General standing up beside the driver and towering over this scene, he let forth a shattering blast from this horn to clear the road.

This was too much for the captain's frayed nerves. Without turning his head, he shouted back, "Shut up there, you sonuvabitch."

Then he turned around and saw the apparition above him. This was enough to startle anyone, and the General's face completed the terrifying picture. The horrified captain took off; crashing through the sumac bushes as he disappeared from the scene of his enormity.

The General's car pushed on through the traffic and nothing could have amused him more.

Even his aides were as vivid as his other adjuncts. Who but he would have an epicurean sophisticate, a prominent surgeon, and a Texas Ranger as aides? Each had his special use and the general kept them all busy. Codman was an old acquaintance from Boston and as suave and diplomatic as they come; Patton called him a "valiant gentleman." Odom was a prominent New Orleans surgeon and acted as medical aide—he also located those forward field hospitals which gave the Third Army its superb medical service. Stiller was an old World War I tanker under Patton, and was as hardboiled and cool a man with a gun as ever came out of Texas. Whenever Patton went forward, Stiller was with him.

General Patton lived his own life with utter contempt for conventions with which he didn't hold. Politics was a low form of life to him, but when his position demanded that he receive visiting congressional committees, he was gracious and charming. The do-gooders and the eggheads he completely ignored. They just didn't talk his language or know his way of life.

He was first and always an exhibitionist. He played to the galleries. His dress and pearl-handled guns were largely stage props that became his trademark in the public mind. He was spontaneously bold and witty in his sayings, and again this was part of the show. Quick repartee was his stock in trade; he strove for it and for the most part was amazingly good at it. But sometimes he overreached and was pathetically inept.

One night the Pattons had Secretary of War and Mrs. Stimson to dinner. It was very fancy, black tie, six courses. Patton, as usual, took his black patent leather pumps off under the table. Punch, Bea's fox terrier, was also under the table, and when Patton got up to join the ladies he couldn't find his shoes. The Secretary was waiting, so he had to go in his black silk socks. He walked in with great poise and was just taking a liqueur when Punch came in with one shoe in his mouth. Mr. Stimson leaned over, took it from Punch, handed it to Patton without cracking a smile and said, "Yours, I believe?" The General thanked him, and spent the rest of the evening in one shoe. When they finally left Mrs. Stimson said, "George, such savoir-faire must be invaluable in battle."

Patton's theory that made him voluntarily accept risks, such as sailing the *Arcturus* to Hawaii, was this: He felt you were born with luck and could develop it, like any gift. He believed that in time luck wore out, or perhaps you got to counting on it too much and weren't psychologically as careful. He said luck was a psychic quality, an ability to recognize a winning chance and take it before it really emerged. He said the other side of it was the law of averages, and that the luck of a front-line infantryman wore out faster than the luck of a rear echelon cook. He believed in testing his own luck periodically, because he said it meant he would be famous if the tests showed his luck was lasting.

In sports Patton played with the same debonair contempt for stodgy rules that later charactertized his action on the battlefield. He played to win gallantly and boldly.

On his second tour in Hawaii, he carried over his ponies. Being a high goal player and having previously captained the only Army team to win the Inter-Island Championship, he was elected to captain the Army team.

In the championship week of play, Patton's team was pitted against the best civilian teams on the island, composed of the old influential Hawaiian-Americans, who were dominant in the social and business world there. Though they were all ten years older than on Patton's first tour there, they still put on a showy game and had a wonderful time. The championship week was *the* big social event of the whole year. There were fabulous parties.

About the fourth game of the tournament Patton and Mr. Walter Dillingham were riding each other off in quite a scrimmage. Patton was screaming and cursing in a loud voice. "Goddammit, Walter, you old son-of-a-bitch, I'll run you right down Front Street." When the period was over, General Drum stood up in the front row of the grandstand and summoned Patton in front of the assemblage and relieved him of the captaincy of the team. He forbade him to play for using "offensive language in front of ladies and insulting his competitors." Patton said, "Yes sir," saluted and started to lead his pony off the field. Mr. Dillingham and the rest of the Oahu team rode up and the Maui team, who were exercising, drifted near. Mr. Dillingham asked General Drum if he had just relieved Colonel Patton. General Drum said in effect that—yes he had—he wasn't going to have any such language. Mr. Dillingham got off his horse and threw the reins to the groom and walked up to Mr. Baldwin, the captain of the Maui team, and said, "Well, Frank, that's the end of the Inter-Island tournament for this year." Mr. Baldwin said, "It certainly is, Walter, I've never heard George Patton use foul language of any kind." He dismounted and they walked off and caught up with Patton. General Drum relented and the tournament went on, but he never forgave him. It might be said that Patton never forgave Drum either.

Sentiment, Humility, and the Luxuries of Army Life

After the Armistice in World War I, several of Patton's officers left to come home early. They had been wounded and were still somewhat incapacitated. The war was over and they were anxious to return to civilian life. So they were on their way to a hospital en route to a port of embarkation, under orders which took them through Paris. They knew that Colonel Patton was in Paris that day on military business. The officers, of whom I was one, found that he was staying at the Crillon Hotel so we went to call on him. Patton was greatly touched by this show of regard from his old officers, who had campaigned in the 1st Brigade, Tank Corps, under him, and his eyes filled with tears. After a few minutes, he said, "You officers had better go. I will make a spectacle of myself if you stay too long."

During the twenties Mrs. Patton insisted on going to Fort Meade with her husband, but there were no quarters. Finally he wrangled a barracks, into which they moved, bag and baggage. To brighten it up as much as possible they painted all the rooms, but the only paint the Quartermaster had was blue and yellow—so the living room was blue with a yellow ceiling, the dining room was yellow with a blue ceiling, and so on. The barracks were wood and tar paper so they were highly inflammable and no cooking was allowed. Mrs. Patton went to the mess three times a day for ten days and then struck. Patton said he didn't know what to do but she just answered, "Do something."

Late that afternoon there was a terrific rumbling; the family looked out to see he had found an abandoned one-room shack and dragged it behind a tank to within fifteen feet of the barracks. "Here's your goddam kitchen," he said.

Beatrice Patton was perfectly happy. She put down duck-boards between the kitchen and the house, and proudly reminded her friends of the outdoor kitchen at Mt. Vernon. There was no grass anywhere and the sand blew into everything, so Beatrice planted oats and they had the only lawn at Meade. In fact their house had a Number 1 priority by the time they left, what with painted walls, a kitchen, and a lawn.

A close friend of Patton's got the house and moved in, much to his and his wife's delight, for they had been apart for two years because of the war. Her mother loathed army life and thought it would wreck her daughter. The Pattons went out to Meade for dinner with them. The mother-in-law was delighted because she felt that Mrs. Patton, being from Boston, would appreciate the True Horror of Mary's life. She started in complaining and worked up to her grand climax, "*And*—my dear Mrs. Patton, the worst of all in this army life is the people—the *hoi polloi*—poor Mary is forced to associate with! You won't believe this but I *assure* you it's true! When we moved into this house the former occupants had painted the walls *blue* and *yellow!*" At that, the host had such a coughing spell Patton had to help him from the room.

Ruth Ellen Totten, General Patton's daughter, tells a story that reveals his sentimentality and his family's modesty. This occurred after the slapping incident of the Sicilian campaign.

"During 1944–45 while my husband was in the Pentagon, I was a Red Cross aide at Walter Reed and helped in Occupational Therapy. I ended up in the double amputee ward for enlisted men. I was Mrs. Totten to everyone out there and didn't mention my maiden name, thinking that I might embarrass some of the men. One day I was helping out in the heart ward and an old Third Cavalry sergeant spotted me. We had a wonderful talk about the old days. I thought no more about it but next time I got back to my own ward there was a certain stiffness, and finally one of the patients who had been there longer asked me why I hadn't told them. Out of an empty head I babbled, 'How would these headlines have looked, Wounded Private Slaps General's Daughter?' That broke the ice and we were all friends again.

"When Daddy came back in '45 on that quick tour, I asked him to come to my ward on the day he visited Walter Reed. He loathed visiting hospitals but he said he would, and he got in there with Mother, two doctors, and myself. I had worked there so long I didn't realize how pitiful my patients looked. There was not a man in there over thirty-five and everyone was missing all or part of at least two limbs. Daddy marched in looking magnificent and stood right in the middle of the ward. There was a throbbing silence and then he began to bawl, hauled out his handkerchief, mopped his eyes and said, 'Men—all I can say is, if I had been a better general most of you wouldn't be here.' Then he marched out. There wasn't a dry eye in the ward."

One last picture comes to mind. He was leaving the 2d Armored Division for a corps command. It had all the theater dear to his heart, and all the spontaneity he could wish for. The entire Division was assembled in a natural amphitheater. In came the old and new commanders with blasting sirens, roaring motorcycles, and the Division at the salute. The new Commander, as fitting, spoke his piece and then turned to General Patton. From then on it was without words. General Patton stepped forward and stood rigidly at attention. There was no need for him to speak, and probably he couldn't, for his face showed the emotion of leaving his own Division that through long association had become a part of him.

The Division answered for him as it leaped to its feet and roared out its admiration. This huge bowl of humanity vibrated with its tribute to their leader. He turned quickly to hide his feelings and walked off the platform.

2. West Point—Early Posts— Chasing Villa

FROM school in California, Patton went to Virginia Military Institute where both his father and grandfather had graduated. After his first year there, he received an appointment to West Point in 1904.

At the time Patton entered West Point the position of Cadet Adjutant was given to the cadet who had the best military discipline and was the smartest soldier in bearing and uniform by the time he entered his first class (senior) year. Patton announced, upon entering the Academy, that he would be the Corps Adjutant in his last year. He made good this boast.

Patton took five years to graduate because he failed in mathematics by a fraction of a point one year. He was a good student in other subjects and for his entire five years he was at the top of his class each year in military discipline and deportment.

In athletics he showed notably the will to win. He never got his letter in football at West Point because of injuries, but he was an outstanding track star, specializing in the hurdles. He later married into a family who were keenly interested in horses and sailing. Mrs. Patton's father rode daily up until two weeks before he died at the age of ninety-five.

George Patton and Beatrice Ayer met when they were sixteen. They were married a year after he was graduated from West Point. On this occasion he told Beatrice that he intended to be a soldier, and that the only thing that could possibly prevent it would be the "Call." When she asked him to explain, he said that cousin Robbie Patton, later head of the Church Institute for Negroes, told him that when he was a student at the University of Virginia, he had no intention of being a minister, but that he had the "Call" and was obliged to answer it. So George prayed every night that he would not have the "Call."

On his first leave from West Point in his plebe year (first year), he wrote to his father about seeing Beatrice Ayer at the time of the presidential inauguration in Washington. The letter, dated March 13, 1905, reads in part as follows:

When I arrived at the hotel I was just going to send up my card when Bea grabbed me. She seemed really very glad to see me. Of course I was similarly affected. Pretty soon Mrs. Ayer came and made me go in and get some more dinner while they dressed for the inaugural ball. As I was by myself, I ordered all the desserts there were and nothing else.

Then we went to the ball, or rather, squash, and saw "Teddy" and the royal family. It was very pretty and gay. Bea and I had a dance, but it was pretty hard work and the floor was of stone. Still in my then state of mind, I would have danced with equal eagerness on a hot stove; that is, if the stove was not burning my partner. After the dance, we went back to the hotel and had supper, and then twelve o'clock came and with it ended my permit, so, like Cinderella, I had to go, although if she was having half as good a time as I, I can't blame her had she lost both her slippers.

On January 18, 1909 before his graduation from West Point in June of that year, young George Patton wrote a letter to Beatrice's father, which shows that military life was part of him:

With reference to the profession of a soldier, I think I appreciate most of its drawbacks. As you say, it is very narrowing, but don't you think that a man of only very ordinary capacity, in order to succeed against great competition, must be narrow? That is, have only one motive. I have no experience but from what I have read of successful men, they seem to be of the one-idea sort.

It is hard to answer intelligibly the question: "Why I want to be a soldier." For my own satisfaction I have tried to give myself reasons but have never found any logical ones. I only feel it inside. It is as natural for me to be a soldier as it is to breathe and would be as hard to give up all thought of it as it would be to stop breathing.

But being a soldier and being a member of the army in time of peace are two different things. I would only accept the latter as a means to the former.

Let those who criticize the Regular Army give pause to consider its contribution to this country in times of peril in all the wars since the Revolution. It has been the base for expansion through absorbing untrained citizen soldiers or has been used as the cadre for the training of the wartime soldiers.

Without the dedicated core of the professional soldier, this country could not have survived six wars. Between World Wars I and II, the officers of the regular establishment, as in other periods of peace, were subject to constant criticism by civilians. They were the forgotten men in the government service. Many remained in the grade of lieutenant for fifteen years. Their lot was unrewarding financially but they held to their chosen profession. They attended their numerous schools, kept their professional skill polished and enhanced against the time when their country would need them again.

There is a source of this inspiration, this dedication, this tireless energy. It is a school on the Hudson called West Point. Our Regular Army has had to swim upstream against the current of civilian opinion most of the time. American citizens felt sure there would be no more wars.

No one wishes to insinuate that there is any difference between the regular officers who attended West Point and those regulars who did not. A very small percentage of the regular officers are graduates of West Point, and some of the greatest soldiers of our generation never attended the Academy. General of the Army George C. Marshall, Generals Walter Krueger, Thomas T. Handy, John E. Hull, and Charles L. Bolte and Lieutenant Generals Clarence R. Ruebner, Leonard T. Gerow, Manton S. Eddy, Lucian K. Truscott, Edward H. Brooks, John R. Hodge and many more were not graduated from West Point.

But the ideals, the training, the spirit of that school have permeated the army. No task is too great for them, and they have been successful in a measure beyond duplication in two world wars, and the Naval Academy at

Annapolis is the source of the same devoted ideals that have always animated the Navy.

Many other institutions have contributed greatly to our regular officer corps. Norwich University, Virginia Military Institute, Virginia Polytechnic Institute, The Citadel, and the Agriculture and Mechanical College of Texas are only a few of the outstanding schools across the country.

Many of the combat leaders of World War II were educated at West Point at the time Patton attended. The names of a few are well known. Among those are: Generals Jacob L. Devers, Willis D. Crittenberger, J. C. H. Lee, C. A. Baehr, Everett S. Hughes, Robert L. Eichelberger and W. H. Simpson.

Getting acquainted at West Point, those officers, destined to command, knew the personal characteristics of many who would serve under them. They had made their initial contacts at West Point. Patton kept a little black book of those he would like to have in his command. Not only were his contemporaries at the Academy in that book, but as he made new acquaintances names were added. Regular officers that did not go through West Point and many from civilian life were on that list and served with him in World War II. Patton was looking for battle leaders wherever he could find them.

Thus he built his fighting team; for armies are made of individual men; they are not tables of organization. It was Patton's ability to select, and his faculty of binding his subordinate commanders and the troops to him with fanatical loyalty, that in large measure were responsible for the phenomenal accomplishments of the units he commanded in both World Wars.

Patton always forced himself to do the things which were hard to do. Just before he was married, he thought that since he had never been under fire, it was necessary for him to stand up between the targets during troop firing exercise.

His first post was Fort Sheridan, Illinois. There he first played polo at the Onwentsia Club at Lake Forest. He was a cavalryman and those were the days when the cavalry was a glamorous service. The horse had not yet been deposed by the machine gun and tank. Though later World War I showed that the cavalry was not suited to modern war with the high fire-power of modern weapons, it still existed in the United States Army until near the time of our entrance into World War II. In Russia, with vast underdeveloped regions, it played a considerable role in World War II and still survives.

The horse was an excellent medium for training officers and men. It kept the rider physically fit and alert. It developed the ability for quick decision. Many armored leaders were horsemen, either cavalrymen or artillerymen. It is essential to keep the physical and mental alertness that were fostered by the horse. Polo and cross-country riding lend a spice of danger to peacetime military life. Lovers of the horse regret its passing, though the automatic weapons, the tank, the jeep, the scout car and the airplane, made this inevitable under conditions confronting the United States Army.

At Fort Sheridan, General Paul B. Malone, then a captain, taught a school for officers. At that time, the teaching of tactics was looked upon as of doubtful benefit and was on a voluntary basis.

There was a regular garrison school for lieutenants, but Malone's school was different. The command and staff school established at Leavenworth was the first school of its kind in our army. Malone was one of its graduates and his course in tactics at Fort Sheridan was patterned on the problems taught at Leavenworth. Malone had only two or three volunteers for his school.

Some considered such schools as factories that would rob an officer of his individuality; others held that only by teaching and the mental drill of solving tactical problems could an officer be grounded in the fundamentals. Patton was one of the latter class, as he felt that no opportunity to perfect himself for his avowed military goal should be overlooked.

There was not much to do at this peacetime post and as a consequence the soldiers had much leisure time. George and his wife, Beatrice, organized a football team for the soldiers and bought them suits and equipment. Patton played end on the team. It is believed that this was the start of organized post football teams.

In January 1912 Patton was transferred to the 3d Cavalry at Fort Myer, Virginia. Shortly after, he became *aide de camp* to General Leonard Wood, Chief of Staff of the Army. It was there also that he first knew Colonel Henry L. Stimson, later Secretary of State and Secretary of War in World War II. His friendship with these two outstanding men had a lifelong influence on him and upon his career.

At that time he owned several race horses and was listed as a gentleman rider, having reduced his weight by over forty pounds so that he rode, in a silk uniform, at 151½ pounds. General Wood used to tell him "Don't get fat," and recommended a diet of scraped raw beef by the tablespoonful washed down with citrate of magnesia. This was rather debilitating, but nevertheless Patton won many steeplechase trophies.

That spring "Colonel" R. M. Thompson, of copper fame, undertook to send a team of American athletes to the Olympic Games at Stockholm. The athletes, including Jim Thorpe, were recruited from all sorts of clubs and schools. There was an army riding team composed of Captain (later Major General) Guy V. Henry, Captain (later Lieutenant General) Ben Lear and Captain "Cit" Montgomery.

Patton was asked to go in the Modern Military Pentathlon which included pistol shooting, swimming, fencing, riding and running three miles cross-country. He finished fourth behind three Swedes in the Military World Olympics. He broke the pistol record the day before the competition. However, when he fired for record he was charged with a miss and finished 27th. Some of his competitors claimed that one of his shots went through the same hole in the target. In 1945 the entire Swedish team invited him to Stockholm. Here he competed with some of his old competitors in Sweden after VE Day, and made a better score than he did in 1912.

In practice for the swimming event he trained in an eight-foot-square tank, pulling against a rope around his waist. He finished second or third in that event.

In cross-country riding he finished third. His U.S. Army horse was hurt on the trip over, and the city of Stockholm gave him another mount which performed better than any of ours, for it was accustomed to the small sunken ditches.

He was first in fencing, conquering the champion of the French army.

In cross-country running he took third place, fainting dead-away at the end in front of the King's box, in a spectacular finish.

Of the twelve Swedish officers who competed against him, several became his "Blood Brothers" and still regard themselves as such. He always considered the Swedish the world's greatest sportsmen.

Patton was the first American to enter the Military Pentathlon and at that time there was no provision for sending a representative from this country, so he paid his own expenses.

Having a bit more leave after the Olympic Games in 1912, he and Mrs. Patton went to the French Cavalry School at Saumur and he took épée fencing lessons from Adjutant Cléry, a famous escrimeur. The French have placed a plaque on the school where he studied and on the hotel where he and Mrs. Patton stayed.

From Saumur he went to Fort Riley, Kansas, to the Mounted Service School and was picked for a second-year advanced equitation course. He was asked to be the Army's first Master of the Sword. To do this well, he asked for a summer leave in 1913 and he and Beatrice went back to Saumur. This time they took a roadster and reconnoitered all the "Bocage Country" from Cherbourg south, using only the back watershed roads used in the days of William the Conqueror. He knew these watershed roads would always be firm enough to carry military transport no matter how much it rained. He had a feeling that he was destined to fight there some day and in this he was right, for he took his historic Third Army over the "Bocage Country" in World War II. He reconnoitered every bit of country from Cherbourg to Saumur: St. Malo, St. Lô, Bayeaux, Falaise, Caen, Chartres, Melme and Le Mans. The factors that led to this reconnaissance were a knowledge of history, imagination, and the everlasting urge to perfect himself in the science of war. The last factor was undoubtedly the dominant thing in his life.

Adjutant Cléry, his old friend of Saumur days, became devoted to Patton, and was anxious to come to the United States as his assistant. Cléry had a wife and three sons, and the Pattons talked it over and decided that he would be too homesick in America, George did not speak much French at that time, so Beatrice was detailed to persuade Cléry not to go. The translated conversation between Beatrice and Cléry was as follows:

Beatrice: You cannot take Madame and the boys with you—you could only send for them—after you have been at Fort Riley some time.

Cléry: We have discussed that and she is quite willing to wait.

Beatrice: But Lt. Patton's job is not permanent—we would have to leave you there after a year or two.

Cléry: If the Lieutenant is there for a year, then I shall become accustomed.

Beatrice: America is so different . . . it is very isolated —there is no village at Riley, only the post, and the town is six kilometers away.

Cléry: What? No church bells to wake me in the morning?

Beatrice: No, just the reveille trumpet, and the food is different.

Cléry: Yes, I have heard that your bread is only crumb.

Beatrice: Also, we do not drink wine at meals. It is too expensive.

Cléry: No wine? Then how does one make the water potable? Well, after all, Americans are very healthy. Nevertheless, I will go! It is decided.

A thoughtful pause—then;—

Beatrice: Let me tell you about the journey—after debarking from the ship in New York, we go on the train for two days, across a part of America. There is a restaurant car where we go to eat, and the rest of the time we sit in a long car without compartments. At night a black porter—you know, like a Senegalese— comes through the car and makes the seats into beds with curtains and that is where we all sleep.

Cléry: What, and the men and women and the jeunes filles, all sleep in the same car, with only curtains between them?

Beatrice: Yes, that is how we travel in America.

Cléry: Then, I cannot go to America, Madame. It is no place for my sons.

Beatrice spent the summer of 1913 translating the French instruction books on fencing, and the Pattons bought the fencing equipment and, regretfully, left Cléry behind.

The men of this regiment wore the steel cuirass and helmet with yellow horsehair crest. Mrs. Patton kept her husband's helmet, which their cook used to call "the Lieutenant's Coat of Arms."

During the same summer they became friends with Lieutenant and Madame Jean Houdemon of the French Army. Houdemon promised Patton that if the United States did not get into war before the French did, he would try to enlist him in his cavalry regiment, and endeavor to see that he got the first officer vacancy.

The French expected the Germans to attack in 1913. When they did attack in 1914, Patton asked for "leave-to-go-beyond-the-sea" and was turned down. Houdemon fought in the cavalry for a while, then joined the air force before the end of World War I. When Pétain took over the government of France in 1940, Houdemon, who had been in the French Air Force since the end of World War I, was air chief of Southern France. Pétain fired him and he went to Pont-à-Mousson as mayor of his home town in the German occupation. He had suffered a bad air crash flying a fighter plane in combat at sixty, and walked with two canes. The Pattons heard he had died. But Patton hopefully searched for him everywhere. At last a French G-2 was assigned to Patton in 1944. This French G-2 was known by the name of Colonel "Bilbane." "Bilbane" is now General Jean Rethoré, Armor, in the French Army. When "Bilbane" joined Patton in 1944 he said of Houdemon, "He is my father-in-law." As this is written, Houdemon is governor of the Invalides in Paris.

After the summer of 1913, the second summer Patton had spent at Saumur, he returned for his second year at Riley. He was the first officer at Riley ever to be a pupil and instructor at the same time, for he was then taking advanced equitation and teaching fencing. Some of the pupil officers disliked the addition of fencing to the curriculum, and as they were very senior to Lieutenant Patton (some even majors), it could have been embarrassing.

The classes were not so eager, as the fencing increased the already crowded curriculum, and George was concerned as to how he should approach the class.

On the first day of the class, Beatrice sat in an inconspicuous seat. The lecture started with a statement by

Patton which ran something like this: "It is an honor to have been chosen by the Cavalry School to practice with you gentlemen the elements of fencing, even though I am so junior to you all; that is, junior to you in everything but fencing. In that I am senior—very much your senior, for I started my fencing career at the age of six with these swords." He brought out a curved wooden saber with a rawhide hilt, and a straight wooden sword like those the Crusaders carried. "This ticking scabbard was made by my nurse." From then on, the class was with him.

That year he made the first straight sword, which was later adopted and replaced the old curved cavalry saber, hammering it out and tempering it himself.

A young officer who was at Fort Riley with Patton at this time, later remarked when Patton was a general in World War II, "You know, looking back on Patton, he has been a general all his life."

After their tour of duty at Riley, the Pattons were transferred to border duty at Sierra Blanca, Texas, in the fall of 1915, the year of the Fair. He was to report to Sierra Blanca for cavalry border patrol duty. George and Beatrice had driven west from Fort Riley to California over the Santa Fe Trail that his grandfather, B. D. Wilson, took in 1837. Mount Wilson is named for him.

Beatrice left him at Sierra Blanca and went back to pick up the little girls and take them to Lake Vineyard. When she arrived, early in November, she found her husband living in their three-room house with Major George T. Langhorne and a Chinese cook. George warned her not to notice anything some of his odd friends did, and she realized what he meant when they gathered together in the evenings and punctuated their stories by long-range spits on the airtight stove.

The following is from a letter written on October 20, 1915 by him to Beatrice before she joined him at Sierra Blanca.

This is the funniest place I have ever been. It is supposed to be very tough and at least half the men wear boots and spurs and carry guns. I met a Mr. Dave Allison yesterday, a quiet-looking old man with a sweet face and white hair. He is the most noted gunman here in Texas and just at present is marshal. He alone killed all the Orozco outfit, five of them, about a month ago.

37

He shot Orozco and his four men each in the head at sixty yards! He seems much taken with me and we go hunting together.

Another noted man I met is Mr. English, a hired fighter for T-O Ranch across the border. He is about sixty and has two grown daughters, cowgirls, who are very dashing ladies. He is the only American who can bluff the bandits over the river and he does.

Each of these men gets about $100 a month for risking their lives daily.

There are seven Love brothers here who run the whole country and are supposed to be worth millions. They own the town and all work either on their ranches or in the store. To look at them, they would appear like laborers, but all seem very nice, like Mr. Yarnley. [A shooting companion at Fort Riley.] I think I will get on with them well, as I usually do with that sort of people.

There are not over twenty houses in the town and one saloon. Yesterday a Ranger jokingly threatened to shoot me for not taking a drink with him, so after I had refused, I bought him a bottle of beer and drank one myself. Don't get worried, he was only trying to be hospitable according to his views, and had not the least intention of being rough.

We have a three room house and a stable and a garage, so are very comfortable. I would not miss this opportunity for the world. I guess there are few places like it left. We have two outposts about thirty miles from here and sixty miles apart, one at Love's ranch and one at Calderon. There is no wagon road to the latter place as it is in the mountains. So is this; 4500 feet up.

In another letter written October 30, 1915 he describes some incidents with the Mexicans. At this time Mexican bandits were causing trouble with the Texans, but Villa had not yet made his Columbus raid.

This is the greatest side show you ever saw. Yesterday a circus came through, followed, during the afternoon, by two trains of Mexicans. The first train had the damnedest bunch of ancient coaches you ever dreamed of, most of them of the vintage of 1850. There were also several good French autos and one car had an armored gun on it. The second bunch started through at about four A.M. I had to get up at two-thirty and ride them to a bridge. I sent some men the other way also at the same time. I had only four privates with me and it was cold as could be. When we got near the bridge, we dismounted to lead. One man was 200 yards ahead, then myself and two men, then one one hundred yards behind, the object being that if we were jumped, someone would be clear to carry the news or act as a reinforcement.

The bridge is in a sort of wash on a curve and as I neared it the man in front galloped back and said he heard Mexicans on the bridge. So I mounted the men and we trotted to it with our pistols out. I could see no one, so when about two yards from the bridge, as near as I could get on account of the fence, I called, "Who is there?" and a voice which to me sounded foreign said, "Friend," and at the same moment six heads with rifles stuck over the bank. Strange to say, I did not think of running, but wondered if I could get one before I was got. I called, "What are you doing there?" and to my surprise and delight they answered, "Patrol, 13th Cavalry." They should not have been there as I was covering the bridge.

The rest of them came by tonight so when you get this I will be back at Sierra Blanca.

About half the necessary troops are, in the words of Macaulay, "Ancient men on crutches and women great with child."

The gent on the envelope is my chief armorer here. More of him later.

The gent he referred to was Mr. Hackett, telegraph operator and dead shot at Hot Wells, Texas, where he was very anxious to have George and Beatrice Patton settle and run a sanitarium with him as director. Hot Wells is an old Indian spring with very pure water even for this alkali country. In fact, all the drinking water came from there in a little cart with railroad wheels which was sent twenty-two miles up the track. Mr. Hackett was an impressive-looking man who had not cut his curly gray hair since his wife left him fifteen years before. She evidently did not care how he looked, since he had made the vow he

39

would not cut it until she returned. It hung to his waist and he ordinarily caught it up in a chignon tied with a black silk handkerchief under his black Texas hat. So that he would not be ridiculed, he had become a dead shot and he and George Patton spent many happy afternoons making hair triggers and shooting cigarettes at fifty yards.

Sierra Blanca was a tough town and the camp of the Rangers there was probably the toughest part of it. There were thirty-seven voters in the town but after the Pattons were ordered back to Fort Bliss they found that Area Headquarters had received a petition from the town signed by two hundred people asking that the Pattons be retained for another four months, as they were the "commonest people" who had ever served there. When they finally left, the Rangers gave a ball.

Their service at Sierra Blanca was an interesting interlude that made many lasting friends. After they moved on to Ft. Bliss they were often visited by their Sierra Blanca friends.

The ranchmen would come to town intending to present live quail to Mrs. Patton. They would take a room in a hotel, get drunk for several days, forgetting about the live quail, and then come out of the fog enough to realize that the present for Mrs. Patton had not been delivered. She always remembered the many gifts of undernourished quail she received at that time.

One day Mrs. Martin Hogan, wife of the saloonkeeper, came to call, and Beatrice asked her about a shocking killing which had occurred there shortly after they left.

"Well, you see, it was this way. Mr. Boykin had some cattle to ship and he put his steers in Mr. Tuppy's pen. Mr. Tuppy was not using the pen as he had no steers to ship, but he did not like Mr. Boykin so he told him to get out or he would shoot him. Mr. Boykin said the train would be there in a couple of hours, and 'you would not shoot me would you, with five children, and me unarmed?' But Mr. Tuppy did, that is, he tried, but instead he got Mr. Sitters, who was perched on the fence watching the quarrel. The second time, he got Mr. Boykin, and now there are no men left in Sierra Blanca because they are either the chasing or the chased."

"But," said Beatrice, "there must have been something behind such a killing—some sort of a grudge."

Mrs. Hogan settled herself more comfortably in the

chair. "Oh, no, Mrs. Patton. There was no grudge, you know how the gentlemen are."

In 1916 the Punitive Expedition into Mexico in pursuit of Villa, the Mexican bandit leader, was forming. Patton, knowing that action was imminent, went to Brigadier General John J. Pershing's quarters and camped in his front hall. For two days every time General Pershing went in or out of his quarters, Patton begged to be taken along on the expedition. After several refusals, Pershing's defenses weakened and he took Patton with him, as Headquarters Commandant and acting aide.

General Pershing on May 14, 1916 ordered Lieutenant Patton to take some army automobiles, an interpreter, Mr. W. Lunt, six privates of the 16th Infantry, and a corporal, and buy corn in the vicinity of some haciendas near Lake Itascate.

Several places were visited and contacts made for the delivery of corn to the American Army. Finally the party reached a village named Las Cienegas. There in a hacienda lived the uncle of General Cardenas. Cardenas was a Mexican bandit general, and an important member of Villa's staff. He commanded Villa's bodyguard, "The Dorados." Patton had been to this particular hacienda before and was familiar with it.

He thought there might be some Mexican bandits in Las Cienegas, and asked the uncle of General Cardenas if Cardenas was home. The frightened appearance of the uncle led Patton to believe that Cardenas was there.

Patton ordered the cars to assemble at a sunken road about a mile from the house, and left them in charge of the corporal, because it was anticipated that there might be a number of enemy in the hacienda.

On foot, Patton and the six soldiers approached the house. Patton ordered all sides of the house to be covered to prevent escape of any bandits inside. Patton, because of his familiarity with the locality, was the first to arrive at his station on the east wall of the house. There at the gate was an old man and a boy skinning a steer. The other members of the party had not yet arrived at their stations. A moment after Patton's arrival, three Mexican horsemen armed with rifles and pistols appeared at the gate. They saw Patton, turned and galloped to the southeast corner of the house. The horsemen then saw the other soldiers coming along the south face of the hacienda, and wheeled north immediately.

The Mexican Punitive Expedition was under strict orders not to shoot unless they were sure of identification. No firing was done by the Americans until the bandits, after turning north, opened up with their pistols, shooting at Patton and Mr. Lunt, the interpreter. Patton then pulled his pistol and knocked one of the men out of the saddle. This man crawled through the gate.[1]

By this time, the pistols had been emptied and both sides reloaded. Just as Patton finished reloading, the two remaining Mexicans on horseback galloped by, about ten yards away, firing at Patton and Lunt. Neither was hit, but Patton fired again and killed the horse of the nearest Mexican, which fell on his rider. The Mexican extricated himself, and raised his gun before Patton blazed away again and killed him.

About this time, the bandit whom Patton had knocked off his horse and who had crawled through the gate was seen running along the south wall of the hacienda. The bandit stopped shooting, held up his left hand as if surrendering, then quickly drew his pistol with his right hand and fired. This was his last act, as Patton killed him, although shooting second. It was General Cardenas. Another bandit was also killed during the fighting.

All this time the old man and the boy continued skinning the steer, probably thinking that this would save them from becoming involved in the sudden death that charged the atmosphere.

As part of the operation, it was necessary to make certain that there were no more bandits at the hacienda. Patton found a piece of timber, near at hand, and moved it against the wall. He was the first one to climb to the roof to prevent the possibility of hostile fire from snipers. Upon arrival at the dirt roof, he stepped on it, and fell through the flimsy structure to his armpits. Fortunately, there were no bandits in the room beneath and he was able to extricate himself without getting hurt.

The bag of Mexicans was three. Patton brought back to the American camp the bodies of two on the running

[1] Patton was one of the best shots in the U.S. Cavalry. He wrote the pistol regulations for two years.

board of his car, including General Cardenas. These two were the ones he himself had killed.

Beatrice received a letter from Patton, written on May 17, 1916, which in part reads:

Here we are back at the windiest place in the world. I just killed two snakes outside my tent. All the men are teasing me because I used a pistol instead of a sabre the other day, but it simply goes to show than an officer should be able to use all arms, for being on foot I could not have used a sabre. The general [Pershing] has been very complimentary. He calls me the "Bandit." There is another bandit here that I wanted to take a try at, but he would not let me. It is just as well as my luck might change and I might not hit this one. You are probably wondering if my conscience hurts me for killing a man. It does not. I feel about it just as I did when I got my swordfish: surprised at my luck. From the latest news we may stay here some time. I hope not, as it is very stupid unless we have war.

After this adventure, Patton rode out of Mexico with General Pershing. He had had eleven months of arduous, active service, often dull but interspersed with valuable experience and excitement. He had won his spurs in the hard ways of war and henceforth was a proven soldier. Having had his Mexican service, he resigned from Pershing's staff and joined the 7th Cavalry.

When General Pershing was selected to command our American Army in France when we entered the war on the side of the Allies in the spring of 1917, he asked for Patton to come with him. Patton left the 7th Cavalry and again joined Pershing's headquarters, sailing to France on the *Baltic*.

3. World War I

France

PATTON went to France with the first U.S. contingent in World War I. He was made Headquarters Commandant of General Pershing's headquarters and served in that capacity as well as that of aide until early in 1918 when Pershing decided we would have an American tank corps. Brigadier General Samuel D. Rockenbach was made head of that arm of the service. Captain Patton was under him.

Before deciding to join the tank corps Patton asked his father-in-law, Mr. Frederick Ayer, for his advice. Mr. Ayer counseled him to "select the weapon with which you can inflict the most punishment while suffering the least casualties." That advice may have been the deciding factor in launching the career of the greatest exponent of the tank as a quick method of destroying the enemy with the least loss of American lives.

In November 1917, when Patton left General Pershing's headquarters in France to take the tanks, General Pershing wrote to Beatrice Patton: *This is the second time Patton has left my staff. I am writing to tell you he has not been fired.*

One battalion of U.S. soldiers manned heavy British tanks, trained, and fought with the British. Captain Patton was given the assignment of training and commanding the two battalions of light tanks, companies A to F, which formed the 1st Brigade, Tank Corps, U.S. Army. To prepare himself for this new type of duty, he went to the British and the French tank schools. After observing these startling innovations in warfare, he decided he preferred the French two-man Renault tank.

Patton established a training center a few kilometers south of Langres in the Haute Marne. The little villages of Bourg and Brennes were selected as places to billet the troops, one battalion being billeted in each town. The officers and men were quickly assigned to the 1st Brigade, Tank Corps, for there were many applicants when the word spread through our American Expeditionary Force that the United States was forming such a unit. All tankers were volunteers in World War I.

In 1918 Patton told me this story soon after I had joined the tanks in France as a second lieutenant. Patton was then a captain and had just come to the newly formed U.S. tank corps at Langres, in France, and had been ordered, as was not unusual, to go on a secret mission. His orders read that he should go to a certain railroad station and take the first train running west, get off at the third station, and take the next train running south, get off at the second station, and

44

there he would receive further orders. At the second station he was met by a staff car with a soldier driver. They were driving along at a fast pace at dusk, and he had no idea where he was going.

He had not been in this part of France before but he had an eerie feeling that at some time, possibly in a former existence, he had been familiar with that countryside.[1]

As the car approached the top of a hill, Captain Patton, to whom the vicinity was entirely unfamiliar, reached forward and asked the soldier driver if the camp wasn't out of sight just over the hill and to the right. The driver replied, "No sir, our camp where we are going is further ahead, but there is an old Roman camp over there to the right. I have seen it myself."

The car went ahead in silence and finally arrived at the headquarters to which Captain Patton was supposed to report. He reported and had conversation with the officers and was leaving through the side door of the headquarters when he turned to an officer there in the room and said, "Your theater is over here straight ahead, isn't it?" and the officer replied, "We have no theater here, but I do know that there is an old Roman theater only about three hundred yards away." This conversation took place well after dark and it was impossible for Patton to see the theater.

On February 21, 1918 Patton wrote in a letter to his wife:

> We have been having some interesting lectures on special subjects and all of them go to show what a complex war we are in and how much we have to learn. It seems more and more certain to me that we cannot punch a hole without tanks. There are too many instruments of death in the way but I believe that tanks well worked up will do the job. I hope the war lasts long enough for us to try our hand. The tanks have attracted a lot of good men and I get requests from them to transfer into tanks nearly daily.

For instructional purposes the French let the Americans have twenty-two Renault light tanks and it was with this type of tank our forces trained, and fought in St. Mihiel and the Argonne. When the tanks arrived at the railroad siding near Bourg, Patton drove them off the flatcars him-

---

[1] The psychic phenomenon of "déjà vu."

self because he was the only one who knew how to operate them, having received training from the French.

In a letter to his wife, he said, *We got them all off the flat cars by 2:00 A.M. I was the only one who knew how to drive a tank, but the men helped all they could. It was bright moonlight. All my men had a hot meal afterward.*

From March 1918 until the St. Mihiel show in September these twenty-two tanks were to furnish the schooling for the two battalions that formed the 1st Brigade.

The Renault tank had a crew of two, a driver who sat on the floor and a gunner who stood in the turret and who was also the tank commander. Each tank had either a Hotchkiss machine gun or a 37 mm. cannon. A platoon was formed of five tanks, two machine gun tanks and three 37 mm. cannon tanks. The tank commander gave the driver signals by kicking him; this being the only possible form of communication in those days. A kick in the back told him to start forward; a kick on the right or left shoulder told the driver to turn; a kick on the head was the signal to stop; repeated kicks on the head was the signal to back.

Each company had 24 tanks; a captain's tank and three platoons of five tanks each, each platoon being commanded by a lieutenant. Eight tanks from each company were turned over to brigade reserve.

Tank tactics in those days did not encompass the breakthrough, now the ideal function of armor. The tanks were supposed to precede the infantry. A common tactic was to have a rolling artillery barrage precede a line of tanks by 100 yards and the infantry follow the tanks by 100 yards. If any machine guns or other fire held up the infantry, the nearest tanks were to destroy the source of the enemy fire. These tanks could only go four miles an hour at top speed with ordinary gasoline. With aviation gasoline they could go five miles an hour. Their ordinary cruising speed was supposed to be that of the marching infantry.

The tank companies used the training tanks in rotation. The Repair and Salvage Company of the old 1st Brigade Tank Corps worked day and night to keep as many as possible of the twenty-two Renaults running. Ordinarily there were enough tanks to train two platoons at a time. The World War I Renault tanks were prone to breakdown, and the officers became accustomed to starting a maneuver with ten vehicles and ending it with half that number.

Officers were sent to a French tank school to learn

tactics. This school was run by the Douzième Groupement of French tanks which had just been in action and were pulled out of the line in April 1918 to a rest area. After the school, which involved drinking of considerable champagne, the singing of the "Marseillaise" and "The Star-Spangled Banner," as well as some tactics, the U.S. officers returned to Bourg and Brennes.

Patton thought it would be well to train these green officers by actual combat, so he arranged to send groups to the same Douzième Groupement, now returned to the front and located in the Somme near Amiens and Villa Coublai.

As a second lieutenant, far down the list, I was sent to campaign for a short time with a first lieutenant, Charles Murat, who in civilian life was Prince Charles Murat, then amateur welterweight boxing champion of France. His forebear was Marshal Murat who rose from private to Marshal in the Napoleonic Campaigns. When Napoleon said, "Every French soldier carries in his knapsack the baton of a Maréchal of France," it was no idle statement.

At one time the company of Murat was given the task of taking the woods called Bois de Hangar near Villa Coublai. I had a place as machine gunner in one of the tanks. These French tanks were ordered to precede a detachment of the French Foreign Legion in taking the woods, but at the last minute the French Foreign Legion had the orders changed. These troops, knowing where the machine gun emplacements were located in the woods, adopted an unusual plan and one which only an outfit highly experienced in war could use. Two zero hours were selected: 12 midnight and 3:00 in the morning. The Legionnaires at 12 midnight infiltrated the Bois de Hangar in groups, crawling noiselessly on their stomachs to positions adjacent to all the machine gun nests—one group for each. The enemy was not alerted by any noise made by the Legionnaires—mute tribute to their infiltration tactics. At 3:00 in the morning, at the second zero hour, the Foreign Legion groups gave a yell and jumped the nests. The woods were taken in ten seconds with negligible casualties and many German prisoners.

After the tour at the front, the American officers returned to the little towns of Brennes and Bourg, near Langres, to continue their training, bringing back with them an admiration for the courage of the French, and a recollection of the Gallic gaiety that survived the hardship of the Somme in 1918.

In 1918 the French had a song of the tank:

> *Voici le char d'assaut,*
> *Voyez comme il est beau;*
> *Il a l'allure guerrière*
> *Même en marchant en arrière;*
> *Crachant du feu,*
> *Ne buvant que de l'eau;*
> *Le char d'assaut*
> *C'est un oiseau.*

(Roughly: "Behold the tank, see how beautiful it is; it looks like a warrior even when marching in the rear; spitting fire and drinking only water; the tank is a bird.")

Patton's discipline became proverbial and the tankers took pride in their soldierly smartness. They knew that his salutes in return to any salute given by a subordinate would be outstanding. It became a byword to call a smart salute: "Give 'em a George Patton."

As the summer of 1918 progressed, the officers and men of the old 1st Brigade, Tank Corps, perfected themselves in the various skills that a tanker at that time should have. There were many schools taught by officers established at the United States Tank Center near Langres. Each officer and each man had to graduate from every school. Some of the schools were reconnaissance, Renault tank driving, Hotchkiss machine gun assembling (the tank was dark inside so it had to be perfected while blindfolded), correcting stoppages, gunnery, map making, map reading, and aerial photograph interpretation. Once every two weeks each company would march to some distant place and camp, generally near a canal so that the men could swim. They then lived on their "iron" rations which were roughly equivalent to the "C" rations of World War II, but not as good.

About September 15, 1918, enough Renault tanks for both battalions arrived and a polish was given to the driving skills of all personnel. Each company went to a nearby trench mortar school at Fort Destain and all practiced driving in shell-cratered ground. The trench mortar shells were called "Flying Pigs" and carried a high explosive charge, making large shell holes into which the Renault tanks drove for practice. Some dud shells were present, so as a precaution a soldier was ordered to walk in front of each tank to search for duds and insure that no tank would drive over them. His orders were to stop the approaching tank in time. An officer fortunately saw an unexploded trench mortar shell the soldier had overlooked and halted his tank a yard short of it. The soldier, when questioned why he had not carried out his orders, said, "Sir, I did not know what you meant by a dud."

St. Mihiel

The tanks were loaded at Bourg and detrained at St. Mihiel in a sector just east of Montsec.

The battalion of tanks that was to cross the German lines at the little village of Richecourt was headed by Company A with B and C Companies in column behind. As A Company commander, I was in the first tank in this battalion column. In this first American show with tanks, I suffered all the qualms that beset a soldier in his first engagement. My tank led and if I failed, the whole effort of that battalion would abort.

My feelings as I sat in the tank waiting for zero hour were a mixture of fear for my own safety, and an added and greater fear that I might be one of the few who cannot perform in battle. Thoughts came to mind of the months of training of the whole battalion; the trust of the men, and particularly of the trust reposed in me by my commander, now Colonel George Patton. What would I do if I discovered I froze under fire?

As this was the initial baptism of fire as a commander I did not know that always every officer, in every show, has these worries. They are greatest in the first show, but they are always there until the battle starts. After the battle commences an officer has little time to think of himself. A private with few responsibilities and duties has a much harder time to do what he should. An officer has less opportunity to think of his personal hazard than the private, because of the press of many matters that need his immediate attention. He is supremely occupied with taking care of his many obligations. An officer in battle is a busy man.

After passing through Richecourt in column, the tanks fanned out in line and preceded the first line of the 1st

Infantry Division, who followed the tanks at 100 yards with their rifles at high port. Casualties were not very heavy, but when an infantryman would fall, his place would be taken by a soldier in the line behind. The 1st Infantry marched on the battlefield almost with the precision of a practice maneuver. It was inspiring to see the steady march of these trained and battlehardened veterans who had been blooded by months of fighting.[2]

Colonel Patton rode on the top of a tank in the leading line of attack until the paint on the tank he rode started to be chipped off between his legs by machine-gun fire.

All objectives were taken the first day. Patton made a personal reconnaissance that day on foot and found himself well inside the outposts of the Hindenburg Line. There he left a small silk tank corps flag that he had in his pocket. Mrs. Patton heard of this by two letters she received.

The first letter was from General Rockenbach of the U.S. Tank Corps [3] who told Mrs. Patton of this personal reconnaissance, and assured her that he had told her husband in no uncertain terms that he should be at his own headquarters, and had a statement from her husband that he would be there.

The second letter was from Colonel Patton who told his wife he had been reprimanded for the reconnaissance, and had promised to remain at his headquarters thereafter. "But you know, Bea, my headquarters is always under my hat."

The following letter was written by Patton to his wife on September 16, 1918, after the St. Mihiel show, and is quoted in part. However, it only covers the action on the 12th and 13th.

DARLING BEA:

The news is out so I can give you a brief account of the Battle of St. Mihiel, etc. At 10 A.M. August 22 I got a telephone message to report to General Rockenbach with my reconnaissance officer ready for protracted field service. I did. At 3 P.M. we were at Army Headquarters and had been told the plans which as you now know contemplated an attack by three Corps. I was to command the tanks in the 5th Corps. The rest of the tanks

---

[2] The 1st Infantry Division in World War II showed the same valor and drive; truly a great division.
[3] Composed of two tank brigades.

were to be supplied by the French. At 8 P.M. I reported to your old friend, General Burtt [captain in Mexico], who was Chief of Staff.

Next day I went to French Corps Headquarters to get permission to visit the front. In going there I was told it was a marsh where tanks could not move. As I did not believe this, I went out with a French patrol that night to the barbed wire and found the ground hard and dry, though in winter it is probably a marsh. We worked hard and got all ready to fight. Also got our tanks. I had to patrol, make plans, and then travel back to our U.S. tank center every other night, a four-hour ride, to arrange things there. We thought that "D" day would be September 7. On September 4 I got orders to leave the 5th Corps and report to the 4th Corps near Toul. Here I got a new job and had to start all over again, which was a bore. Still, it had to be done.

I walked down to the Rupt de Mad by day to the bridge at Xivray which is in no man's land, and was not shot at. I had to do it to see if we could cross the stream.

Then we started to detrain and that was awful. For four nights the French made every mistake they could, sending trains to the wrong place or not sending them at all. The last company of the 329th Battalion detrained at 3:15 A.M. and marched right into action.

We attacked at 5 A.M. on Thursday, September 12 and at 1 A.M. 900 plus guns opened and shot till 5 A.M. It was dark with a heavy rain and wind. I was on a hill in front of the main line where I could watch both of my tank battalions, and the thirty French tanks I had also under me.

I could see our tanks getting stuck in the trenches. It was a most irritating sight. At 7 A.M. I moved forward two miles, and at 9 A.M. I decided I had to get detailed information on our progress, so I took an officer and three runners and started forward.

There were very few dead in the trenches as the Boche had not fought hard, but you never saw such trenches, eight feet deep and ten to fourteen feet wide. At the first town we came to, St. Busant, the Boche were still shelling. I found French tanks stuck in a pass under shellfire. I talked to the major and went on. I had not gone twenty feet when a six-inch shell struck the tank he was working on and killed fifteen men. I went on towards Essey and got into the front line infantry who were lying down. As there was only shell fire I walked on, marching with vigor. Most of the shells were high.

Here I met General MacArthur (Douglas) who was commanding a brigade. He was walking about, too, so we stood and talked but neither was much interested in what the other said as we could not get our minds off the shells. I went up a mile to have a look, and could see the Boche coming beyond Essey. Just then five tanks of my right battalion came up so I told them to go back as there were too many shells in the town. The lieutenant in command obeyed. This made me mad, so I had them thrown in front, but there was no danger as the Boche were shelling the next town.

Some Germans came out of dugouts and surrendered to General MacArthur.

I asked him if I could go on and attack the next town, Pannes. He said to move, so I started. All the tanks but one ran out of gas. When we got to Pannes, after moving forward some two miles, the infantry would not go in, so I told the sergeant commanding the tank to go in. He was nervous at being alone so I said I would sit on the roof. This reassured him and we entered the town. Lieutenant Knowles and Tank Sergeant Graham sat on the tail of the tank. I watched one side of the street and they the other. Pretty soon we saw a Boche who threw up his hands. I told Knowles and Graham to dismount and go get him, and I rode on outside the town towards Beney. I saw the paint fly off the side of the tank, and heard machine guns, so I jumped off and got in a shell hole. It was small and the bullets knocked all of the front edges in on me.

Here I was nervous. The tank crew had not seen me get off and the tank went ahead. The infantry was about two miles back of me and did not advance. One runner on my right got hit. If I went back the infantry would think I was running; if I did not they would not support the tank and it might get hit. Besides, machine gun rattles are unpleasant to hear. Finally I decided that I could get back obliquely. So I started and as soon as the machine gun fire opened up I would lie down, and beat the bullets each time. The captain of the dough- boys said he could not advance as the troops on his right were not up. I asked him to send a runner to the tank I had operating to recall it, but he said it was "not his tank," so I went and I burned the breeze too; so did the bullets. I kept the tank between me and the fire as much as possible and finally got it back.

By this time four more of our tanks had come up, but there was no officer with them. I put Lieutenant Knowles, who had taken thirty Boche prisoners instead of the one I sent him to get, in the tank, and asked the infantry if they would follow. They said yes, so I started the tanks. In the main line some of our machine gun crews had pushed out front and one of our tank crews thought they were Boche and began to shoot at them. I had no time to get someone, so went out again to stop the tank crew from firing on our machine gunners. The tanks went on to Beney but the infantry swerved off to the right and I sent a lieutenant out to change direction of the tanks. Then I followed the advance in front. There was not much shooting for our tanks had scared the Boche away.

From here I walked along the line of battle to the left flank at Nonsard where the other battalion was. The captain who would not send the runner was killed at this time. I was very tired indeed, and hungry, as I had lost the sack with my rations and my flask of brandy.

At Nonsard I found twenty-five of our tanks. They had taken the town and only lost four men and two officers, but they were out of gas. All my runners were gone so I started back seven miles to tell them to get some gas. That was the only bad part of the fight. I had had no sleep for two nights and nothing to eat the night before except some crackers I got off a dead Boche. I would have given a lot for a little brandy, but even my water was gone. When I got to Seicheprey it had been raining two hours and the mud was bad. Here I met an officer sightseeing and he gave me a lift. This was lucky as the car got stuck in a jam and went slower than the men on foot in front, and an airplane dropped a bomb on the road and killed two soldiers who had been walking just back of me. I got a motorcycle and got the gas and reported to the Corps.

The 13th we did nothing. I will tell you of the 14th later.

This is a very egotistical account of the affair, full of "I," but it will interest you. I at least proved to my own satisfaction that I have nerve. I was the only officer above the rank of major on the front line except General MacArthur, who never ducked a shell. I wanted to, but it's foolish as it does no good. If they are going to hit you, they will. I had in this action 144 tanks and 33 French tanks. Quite a command. We lost two tanks with direct hits and eight men and three officers; only one killed and one lost an eye.

All the losses were small; absurdly so. The great feat the tanks performed was getting through the mud and trenches. The conditions could not have been worse. Only 40% did it the first day, but we had 80% up by morning. The men were fine, nearly all the officers led the tanks, marching on foot in front of the tanks.

General Rockenbach gave me hell for going up, but it had to be done. At least I will not sit in a dugout and have my men out in the fighting.

I am feeling fine and at present have little to do.

I saved my little map for you as a souvenir. Here are some cap ornaments I got off a dead German. Personally, I never fired a shot except to kill two poor horses with broken legs.

St. Mihiel, the first U.S. tank show, was not a very difficult engagement. The defending German troops were not their elite troops and by the third day the Germans had pulled back to the Hindenburg Line, leaving between our forward lines and the Hindenburg Line a wide no man's land. On that day, the 14th of September, Colonel Patton decided to make a reconnaissance in force in this no man's land, and sent a large force of his light Renault tanks down a ridge running northeast from the little village of Nonsard.

The tanks marched on at a brisk pace for about half a day and came into a wide plain at the end of the ridge. There appeared a provisional squadron [4] of the 2d U.S. Cavalry Regiment [5] on a like mission under the command of Lieutenant Colonel O. P. N. Hazzard. Captain Ernest Harmon, later destined to command the 2d Armored Division in combat in Africa and in France in World War II, commanded a troop in this squadron. This was the

---

[4] A squadron of cavalry was the equivalent of a battalion of infantry.
[5] The regiment comprises three squadrons.

largest unit of United States horse cavalry used in action in World War I. No U.S. horse cavalry units were used in World War II. The 3d U.S. Division in World War II improvised some mounted units in Sicily and used them effectively in the rough terrain of the northwestern part of that island.

Half a mile away toward the Hindenburg Line were spied some German pot-helmets bobbing over the high ground in front. Colonel Patton ordered me to capture these Germans. Trying to recall the best training-camp infantry tactics, I took a squad of men and led them by rushes toward the helmets. We arrived well winded to find that they were already prisoners, and that some dismounted 2d Cavalry soldiers were marching them to the prisoner of war cage. The 2d Cavalrymen had been a little further down the reverse slope of the high ground and could not be seen. This is what might be expected of a tanker trying to act like an infantryman.

In a few minutes, Colonel Patton ordered me to send out a patrol of three tanks. Lieutenant Ted McClure, from Richmond, Virginia, was given the detail and disappeared toward the German lines with his three tanks.

In about an hour, much firing was heard from the direction in which he had gone.

In another hour and a half, McClure returned with a breechblock of a 77. He had hit the Hindenburg Line far ahead of any supporting troops and had come under the direct fire of a German battery. He had charged the battery, putting the guns out of commission, bringing back the breechblock of one of the guns of the battery to substantiate his story. It was a courageous exploit and in keeping with other acts of this officer.

Late that afternoon, the enemy artillery started ranging in on our tanks in no man's land. Orders were received from General Rockenbach to return to our lines. As we passed back along the ridge we had used before, we noticed the towns were burning from enemy artillery fire. Our tanks clanked through burning towns all night long, finally reaching a position at daylight out of enemy artillery range.

Argonne

After a day or two of rest, the tankers from St. Mihiel under Patton's orders entrained for the Argonne show, the

Battle of the Argonne Forest, which was destined to be the last engagement of World War I. The troops were in the usual 40 and 8 cars (forty men or eight horses). The tanks rode lashed in place on flatcars. The destination was a railroad siding a few kilometers south of the little town of Varennes, which lay just east of the Argonne forest.

The tankers arrived at night, and the unloading of the cars in the rain and pitch-black darkness was difficult, though Patton's personal supervision made possible what might have been an impossible feat. As the tanks were driven down the train to the last flatcar to run down the unloading ramp located there, each car would jump off the track at the end opposite the weight of the moving tank. The men learned to take this in their stride, and to lift the ends of the cars back on the tracks if their wheels failed to come to rest on the rails when the tanks had passed.

The unloading ramp was a makeshift sloping pile of railway ties bound together by ropes. One soldier formerly had been a sailor and subsequently a timber topper from the Oregon lumber camps. He was invaluable in making the ramps and would jump in under the moving tanks to throw a half hitch on logs that were slipping under the weight of the vehicles as they moved from the last flatcar to the ground.

When the unloading was completed, the tanks proceeded to a small woods about three kilometers north of the railway siding. This move was made at night and it was impossible to obliterate entirely the tank tracks before daylight came. Colonel Patton sensed the danger of enemy aerial photographic reconnaissance, and moved the tanks to another woods closer to the front, taking great care to have the men strew small branches of trees on the tank tracks leading to the new location. This move saved many casualties, for the first woods were saturated by German artillery shortly after the tanks had left.

Reconnaissance for the Argonne battle was started immediately. The routes of march of the tanks were planned and the terrain over which the battle would be fought was studied from observation posts and by walking over some of the ground near the points of departure.

The Argonne sector had been a quiet one since early in 1914, the start of World War I. It was a rest area and the Germans and French both had sent to this area fatigued

56

troops to recover from the exhaustion of combat. Often in the no man's land between the lines, parties of French and German troops would be seen shooting squirrels.

Some of the tankers' reconnaissance took them into this no man's land and though it was under direct observation by the Germans, and within enemy machine gun range, not a hostile shot was fired. Several patrols, both French and German, had been shot in this no man's land in 1914. They lay undisturbed as they fell nearly four years before. The clothing they wore and the arms they had carried were recognizable, but they were uniformed skeletons. It evidently was not a quiet sector in 1914, and the Americans were to change its character back into its 1914 mold. The Argonne was desperately fought and was the last and most vicious battle the United States Army had in World War I.

Tapes were laid to show the route of march of the tanks to the front line. This was the practice then, for, in general, advances were small and accurately coordinated with pre-designated artillery barrages and the movement of troops on the flanks. Until the final drive came in 1918, a gain of an objective 500 yards in front of the lines was considerable, and might cause as much as 25 per cent casualties to the attacker. The Argonne altered this method of warfare from a static type to one of fluidity similar to that of World War II.

Warning orders from the higher command were received about twenty-four hours in advance of the Argonne jump-off schedule for first light on the morning of September 26, 1918. The battle was bound to be a hard one and I prepared written orders for "A" Company which might be useful if the company commander was an early casualty. This proved to be sound as I was a casualty within an hour after the jump-off.

In World War I the supply of gasoline for tanks was a difficult problem and so tanks carried, up to the very last possible stop, *bidons* (small barrels) of gasoline lashed to the tails of the tanks. Many tanks were hit and burned. On the whole, however, their efficiency was greatly increased by the system of carrying the gasoline forward with the tanks.

Sometimes the best ideas in combat are furnished by enlisted personnel. One of the greatest ideas of World War I, which increased the effectiveness of the tanks at least

25 per cent, was furnished by a private of one of the companies of the old 1st Brigade, Tank Corps. This soldier noticed at St. Mihiel that our tanks were continually breaking down, and were out of action for a long time because repair only took place well behind the lines, and after the lines had moved far ahead. He conceived the idea that it would be desirable to have a repair and salvage tank follow the combat lines of tanks at a distance of about a mile and a half.

The repair and salvage tanks (having duties similar to the modern maintenance tank) carried extra fan belts. Breaking of fan belts was one of the main causes for the Renault tanks being put out of action. Each repair and salvage (maintenance) tank also carried other minor repair equipment. This idea came as a result of the experiences of the St. Mihiel battle and was tried first in the Argonne. Today the modern repair tanks, indispensable to modern tank combat, stem from that soldier's inventive contribution. It is believed that this was the birth of the tank company maintenance section which was used so successfully in World War II and in Korea—the tank retriever concept.

Patton in World War II continually asked junior officers and men for suggestions for improvements because he knew that those intimately working and fighting with tanks would furnish worth-while ideas.

The company orders for "A" Co., 1st Brigade, Tanks, showed some interesting features. They provided for six runners to be with the captain. Runners were used up fast.

Supply was difficult so the tanks carried as much fuel as possible.

All first string tanks with oil and gas on tails. 2 Bidons of 13 gallons on each tail, of each tank. Reserve tanks in addition to oil and gas to have turret filled with bidons of gas.

Here is the reference to the use of the repair and salvage tanks in this the first battle where they were used.

One repair tank with platoon mechanics to follow with repair tools, extra treads, pins, etc. at a distance of 2000 m. behind attacking tanks.

On the night of the 25th of September, the tanks had difficulty getting over a bridge that was under fire about a kilometer south of the jump-off point for the morning attack on the 26th. Colonel Patton, as might be expected, was at the bridge ahead of his tank column, timed the salvos of German 77's and found the rhythm of the fire. By being there personally and in charge, he was able to get the tanks over the bridge in rushes of small groups without a single tank casualty. The military policeman in charge of the bridge was killed just as the last of the American tanks cleared the bridge.

Some of Patton's command lay in waiting the night of the 25th to 26th on a hillside at the Côte de Fourimont. "B" Company attacked in front of the 28th Infantry Division from Pennsylvania; "A" Company in front of the 35th Infantry Division from Kansas, in which former President Truman commanded a battery of artillery.[6]

The barrage that poured down on the Boche for over an hour before the dawn attack was an amazing sight. The flashes of the guns and in some cases the visible explosions of the shells on impact gave a lurid light. The Allied 75 mm. guns extended almost hub to hub for miles, and were firing at a rate that must have been appalling to the Germans. All Allied soldiers offered up thanks that they were not on the receiving end.

"B" Company's tanks got ahead of their infantry and entered the town of Varennes. The battlefield was covered with fog and smoke, making it difficult for the tanks to keep in touch with the doughboys of the 28th Infantry Division, who were attacking north on the eastern edge of the Argonne forest.

One of the officers, Lieutenant Johnny Castles, had his tank hit by a 77 mm. shell from a battery in Varennes, shooting over the sights at point-blank range. His driver, Don Call, escaped to a nearby trench, saw Castles' predicament, and returned under the fire of the German battery. He rescued Castles, who was badly wounded and could not extricate himself from the tank turret, dragging him into the trench and safety. Call received the first Medal of Honor given in the United States Armored forces for this valorous act. Castles recovered from his wounds

---

[6] Both of these divisions were National Guard Divisions.

and practiced law in New York, returning to the Army as a G2 with Armor in World War II.

"A" Company's tanks moved into position on the crest of Vauquois hill. If it had not been for the tapes placed by the Brigade reconnaissance officer it would have been impossible to find that jump-off point because of the fog and the smoke. The tanks, and those on foot leading them, moved through a prepared German machine gun barrage which though disconcerting was not deadly, because Vauquois hill defiladed the line of march. The bullets sounded close and those on foot really crouched as they walked, for they did not know how much margin of safety this defilade gave them.

On arriving at the top of Vauquois, it was found that the hill was half blown away by mines that had been set off by German troops to halt the attack. Later, after the armistice on November 11, 1918, Vauquois became a military curiosity. As has been said, the Argonne front was static for years, and the Germans had made Vauquois an underground hotel. There were many stories of dugouts, some with shower baths, and some with pianos. There was one particular dugout called "The Crown Prince's Dugout." This was furnished in the style of a guest room in a fine hotel.

Resistance of the Germans was fanatical, for these were elite troops, the famous 1st Prussian Guard. In some instances they continued manning their machine guns trained on our infantry while our tanks ran over their machine gun nests and crushed the German crews.

There were snipers on Vauquois hill who had heavy armor plate that was hung from their shoulders and would turn shell fragments and even rifle bullets if they struck a glancing blow. This German sniper's armor weighed twenty pounds and only protected the front upper portion of the body. It was useful to a sniper shooting from a trench with his body only half out of the excavation.

Lieutenant Ted McClure some days later was fighting his tank on the plateau near Cheppy. His driver was green, and when a German projectile from an "elephant gun" [7]

---

[7] An enlarged shoulder rifle shot from a bipod support. It weighed about fifty pounds and fired an armor-piercing shell the approximate size of a man's thumb. It was capable of piercing the armor of a Renault tank.

went through the turret, he panicked and stalled the engine. McClure cranked the motor from inside the turret, a difficult feat. Before he accomplished this, the tank was twice more pierced by the "elephant gun," but neither McClure nor his driver were hit.

Many of General Patton's old officers of World War I were anxious to serve again with him in World War II. Some were lucky enough to get under his command the second time. He helped many others to get back in the service from civilian life, even though he could not find a place for them near him.

It was characteristic that through the years between the World Wars his old officers held him in friendly esteem, and that he kept in touch with those who had served under him. Like old fire horses at the sound of the bell, those who could serve asked his help in getting back into the service. Some of those old tank corps men who kept in close contact with him are mentioned here.

David M. Bowes was one who had distinguished himself for valor in World War I.

Another, Arthur Snyder, commanded a tank in the Argonne battle. The tank in which he had two successive drivers killed in one day at the Argonne in the fall of 1918 now stands as a monument in the street that leads to headquarters at Fort Meade, Maryland, the home of Second Army Headquarters. This battle-scarred old machine looks like a sieve. Snyder commanded a tank battalion in World War II in Italy.

From Washington, D.C. there was an upstanding young lieutenant, James P. Nolan, whom the old officers of World War I tanks always contact when passing through town.

There were two other young soldiers who received battlefield commissions for leadership in the face of the enemy. One was Dave Winton who has served the Armed Forces in a civilian capacity on many occasions in the last ten years. Dave Winton was unable, because of the disability resulting from wounds, to get back into the service. The other young soldier was Horatio Rogers, who received a battlefield commission in 1918 for outstanding performance. In 1918 he was too young to receive his commission and had to wait a month or two for his battlefield promotion from sergeant to lieutenant to come under the law. He was, in 1942, Dean of the Law School of

61

American University in Washington, D.C., but returned to the Army in that year.

Lieutenant Leslie Buckler, who succeeded the author as company commander of Company "A," is now a professor in the Virginia Law School, Charlottesville, Virginia. Buckler, who fought "A" Company with great skill until he was evacuated as a casualty, tried to get into the service during World War II but his age prevented it.

Two outstanding tank drivers of the old tank corps, who are now living in Washington are Norman Cann, a successful lawyer, and Bathurst Chambliss, a businessman. Chambliss served in Armor during World War II.

Loyall F. Sewall, an officer under Patton in World War I, returned to serve under him again in World War II in the Third Army.

In World War I there was no radio communication between the tanks, and the only way that messages could be transmitted to tanks was by word of mouth, which involved considerable risk when they were in action. The officers had to be on foot to be heard. A planned method of communication was by flag signals, but unfortunately this failed to work. It was found when the flags were poked out through the hole in the turret of the tank, machine gun bullets shot off the flag as fast as it appeared. The would-be signaler invariably ended up with spinters in his hand.

One planned way for a tank in action to communicate with headquarters at the rear was to release a pigeon with a message tied to its leg.

The officers of the 1st Brigade, Tank Corps, which was previously explained, comprised Companies A to F of light Renault tanks, were supplied at the beginning of the Argonne show with wicker baskets containing two pigeons for each command tank. The wicker baskets were about six inches high and over a foot square. The only place to put these baskets in the interior of the little Renault tank was on the turret floor. The gunner, crowded by everything in the turret, including guns and ammunition, was forced to stand on the wicker baskets. Unfortunately, the designers had not planned for such an eventuality so nearly every pigeon basket in the first five minutes of action was flattened out, and, of course, the pigeons were flattened with the baskets. Thus, no pigeon messages got back from the tanks to headquarters.

Pigeon gas masks were issued—impregnated Bull Durham sacks. It would have taken Houdini to have put one on a pigeon in the dark and crowded turret of a tank in combat.

Pigeons survived in one tank. This tank was found by an officer in the Argonne show, broken down. The crew had had no food for two days. The lines had moved far ahead. The sergeant tank commander said, "Sir, may I release my pigeons? They are starving."

A pigeon's life in the old tank corps was risky.

One story that was going the rounds tells of a British headquarters group crowded around the dovecot waiting for word from the tanks. Finally a pigeon flew in; the message was eagerly removed. It read: *Fair fed up with carrying this bloody bird.*

Major Sereno Brett, U.S.A., who commanded one of the battalions of the Renault tanks in Patton's 1st Brigade Tank Corps, through great effort saved one pigeon to dispatch to the dovecot at U.S. Army Headquarters. The message was written, tied on the pigeon's leg, and the bird released. It was confused by the rough tank ride and resentful of the firing in the tank and flew into a nearby tree. Major Brett threw sticks at it. It finally took off and flew toward Germany.

Patton was on foot directing the tanks the first day of the Argonne battle. Our infantry was not moving forward. He ordered those near him to charge a machine gun nest that was holding up the advance. Patton led the charge. He found after a short time that he and his runner, Angelo, were all that were left. It was a suicidal mission and he was hit in the leg by the machine gun and fell in a shell hole. He said that on this charge he seemed to be looking at himself as if he were a small detached figure on the battlefield, watched from a cloud on high by Confederate kinsmen and his grandfather whose daguerreotypes he had studied as a boy.

Angelo used his own first-aid packet to staunch the blood from the severe thigh wound made by the machine gun bullet. He and Patton lay nonchalantly in the shell hole taking potshots at German planes until the medicos came.

Patton and the writer were hit early the same day and finally evacuated to a base hospital about fourteen miles south of Dijon.

On October 2, 1918 Patton wrote to his wife a letter which reads in part:

Here I am at Base Hospital No. 49, missing half my bottom but otherwise all right.

We stayed at the evacuation hospital just back of the line from the night of the 26th till the night of the 29th. Then we left by ambulance to the train. The train was composed of boxcars and we were put in racks three high. I got a top. We were in stretchers and they are not comfortable. We left by slow freight at 7 P.M. and got here at 11 A.M. on the 30th. It was a pretty tiresome trip but as it was raining there was no dust. They fed us once during the trip on coffee and molasses and bread. It was good enough but not up to the pictures of Red Cross trains. This hospital is pretty nice, but there are only two nurses for 50 officers. I got washed today for the first time and I am the senior.

Still it might be worse, though how I can't see. The hole in my hip is almost as large as a teacup, and they have to leave it open.

I just wrote Boyd to come and have a look at this place and get some books to the men and let them smoke.

A lot of funny things happen. One of my captains came to in a first aid station and saw a chaplain leaning over him and a man with a big hypo sticking stuff into his stomach. He thought he was dead and they were embalming him. One fellow died in the next bed to mine, his back was broken. It is strange that the "gentlemen" make less noise over their wounds than the others. But there is little howling. Even in the train I heard hardly any noise.

There is a fellow next to me with a smashed hip. He suffers a lot but jokes. I suffer none at all except when they dress the wounds.

Still, we broke the Prussian Guard with the tanks, so it is all fine.

War produces fantasies as well as facts, and the tank captain who thought he was being embalmed, and who later recovered, got many a good laugh at his own expense from his friends in the tank corps. I have no definite recollection of this incident, because at the time I was out of my head from the concussive effect of a sniper's bullet in my skull, but I was informed that I was this confused officer.

As soon as Patton's wounds and mine were sufficiently healed to permit them to be sewn up, Patton got a car and together we deserted from the hospital to return to troops. Together we were forgiven by Pershing upon Patton's personal report to him.

While we were in the hospital together, Patton often talked over Lt. McClure's exploits at St. Mihiel, when he had broken through the main resistance and could have slashed into the enemy's rear if he had had sufficient strength. He decided that the next time we would employ more tanks than the three under McClure on his reconnaissance at St. Mihiel, when he captured the battery in the Hindenburg Line, and achieve a real break-through. The war ended before this could be tried, for the opportunity did not come in the Argonne, the last battle of the war. Because of casualties, never did the 1st Brigade, Tank Corps, have enough operative tanks, or men to man them, for a break-through.

The last of World War I saw open tactics come into their own again. The Germans were withdrawing too rapidly to build a formidable trench system and the Allies were pushing them to the utter exhaustion of the attacking troops. The casualties of the 1st Brigade Tank Corps in this one battle were close to 90 per cent, but the Germans were in worse condition. However, our 1st Brigade Tanks were so depleted they could not exploit this ideal situation for a real tank break-through. This was their last action in World War I. The American troops continued to drive forward and with their cutting of the Sedan-Metz railroad the war ended.

The Germans in the 1st World War were not quick to grasp the potentialities of the tank, and one of the reasons was that the tank they developed and used to a limited extent was not efficient. It was called the Elfrieda, and at the allied counter-attack at Villa Coublai near Amiens in the Somme during May, 1918, some of the Elfrieda tanks were overrun and we had a chance to study them. The Elfrieda was about as maneuverable as a mechanical hippopotamus. It was unwieldy and bogged down in country where a good tank should not get stuck. The British and the French were far ahead of the Germans in tanks and in their employment at that time.

Near the end of the war, and at the start of the Argonne show, as has been said, the Americans threw in the six companies of tanks under General Patton, then Colonel, which comprised the U.S. 1st Brigade, Tank Corps. The Germans by this time had evidently changed their minds, but it takes some time to develop armored units, and until then they had not taken the tank in earnest. In one of the reports of the Argonne made by a German officer to his higher command was this statement: *The battle started with the allied infantry preceded by myriads of baby tanks spewed from the broth of hell.* Patton's tanks engendered this report.

The portrait of Patton would not be complete without the story of his battles of World War I, for he here displayed the leadership that later was to spark the magnificent campaigns of the United States Third Army in World War II.

He was always more interested in combat leadership than rank. The quotations from a letter written November 18, 1918 to his wife are revealing:

> The most terrible thing has happened to me. I heard last night that I will not get the D.S.C.
>
> I woke up all last night feeling that I was dying, and then it would occur to me what had happened. I cannot realize it yet. It was the whole war to me, all I can ever get out of two years away from you. But I will be God-damned if I am beat yet. I do not know what I will do, but I will do something.
>
> General Rockenbach thinks my colonelcy is a compensation, but it is nothing. I had rather be a second lieutenant with a D.S.C. than a general without it.
>
> I am sorry to bother you, but I had to get it off my chest and onto yours even at long range by letter.

However his gloomy thoughts were unfounded, for he got the D.S.C.

We felt that we were making the world safe for democracy in winning World War I. When the allied nations won World War II again in 1945, we were not so sure that there would be no further wars. But we are not a military nation; war is a headache; we had taken our aspirin so we allowed the most powerful military force that any nation in the history of the world had ever built to disintegrate. Professionally we are not military-minded. We are businessmen, hence, we quickly returned to business as usual.

In the foreseeable future, officers will be needed who can win in fighting modern war; tough, aggressive, skillful killers who can lead our soldiers in battle to destroy the enemy with a minimum of casualties to our own men. War is not pretty; it is not pleasant; discipline and drive are uncomfortable; but we should be thankful that our country produced a Patton for World War II.

There is a manuscript book of poems which were written by Patton while he was on active duty in the U.S. Army. In the short preface of these poems he said, "These rhymes were written (over a period of years) by a man who, having seen something of war, is more impressed with the manly virtues it engenders than with the necessary and much exaggerated horrors attendant upon it. They are offered to the public in the hope that they may help to counteract the melancholy viewpoint of many of our poets of the great wars." Generally, they were written for the definite purpose of urging preparedness and for glorifying the deeds of soldiers. He felt that in the troubled times in which he lived the sacrifices of soldiers to preserve the freedom of mankind should be exalted. He said, "We should not dwell on sorrow that those slain in battle have died, but rather be thankful and happy that they have lived."

The two Patton poems that follow were inspired by incidents that occurred during action in World War I. The second poem was based on an incident that occurred in the action of the 1st Brigade, Tank Corps.

TO OUR FIRST DEAD

(Three soldiers killed by the Germans in a Trench raid in the St. Mihiel sector, November 1917.)

They died for France like countless thousands more
Who, in this war, have faltered not to go
At duty's bidding, even unto death.
And yet, no deaths which history records,
Were fought with greater consequence than theirs.
A nation shuddered as their spirits passed;

And unborn babies trembled in the womb,
In sympathetic anguish at their fate.

Far from their homes and in ungainful strife
They gave their all, in that they gave their life,
While their young blood, shed in this distant land,
Shall be more potent than the dragon's teeth
To raise up soldiers to avenge their fall.

Men talked of sacrifice, but there was none;
Death found them unafraid and free to come
Before their God. In righteous battle slain
A joyous privilege theirs; the first to go
In that their going doomed to certain wrath
A thousand foeman, for each drop they gave
Of sacramental crimson, to the cause.

And so their youthful forms all dank and stiff,
All stained with tramplings in unlovely mud,
We laid to rest beneath the soil of France
So often honored with the hero slain;
Yet never greatlier so than on this day,
When we interred our first dead in her heart.

There let them rest, wrapped in her verdant arms,
Their task well done. Now, from the smoke-veiled sky,
They watch our khaki legions pass to certain victory,
Because of them who showed us how to die.

BILL

(The incidents recounted below are true, and occurred in
one of the tanks of the 1st Brigade, Tank Corps, during
the Argonne offensive, September 1918.)

Bill, he kept racin' the motor,
For fear that the damned thing would die,
While I fiddled 'round with the breech block
And wished for a piece of your pie.

It's funny the way it affects you,
When you're waiting the signal to go
There's none of the high moral feeling
About which the newspapers blow.

For myself, I always is hungry,
While Bill thought his spark plugs was foul.
Some guys talks o' sprees they has been on,
And one kid, what's croaked, thought of school.

At last I seen Number One signal: [8]
I beat on the back o' Bill's neck.[9]
He slipped her the juice and she started,
—And Bill he ain't never come back.

The first news we had of the Boches
Was shot splinters, right in the eye.
I cussed twice as loud as the Colonel,
And forgot all about the old pie.

A Boche he runs out with a tank gun:
I gave him H.E.[10] in the guts.
You ought to have seen him pop open!
They sure was well fed, was them sluts.

We wiped out two nests with caseshot,
And was just gettin' into a third,
When we plunked in a hole full of water.
—That God-damned Bill sure was a bird.

He hollers to me: "Frank, you're married:
If only one gets out, it's you,"
And he rammed me up out of the turret . .
I guess that's about all I knew.

A stinkin' whizz-bang beaned me,
Or I might of rescued Bill,
But it's too late now. He's sleepin'
By our tank, on that God-damned hill.

---

[8] Number One is the platoon leader's tank, from which all signals are given. Arm signals from tank to tank were used when the enemy fire was not so deadly as to preclude this method of communication. Often an officer would have to dismount and give orders verbally to another tank crew, for it was difficult to attract the attention of the crew of another tank in battle.

[9] The tank corps signal to move forward is repeated kicks on the back of the driver's neck or back. The noise in a moving tank is so great that the voice cannot be heard; hence, all commands are given by touch signals.

[10] High Explosive.

They give him a Medal of Honor,
For savin' me for you,
So if it's a boy we'll name it Bill.
It's the least and the most we can do.

4.   Between the Wars

The Tank

PATTON returned with the 1st Brigade, Tank Corps, to
the United States in 1919 and went with his tanks to
Camp Meade, Maryland, now a permanent fort. He was
eager to continue his work on the development of the concept of armor, mobile warfare, and the tactics and technique of tank employment in combat. This was premature,
however. Patton struggled for about one year with his
rapidly deteriorating organization; then he decided to return to his beloved horse cavalry. Since the appropriation
for the year 1920 had been cut to the absurb amount of
$500, and since he felt that to stay with armor would
"break his heart," he made this move. The Army, Congress, and other related agencies, were unable at this time
to visualize the tremendous potential in this new arm.
However, he never lost touch with armor and for the next
five years, until he was transferred to Hawaii, he was an
unofficial member of a tank board.

During the time Patton worked actively with a tank
board, an inventor named Christie produced the chassis
with sprocket wheels that bears his name. Patton was delighted with it from the first, and after he tested it, he invited seven generals to Camp Meade to try it out. Mrs.
Patton went with him to watch the test, in a big hat and
organdy dress, as they were to have the generals to lunch
afterwards.

On reaching Camp Meade, George Patton gave a short
talk, saying that the tank would go at thirty miles an hour
through sand, would knock down a tree, break through a
small building, and end the ride by sliding down over a
sand bluff. The tank itself had no armor and little super-
structure, but was in effect a platform mounted on the

famous sprocket wheels. He asked who would like to ride first, but no one answered. After waiting a suitable time, he said, "Very well, Mrs. Patton will be glad to demonstrate it." She was hoisted onto the platform between the outspread legs of the fattest sergeant who could be found, who put his arms around her waist. Two other soldiers held her feet, and they started on the ride. The dust was thick and the organdy dress and big hat were casualties. At the end Patton asked again, "Now, who would like to ride?" Finally one general spoke up, "Thanks, we have seen enough, we shall recommend that the Christie be adopted."

The Germans were far behind the Allies in World War I, and slow to realize the value of the tank. The French then had a well-developed tank corps with their heavy Schneider tank and their Renault light two-man tank. The British had the Mark 8 and Mark 4 heavy tanks, and a somewhat lighter Whippet tank that could cross a wider trench than the light tank of the French.

The late General Heinz Guderian, World War II Panzer commander, published a book called *Panzer Leader* which shows how the Germans got ready between World War I and World War II to use the break-through of the tank. The Germans at the beginning of World War II were highly successful in their use, and the Battle of France was won in the break-through of the German tanks to the coast. This was accomplished despite the fact that the French tanks were superior in quality and quantity at that time. Here, mass employment of armor proved to be sound doctrine.

The first opportunity afforded Patton to give expression to his ideas on the employment of armor as distinct from the use of tanks was in the Tennessee maneuvers of 1941. Just prior to these maneuvers a certain opposing division commander was quoted in the press as offering fifty dollars' reward for the capture of Patton. General Patton's reaction was prompt and typical. He accepted the challenge and offered a hundred dollars for the capture of his opponent. So much was this played up in the press and so enthusiastically did the troops, especially those of the 2d Armored Division, enter into the spirit of the thing, that the originator sought out his old friend Patton and suggested that the whole thing be called off. Patton, as always the good sport, readily agreed to do so.

In these maneuvers, so aggressive and so disruptive were his tactics in the employment of the 2d Armored Division that each of the several exercises was forced to terminate from twelve to twenty-four hours ahead of the two- to four-day allotted period.

The lessons to be learned from this debut of American armor were apparently lost to much of the "high command." Instead of seeking to "harness the tide" to our own advantage, every effort seemed bent on "stemming the tide." For example, the epidemic of antitank measures, the doctrine of tank destroyers, and the accentuation of the technical and mechanical weaknesses of tanks and armor were exploited rather than the devastating shock action inherent in armor. Likewise, the remark, attributed to those in control of the subsequent (Louisiana) maneuvers, to the effect that "Armor would be used properly in these maneuvers and Patton won't be allowed to run all over the countryside as he did in the Tennessee maneuvers," was current throughout the maneuvers and came to a climax in the role assigned to the 2d Armored Division in the final exercise of the series. The plan called for the 2d Armored to advance on a single hard road behind an infantry division which was teamed with it in a provisional corps. The infantry division was to deploy and attack during the night, open a gap in the opposing line, and let the 2d Armored through at daylight. The ground, drenched with three days of torrential rain, was almost impassable to foot troops. Consequently, every vehicle of every unit participating on either side was on the single hard road. It was obvious to Patton and to Major General Charles L. Scott, who commanded the Corps, that the armor would never reach the gap, let alone get through it, and they protested strongly against this misuse of armor.

Their protest was rejected and all preparations were made to try to carry out the prescribed operation. A few hours before the start the road had become so congested that even the infantry division could not get through to its appointed place and it became apparent at last to the "high command" that the armor could not be used in that way and they acceded to Scott's and Patton's proposal to move around the flank. In a couple of hours the division was completely regrouped, new orders were issued, and Patton took the 2d Armored Division on a hundred-mile sweep into Texas and came in on the deep flank and rear of the enemy in the vicinity of Shreveport. There again, except for umpire ruling, the maneuver would have ended ahead of time. Again these lessons seemed lost and Patton was criticized for a few stray tanks which, because of mechanical failures, were left marking the path of his decisive flank march.

This was a Pyrrhic victory for Patton. While in the enemy's rear he was completely cut off and out of gas. The none too friendly control headquarters took this attitude, "Now Georgie has gotten himself into this mess, let him stay there out of gas." Never a man to accept defeat, he nevertheless did procure gas in the most unorthodox manner and as the maneuver ended, his division had captured the enemy's capital—Shreveport.

In the next maneuvers, those in North Carolina, with the experience gained in Tennessee and Louisiana, the 2d Armored was a first-class team and it operated intelligently and purposefully under the skillful direction and planning of Patton. Again a negative tone to the appraisal by the "high command," the principal comment was that such tactics resulted in a lot of small fights throughout the entire battle area and that was no way to fight a war!

To show his confidence in his conception of armor mobility and in his division, he marched it back to Fort Benning, some three hundred miles, with only one long halt of two and a half hours, an unequaled feat at that stage of armor. He published an order complimenting the division on its fine performance throughout the combined maneuvers period and expressed his satisfaction with its training progress by saying it had met successfully "every test short of war." This order was signed and published December 6, 1941, the day before Pearl Harbor.

The cool attitude of the "high command" toward armor did not prevent Patton from continuing to develop his ideas and his principles for the employment of armor which were and are still sound. At the Desert Training Center at Indio, California, he had a further opportunity to round out these ideas and to fix them more firmly in his own mind and in the minds of those working under him. The essence of these views is evident in his use of armor in Morocco, in Sicily, and in the Third Army operations in Europe.

In Tunisia, in Italy, and in Europe, other than in the Third Army, the other school of thought often prevailed and armor was employed piecemeal. A realization of what armor could accomplish if properly employed might well have strengthened the operation of the Third Army to the point where the probability of the Battle of the Bulge would never have arisen.

Had he lived, he would have continued, and with reason, to bring about proper realization of the correct employment of armor. He would have been years ahead in his thinking on the proper balance of armor with those other elements so essential in modern warfare. He would have arrived at the proper balance necessary in a modern striking force or task force utilizing air, armor, air-borne, infantry and the atomic weapon.

Because of niggardly appropriations, little was done to develop tanks, or equip armored units, between World War I and World War II by the U.S. Army, though many in the Army wanted to do so. The Germans, however, had become convinced that mobile warfare, whose greatest asset were tanks and mechanization, was to be the foundation of successful modern warfare.

Because of General Guderian's break-through to the coast in the Battle of France, our U.S. Army came into World War II with the memory of that battle vividly in mind. Our high command started to create many armored divisions. Plans were laid in 1942 for at least twenty armored U.S. divisions.

In much of the fighting in 1942 and 1943 in Tunisia, the tanks of the 1st Armored Division were employed in small detachments and piecemeal in support of U.S. and British infantry units. History repeats itself, for this is what happened to our Federal Cavalry for the first two years of our Civil War.

This completely destroyed the true function of armor, the break-through. Policy was reviewed in Washington in the light of the then current Tunisian operations. It was decided not to continue with making more armored divisions. In fact, only 16 divisions of the originally planned 20 were created. Therefore, armor did not perform its expected function. The circumstances already set forth prohibited its proper use.

Then the turn of the wheel—the battle to retake Europe was launched on D-Day—armor again had its field day. Patton with his armored sweeps, achieved after penetrations of the German lines, held the enthralled interest of the public in America and England. Possibly some German again may have referred to our tanks as "spewed from the broth of hell." All wished we had more tanks, for that would have shortened the war and saved our boys' lives. But armored divisions cannot be created overnight.

Then came Korea with terrain similar to the Apennine Mountains in Italy, where a division front in some defile might be one tank wide. That tank front would be the one tank on a road in the pass with the division strung out for miles behind. Hence, based on this experience, value of tanks is again questioned. Memories again grow short. Their worth is forgotten.

But if we are forced again to fight, there is much country on this planet where armor can break through, and there many of the battles of the future may be fought. Armor will again come into its own. The tanks are invaluable life-savers, because they can attack, break through, destroy communications and rear installations, and trap the enemy.

Now that A-Bomb and H-Bomb weapons are available, the role of armor is more important than ever. Armor offers fair protection to the crew against blast and the effects of radiation; at least a tank crew is immeasurably better protected than the foot soldier.

Further, armor is the only arm that can stay dispersed, then quickly concentrate to break through, and then promptly disperse again to fan out and cut the communications of the enemy. This ability to change speedily from concentration to dispersion reduces the time of concentration, and vulnerability to the A-Bomb is in direct proportion to the concentration of the target.

During the Second World War in Italy, where the Apennine Mountains made bad tank country, we had Lieutenant General Willis D. Crittenberger, an experienced armor man, commanding the U.S. IV Corps, and we had a fine fighting 1st Armored Division under the late Major General Vernon Prichard. Armor could not be employed for its main purpose, the break-through, until our troops slugged their way out of the Apennines and into the Po Valley.

But when the 1st Armored Division debouched into the Po Valley, and into good tank country, armor did what it was supposed to do. They charged ahead many miles a day, trapping whole enemy corps. In going into Milan, a complete German corps headquarters passed the vehicles of our IV Corps headquarters on the road. The Germans were going toward the rear to surrender to anyone who would accept them. They were marching in good discipline, but no U.S. troops were in charge of them. It was an amazing sight to behold.

Patton was the greatest modern exponent of armored penetration, where armor is poured through a small gap in the enemy lines and spreads beyond the gap to cut communications and the supply routes of the enemy. One of his officers in Europe nervously asked him, "General, how about our flanks?" to which he replied, "Let the Germans worry about our flanks." Chances of flank attack can be taken more readily with armor than with infantry, for the tank is not as vulnerable to small arms fire.

Peacetime Schools

The American Army had already initiated a rather well thought out scheme of higher military education before World War I. This was greatly improved following that war and Patton benefited from it as did everyone who had the opportunity of participating in the project. As a major he graduated from the Advanced Course at the Cavalry School, Fort Riley, in June 1923. At that school he was very active, participating in polo and hunting, but, never-the less, his interests did include weapons and tactics. Lieutenant Paul M. Robinett, later retired as a brigadier general because of a wound received while leading CCB (Combat Command B), 1st Armored Division in North Africa, was an instructor in the machine gun and recalls that Patton asked for personal instruction on Saturday afternoons because he felt the machine gun was, at that time, the greatest killer.

Patton was given to swashbuckling among the lieutenants, of which Robinett was one, and to keep himself in practice conducted a fencing course for them in the attic of the quarters in which they were living. As they said, he always carried a bucket of blood with him wherever he went, but before the senior officers he was more circumspect. Many admired him greatly and fully expected him to go places.

Patton went directly from Fort Riley to the Command and General Staff School and graduated in 1924. There he became well acquainted with many selected officers with

76

whom he had not previously served. He also saw others with whom he was more familiar and formed a fuller appreciation of their capabilities.

Inasmuch as he was selected for the Army War College, where he graduated in 1932, his work must have shown high promise. At that time the Army War College was the highest military school where selected officers of all the arms and services, as well as the Navy and Marine Corps, came together for schooling in the very highest aspects of national defense and the military art. Barring ill health and accidents, the successful graduates of this college were destined to play an important role in war if it should arise.

Patton never appeared to have any great ambition to work upon the intricate planning problems of the War Department General Staff. He much preferred troop duty. However, he held an important position in the Office of the Chief of Cavalry in the years between the two World Wars and was on the General Staff in the Hawaiian Department. Obviously, Patton preferred the life in camp, drill field, and maneuvers, to humdrum service in an office. Even when he was in the office of the Chief of Cavalry he spent much of his time riding. He was always a strong competitor in numerous horse shows, polo matches, and hunts along the Eastern seaboard.

Peacetime Posts and Sports

Patton served at several Cavalry posts between the wars, including two additional tours of duty with the 3d Cavalry Regiment at Fort Myer, Virginia. One of the frequent duties of the cavalry stationed there was to act as burial detail for officers interred in Arlington Cemetery. This duty involved the escorting of the caisson on which the body rested from Union Station in Washington to the cemetery. There was little excitement in these trips, never made at a faster pace than a decorous trot.

One day Major Patton, on one of these burial details, became bored and ordered the pace increased to the gallop when they arrived at the unpaved roads near the cemetery. The unusual excitement of the gallop became too much for the funeral horses pulling the caisson and they ran away.

In the middle twenties he captained the Army polo team in Hawaii and they won the Inter-Island championship for the first time in the twenty-five years of competition. He was then rated a six-goal man. It was during this period that he seemed deliberately to foster the impression that he was only what was then called "a riding Cavalryman" with no intellectual interests. Yet, he actually was delving deeply into military history and writing prodigiously.

He believed that an officer should play games that involved danger and quick judgment. Polo and fox hunting were training media. He captained many U.S. Army polo teams and fox hunted whenever he could. He has said that the sports most useful to an officer are those with a spice of danger.

At the end of Patton's tour of duty—1925-1928—at Schofield Barracks, Hawaii, the Division Commander, Major General W. R. Smith, called in Patton to read to him a derogatory report. Regulations required all such reports to be read to officers by those who commanded them. The report read, "This man would be invaluable in time of war but is a disturbing element in time of peace." Patton said to his wife that he considered this a compliment.

On a later tour of duty at Fort Myer, Patton gave a talk to the Army officers about polo being a very expensive game, and said that the army was privileged to be able to play it because it was fine training for leadership. This talk was given before the second game that was played that season at Fort Myer. He said, "If you are privileged to have a thing, you must take care of it. Mrs. Patton, the children and I replaced the divots after the first game. Hereafter all players will go over the field and replace the divots after each game." He always told all players to go to the stables after each game and see that their ponies were properly cared for.

George Patton prayed before all his battles. He was in the habit of praying all his life. When things that were important to him arose, he sought the help of his Maker. One day Mrs. Patton found him kneeling at his bedside praying with his boots and spurs on. When he had finished, she asked him what he had been praying for and he said, "I have been praying for help in the polo game."

"Did you pray to win?" said Mrs. Patton.

"Hell, no," replied Patton, "I was praying to do my best."

Sergeant George Meeks came with Patton from the 10th

Cavalry Regiment[1] in 1936 and was with General Patton as his orderly until his death in 1945. Meeks says that after he learned what the General wanted, which only took a short time, he was never reprimanded during his entire period of service with General Patton. Meeks soon learned that General Patton was generous to a fault to those who worked with him, though always extremely strict in connection with the wearing of the uniform. Patton would "tell him what he had to tell him and that was all, he was through with it."

During one tour of duty at Fort Myer in the late 1930's, the Patton's third assignment at that post, Colonel and Mrs. Patton were joint masters of the hard-riding Cobbler Hunt which covered some of the roughest fox-hunting country in Virginia.

I have often seen Patton in the hunting field pass by the low spots in the fence, in favor of a high place with an unknown landing on the far side. He was steeling himself to danger.

After his final tour of duty at Ft. Myer, Patton again served in Hawaii as G2 for General Drum. Scorning both the slow, prosaic Army transport service and commercial liners, Patton decided to sail over in his own boat. Patton bought an old schooner, the *Arcturus,* forty feet on the water line, studied navigation for two months, and he and Mrs. Patton, with the misgivings of their friends, sailed the boat to Hawaii from the West Coast of the United States, hitting the Islands on the nose.

Patton had never studied navigation before making this trip and he felt it was imperative that he, as owner and commander of the boat, should be able to navigate. He went at it with his usual thoroughness and zeal, but to get actual sights of the sun with the sextant and to bring it down to the horizon was impossible where he was stationed at the time. He overcame this, however, by driving sixty miles every morning before breakfast, to a spot where he could get a glimpse of the sun and bring it down to the horizon.

The crew was made up of three friends, Mr. and Mrs. Gordon C. Prince of Massachusetts, Francis P. Graves of California, and Joseph Ekeland, a Swedish sailor and rigger.

---

[1] A former Negro Cavalry Regiment. This was prior to the integration of races within units.

About the second or third day out on the trip to Hawaii, on taking the morning sights Patton could not make his agree with those taken by Gordon Prince. The figures seemed right but Gordon Prince noticed that the observed altitude was quite different. Before taking sights, it is usual to check the sextant for index or reflection error, in case it should have got out of adjustment since last used. Prince checked Patton's sextant and found it was way out of kilter. Patton had never tried to adjust a sextant before, but he spent the whole morning on the cabin roof taking it apart, and would not come down for lunch. By afternoon it was reassembled and in perfect working order with no error whatsoever.

A radio had been installed on board, chiefly to be able to get the time ticks with which to check the chronometer. Patton had spent a good deal of time fussing around with this set, and had a man down to put it in perfect order just before they started. Somehow or other, he could never seem to get a time tick at noon, and there was a good deal of cursing going on, and fiddling around with various dials. Finally Prince tried it one day and found that the machine worked perfectly, but Patton had evidently been expecting an entirely different set of signals from those usually sent out. His sailing companions accused him of expecting the announcer to say, "Good morning, folks, it is now noon!"

The *Arcturus* had a fair weather sail down-wind all the way with the best of weather, and everyone was in top form. Every evening after supper Bea would read to them the Glencannon stories written by Guy Gilpatrick. She had a fine Scottish accent, and by the time the *Arcturus* raised the Hawaiian Islands, everybody aboard, even Joe, was speaking with a decided burr. There was a lot of poetry recited on the trip. Prince thought he was familiar with Kipling, but Patton knew two poems for every one Prince remembered. During this tour of duty in Hawaii they sailed to Fanning and Palmyra Islands and at the end brought the *Arcturus* back to the West Coast where they sold her. Their son, George, then thirteen, was a member of the crew on these two voyages.

The year after he had been to Honolulu with Patton, Prince was working on his boat in a boatyard in Beverly, Massachusetts. Some youngster with a .22 long rifle took a shot at him from a distance and winged him in the neck.

It went in one side, missed the jugular vein, bumped his windpipe hard, and lodged against the other jugular. Dr. Johnson yanked it out at the Beverly Hospital, and Prince was as good as ever except that he had to live on milk punches for two days—a very pleasant convalescence. Somehow or other, this got on the front page of the papers, and Patton saw it in Honolulu. Prince received a telegram through military channels as follows: SORRY YOU GOT SHOT. NEXT TIME MARRY THE GIRL. PATTON.

While G2 in Hawaii, from 1935 to 1937, Patton wrote a paper saying that an attack on Pearl Harbor by the Japanese was feasible and would be disastrous to us. But to the American public war seemed far away.

5.   The Coming of World War II

WHEN World War II descended upon us, Patton again wished to be in command of a fighting unit and had made arrangements, if he was not given a fighting command in the American Army, to transfer to the Canadian Army. There he had been promised a fighting unit with command in the rank of a major.

From his last cavalry station he was transferred to Fort Benning, Georgia, to command one of the tank brigades of the 2d Armored Division. Tank brigades were later called Combat Commands, and each armored division had two Combat Commands instead of one brigade. Eventually Patton was made division commander of the 2d Armored Division. This division was a great incubator for generals. More than thirty generals, at one time or another, served in the 2d Armored Division in subordinate ranks. Patton commanded it a long time, and he impressed his personality on the division. Truly this outfit exemplified the principle that a command quickly becomes the embodiment of the commanding officer. Patton often said to his subordinate commands, "Remember that your command is not only yours, but it is you."

Those who have commanded the 2d Armored Division since World War II wrote frequently to Mrs. Patton, prior to her untimely death, to report to her the news of the division. It was "his" division and those who commanded it felt an urge to report to Mrs. Patton as they would to him if he had been alive.

Patton was an enthusiastic disciplinarian. He knew that the time was short to train the civilians turned soldier. Likewise, he realized that discipline saved lives. On one of the maneuvers in the United States in 1941, his armored columns had gathered in great congestion at a crossroads. Such bunching of vehicles presents a remunerative target for either enemy air or artillery and pays big dividends in casualties. The first that those on maneuvers knew that he was aware of the bunching of the vehicles at the crossroads, was when a puddle-jumping plane dived at the vehicles and General Patton screamed from the plane, "Get those goddamn tanks off the roads and into the bushes." The tanks scattered immediately and the soldiers and officers realized that Patton was likely to appear at any time, and from any direction, and when he did he would speak out.

Patton always admitted mistakes and would give full publicity to his apologies. This was one of the characteristics that raised him in the esteem of all who served with him.

On one occasion at Benning he severely reprimanded two young reserve officers for what he believed to be a failure in their duty. Later the same day he found that he had been mistaken. There was a meeting of all the officers of the 2d Armored Division for a lecture the next day. Patton opened the lecture by saying that he had reprimanded the two officers, naming them, and that he wanted to apologize publicly for his action because he had not known the facts. This is not an isolated case. It is illustrative of a general course of Patton's personal conduct.

Many wanted to serve under him because of his spreading reputation and that of his 2d Armored Division. Mr. Justice Frank Murphy asked for active military status in the spring of 1942 as a lieutenant colonel with the 2d Armored Division. President Roosevelt ordered him back to his duties on the bench of the Supreme Court of the United States, so he regretfully left the life of a soldier to sit again as a judge on the highest court of our land. Also to join the division at this time was United States Senator Henry Cabot Lodge, Jr., a major, who volunteered and was then sent by the division to gain combat experience with the British Eighth Army in Libya. He was one of our first armored officers to engage in tank warfare in World War II. Upon Eisenhower's assuming the Presidency, he was appointed our ambassador to the United Nations.

From the 2d Armored Division Patton was ordered to Indio, in the Great American Desert region of California, in the early spring of 1942 in charge of the desert training of the Armored Force, for at that time the Army believed that most U.S. tank battles would be in desert country, possibly in Libya.

On his departure from his beloved 2d Armored Division, one of his daughters gave a party for him at his quarters. A number of officers of the 2d Armored Division and their wives gathered here after the Easter morning service. Some of his old officers of World War I had found out about the occasion and sent a silver cigarette box upon which their signatures were engraved together with this message: *To a Gallant Soldier whose friendship we cherish. May you go on to further deeds of valor in your country's service.*

When handed the cigarette box, he turned to a window in the room with his back to the crowd. One of the wives didn't understand what the situation was, and approached him to find that there were tears running down his face and he was unable to control himself.

This occurred just about three or four minutes after he had raised his glass of champagne and said: "Here's to the wives. My, what pretty widows you're going to make!"

The wife of an officer present was talking to him a little later, and said, "I understand you have given my husband an interesting assignment?" to which he replied, "He's got a good job, but he's going to get shot!"

He first went from Benning, Georgia, to select the training site for the Desert Training Center near Indio, California. On returning to Benning he elected to fly back to his new station at Indio in his private plane, a Stimson voyageur (he had held a private license for some time). It took him several days, for he had to come down for gas every 200 miles, and when he reached Tucson he wired the Western Defense Command that he was flying himself in. General DeWitt, the Commanding General, wired back, "Civilian planes will be shot down," and much to his chagrin he had to land and leave his plane at Blythe, California. On arriving at the Desert Training Center, he found his "landing field" a cactus-covered mountain side.

The training in the desert was most rigorous. Only one

canteen of water was allowed daily and all officers were ordered to run a mile in ten minutes daily, including Patton himself.

From the training in the American desert, Patton was called to head the Western Task Force that was to land on the Atlantic coast of French Morocco. He left the desert for Washington on July 30, 1942. Despite the many persons involved in its formulation the invasion plan was kept highly secret.

On the fourth of August at 6:00 P.M. General Patton was ordered to fly to the United Kingdom. The following morning he was on his way. General J. H. Doolittle,[1] Colonel Kent Lambert [2] and five air corps officers were also aboard. He noted that all on the plane, although going to war, were talking of fishing and shooting. This is very normal.

After sleeping well on the plane, and twenty-one hours after departing from Washington, they landed in England. Patton was billeted next to General Doolittle at Claridge's. These two distinguished generals were part of the planning group for the African landings, working in London. Also in this group were Generals Eisenhower, Truscott [3] and Clark.[4]

After discussing the operation all day on the ninth of August, Patton had supper with General Eisenhower. They talked until 1:00 A.M. They were both in agreement and it is so stated in the diary.

August 9, 1942

We both feel that the operation is bad and is mostly political. However, we are told to do it and intend to succeed or die in the attempt. If the worst we can see occurs, it is an impossible show, but, with a little luck, it can be done at a high price; and it might be a cinch.

On the fifteenth of August, at a meeting with Eisenhower, Doolittle and Clark, all the aspects of TORCH

---

[1] General James H. Doolittle, Commanding General Eighth United States Air Force.
[2] Colonel Kent C. Lambert, G3 for Patton's Western Task Force.
[3] Brigadier General Lucian Truscott, commanding the Northern Landing Force, later promoted to General.
[4] Major General Mark C. Clark, Commander U.S. Fifth Army, later promoted to General.

(code name for the North African Invasion) were discussed. Here General Patton sold the others on going ahead with this operation and so recommended it to the authorities in Washington. General Patton came away from this meeting with the feeling that he was "the only true gambler in the whole outfit" planning TORCH.

By September, the plans were readied and Patton had returned to the United States. He was to command the Western Task Force that would land on the west coast of Africa at French Morocco. It was in formulating these plans that he came to know and admire Brigadier General John E. Hull, who was on the planning staff for this landing.[5]

Landings were planned on the north coast of Africa in the Mediterranean at Oran and Algiers, in addition to the Patton landing on the Atlantic Coast in French Morocco. He was responsible for landings to be made at three points. The main landing under Patton was to be at Fedala, a small town about ten miles north of Casablanca, the largest city in French Morocco—a city of over a million people—whose capture was a major objective. There was to be a landing at Safi, south of Casablanca, under his subordinate, Major General Ernest Harmon, who commanded the 2d Armored Division. These two landings were planned to pinch off Casablanca. Also a third landing on the northern flank was to be made at Lyautey commanded by his subordinate, Brigadier General Lucian Truscott.

It is interesting to review some of the reasons which compelled Patton to establish the three major points of the Western Task Force landings. The landing near Port Lyautey was decided upon in order to secure as soon as possible an airfield from which the U.S. land fighter planes transported by carrier could operate. Once having taken off from a carrier, these planes could not return. The reason Safi was chosen as a point for landing was because it was the only port outside of Casablanca where heavy cranes were located which would be capable of unloading the medium tanks. This port therefore was assigned as the landing place for the 2d Armored Division.

The selection of Fedala Beach for the main effort provides an interesting anecdote on the planning stage. It was

---

[5] Brigadier General John E. Hull, later General, and as this is written commanding all U.N. troops in the Far East.

on an extremely hot day towards the end of August that Patton's staff, then in headquarters near Norfolk, Virginia, presented the tactical picture of the landing possibilities in Morocco. Available beaches, their defenses, and the French capabilities of bringing up reserves were all set forth. The staff recommended that the main effort be made at Rabat where the French defenses were much less than at Fedala, and where French reserves were more distant. Patton was sitting at his desk, coat off, feet on table, with a pair of brilliant red suspenders supporting his trousers. At the end of the presentation he said: "The main effort will be at Fedala. No landing operation in history has ever succeeded distant from its objective."

As one of Patton's tank officers of World War I, I was again in uniform in the 2d Armored Division. I was overage for my rank. I had not been in the service between the wars because of retirement for wounds received in the Argonne, and I had heard that I was going to be left in the United States. It was common talk that officers over fifty, unless they were general officers, would not be allowed to engage in combat duty, and I was only a lieutenant colonel. This was no idle rumor, because some of the officers of the 1st Armored Division had been taken off the gangplank because of their age. At that time, the plans and thoughts of the British were very important. The British had found that they had too many Colonel Blimps, and had rectified this by getting rid of the older officers without high rank.

I had some leave accumulated and took advantage of it to go to Washington to see General Patton, who was then organizing the Western Task Force that was destined to land on the beaches of French Morocco. In an interview with General Patton, I said that I realized I was but a lieutenant colonel and my rank was not high enough for my age, but that I didn't want to be left behind. General Patton's eyes started to fill up with tears and he said: "I'm not only going to take you but I am going to give you an Armored Landing Team." A lawyer should always try to get the jury on his side, and Patton was the jury in this case. It was this loyalty of Patton to those who had served with him and under him, in addition to his likable emotionalism, which made everybody that worked with him give a supreme effort.

Other officers overage in grade for combat duty were

two regular army officers whom Patton befriended and who fought with him. Both these officers distinguished themselve and performed gallantly for their country. One was Colonel William Wilbur, who was given the Congressional Medal of Honor for heroism above and beyond the call of duty at Casablanca in the Western Task Force landings in Morocco. The other officer was my good friend, Colonel Harry (Paddy) Flint, at one time my commanding officer when he had the 66th Armored Regiment of the 2d Armored Division, whose fabulous performances earned him two Distinguished Service Crosses in World War II, and who was killed in Normandy leading his troops in combat.

Patton's Western Task Force received its amphibious training at Little Creek and Solomons Island up the river from Norfolk in October, 1942. There were many practice landing operations from the ships that were to carry the Western Task Force to French Morocco.

The officers and men had a chance to become accustomed to riding in landing craft and jumping onto the beaches. A large part of the training was in climbing down the landing nets strung over the sides of the ships into the boats, and climbing back from the boats to the deck. In fact, that type of training had been started at Fort Bragg where landing nets were set up on towers and suspended from ropes between trees in the camps established for units that were making the landing.

The APAs (Attack Transport Ships) lowered their little 36- and 50-foot landing boats so that the troops could get accustomed to climbing over the ship's side and down the swaying cargo nets into the boats. These little boats, which were to play such a significant part in all the landing operations of the war, scooted noisily around the mother ships, shoving the water aside with their flat bows, awaiting their turn to load with troops and proceed to the beaches.

While we practiced having the troops hit the beaches, there was no time to practice the landing of armored vehicles. However, the Navy crews were well trained in hoisting the vehicles from the hold of the ships and lowering them into the landing craft; a skill of great value to the expedition. This training by the Navy in loading tanks on the LCMs had been going on for a long time before the troops arrived at Norfolk.

Troops, about two days before departure for the landing operation, were issued bazookas which fired a hollow charge projectile, adapted to pierce armor, from a hand-supported rocket launcher. The maximum distance that these early bazookas would shoot was measured in a few hundred yards and they could be accurate only at distances less than 100 yards. When the bazookas were issued, much ammunition was issued with them and stored on ships, but because of the expediency, in some cases instructions on how to use the bazookas did not arrive.

There was reason for this hurry for it was known by the higher command that there were but a few days in November when landings could be made on the beaches of French Morocco, and November was the month when the landings had to be made.

Normally surf conditions on the coast of Morocco during the month of November were bad. Weather reports indicated that on an average of only three days of the month was the surf less than fifteen feet; impossible for small landing craft. Further, the landing crews were inexperienced and to a large part untrained in landing in heavy surf. Nevertheless the landing had to be made in the early part of November. A weather expert from the West Coast was brought to Washington, and a system of weather forecasting established from which the height of the surf could be predicted, more or less, from the course and intensity of storms originating off Iceland. These storms were followed by photographic reconnaissance from Gibraltar. It was amazing that three days of comparatively calm weather existed between the 8th and 11th of November. Even then the surf ran high at time and many landing craft were overturned and their personnel drowned.

One unit commander and one of his captains sweated it out the hard way. They took a bazooka with a few rounds of ammunition out on a small launch and experimented, guessing how it was loaded and fired. Neither of them knew whether the bazooka was properly loaded, or what it would do when fired. But all worked out satisfactorily. The troops on the ships were instructed all the way across the ocean, firing the new weapon at the crests of the waves from the decks of the ships. The bazooka proved itself in one instance in an important service as a surprise weapon in the Goalpost [6] landing at Mehedya, near Lyautey, Africa.

[6] "Goalpost" was the code name for the northernmost of Patton's Western Task Force landings in Morocco.

War tents for each of the three forces in the Western Task Force were established to house and make available the pertinent information that the subordinate officers should have to accomplish their missions. We had had such tents in training on maneuvers but these war tents now housed the heart of our actual battle information. They possessed an importance and a formality heretofore wholly lacking. This was all enhanced by the cordon of guards at every entrance and walking post at all approaches to the tents. General Truscott, to facilitate the planning for Goalpost, had taken Colonel de Rohan, who commanded his infantry regimental combat team from the 9th Infantry Division, and me, who commanded his armor, into his confidence and told us the secret data about the place we were to land and many of the plans. I do not know how such information affected others, but I would wake up at night in a cold sweat dreaming that I had revealed the plans. When many lives and the success of an expedition depend on absolute secrecy those in the know carry quite a burden. Evidently no one talked for the African landing turned out to be a complete surprise.

In the war tent for Goalpost, which must have been typical of the other similar tents, there were papier-mâché relief maps of the portion of the coast where our landing beaches were to be located and the surrounding country, to give us an understanding of the terrain over which we would fight. There were silhouette pictures showing the appearance of the hill masses near the landing beaches as they would be seen from the sea, so that we could recognize the beach upon which we were destined to disembark as we approached the African shore. In the war tent some information was also available on the general plans, but we were not to get full and detailed knowledge until we embarked on the ships that were to carry us, and we were on our way and well out to sea.

The ships of Patton's Western Task Force convoy, when seen from the crow's-nest, were a beautiful sight. They spread from horizon to horizon and numbered over 100. Occasionally over the loud speakers would come instructions for "general quarters," which meant battle alert. All troops learned how to man their stations and what to do when "general quarters" sounded. Everyone played the game hard because they could never tell whether the call to "general quarters" was for practice or the real thing.

At all times all antiaircraft guns were manned 24 hours a day, not only the 50-caliber guns of which there were a great number on each transport, but also several larger pieces carried by each ship. General Patton named General Lucian Truscott to command the Goalpost force and he was in charge of the operations in the northern landing of the Western Task Force as Patton's subordinate. This landing was to be made at Port Lyautey. The 3d Armored Landing Team was the armor assigned to Goalpost. Truscott had additionally a company or more of light tanks, and a regimental infantry combat team from the 9th Infantry Division commanded by Colonel de Rohan, as well as other supporting troops.

On October 20, 1942, Patton wrote to his brother-in-law, Frederick Ayer, before he sailed on the Moroccan landing. Patton explained that his task force would have to meet and defeat a superior number of enemy on a coast where landings could be made only part of the time. He said:

> The job I am going on is about as desperate a venture as has ever been undertaken by any force in the world's history . . . So my proverbial luck will have to be working all out. However, I have a convinced belief that I will succeed. If I don't I shall not survive a second Donqurque (if that is how you spell it). Of course there is the off-chance that political interests may help and we shall have, at least initially, a pushover. Personally, I would rather have to fight—it would be good practice. However, in any event we will eventually have to fight and fight hard and probably for years. Those of us who come back will have had some interesting experiences.

> And further, when we get back we will have a hell of a job on our hands. I should like to have a crack at the latter part. So far as Bea and the children are concerned, I know that under your supervision they could not be better off.

> I am enclosing a sealed letter to Bea which you are only to give her when and if I am definitely reported dead. I expect you to keep it a long time. Letters even to me will probably be censored, so avoid political and financial statements you don't want others to read.

> This all sounds very gloomy, but is not really so bad. All my life I have wanted to lead a lot of men in a des-

perate battle; I am going to do it; and at fifty-six one can go with equanimity—there is not much one has not done. Thanks to you and Bea, I have had an exceptionally happy life. "Death is as light as a feather, reputation for valor is as heavy as a mountain."

Very affectionately,
G. S. PATTON, JR.[7]

General Patton was always a great admirer of General Pershing. He visited him on the 21st of October. General Patton's diary notes on this significant event are worth quoting.

October 21, 1942

Called on General Pershing. He did not recognize me until I spoke. Then his mind seemed quite clear. He looks very old. It is probably the last time I shall see him but he may outlive me. [He did.] I said that when he took me to Mexico in 1916 he gave me my start. He replied, "I can always pick a fighting man and God knows there are few of them. I am happy they are sending you to the front at once. I like Generals so bold that they are dangerous. I hope they give you a free hand." He recalled my killing the Mexicans and when I told him I was taking the same pistol he said, "I hope you kill some Germans with it." He also said that he hoped I got a chance to kill someone with my sword whip. He said that at the start of the war he was hurt because no one consulted him, but he was now resigned to sit on the sidelines with his feet hanging over. He almost cried. It is pathetic how little he knows of the war. When I left I kissed his hand and asked for his blessing. He squeezed my hand and said, "Good-by George, God bless you and keep you, and give you victory."

I put on my hat and saluted when I left, and he returned it like he used to, and 25 years seemed to drop from him. He said that when he started World War I he was just my age. A truly great soldier.

Just prior to departing the offices in the Pentagon, General Patton was bidding farewell to a few of the civilian secretaries assigned to handle top secret matters. One of

[7] Quoted from *Atlantic Monthly* November, 1947. Copyright, 1947, by Atlantic Monthly Co.

them, a young girl in her twenties who had written all these secret orders for the landing, said to the General with tears in her eyes, "I just can't let you boys go unless you tell me where you are going." The General said, "Gracie, you are the best goddamn confidential secretary in the world."

The General departed by C-47 aircraft from Bolling Air Field at 1400 on October the 21st for Norfolk. There was no fanfare as it was very secret. Aboard the plane besides General Patton were General Keyes, the Deputy Commander; the Task Force Chief of Staff, Colonel Gay; the Deputy Chief of Staff, Colonel Harkins; the G2, Colonel Black; the G3, Colonel Lambert; the G4, Colonel Muller; General Patton's Aide, Captain Jenson (killed in Tunisia); and Captain Stiller, his other aide.

To those aboard it was a very impressive occasion because they knew where they were going. The Chief of Staff has related that he was so tired that, unlike the others who were abuzz with excitement, he went to sleep and had to be awakened after they landed in Norfolk.

On the 23rd of October Patton wrote to his wife as follows:

> Norfolk, Virginia
> October 23, 1942
>
> DARLING BEA,
>
> I must have been considerably upset to have started to leave without saying good-by—I guess I was. I noticed your eyes did not go back on you as we waited for the cars. I hope you had a nice ride back.
>
> We are going to sleep on board [the *Augusta*] tonight and leave this place on shore at 0230 [2:30 A.M.] for the ship. The S.S. *Contessa* at last showed up.
>
> It will probably be sometime before you get a letter from me, but I will be thinking of you and loving you.
>
> GEORGE

As we slid past Cape Henry and into the swells of the gray Atlantic, it began to dawn upon us that we were now embarked on an adventure new to us all. A feeling of exultation tinged with a sense of destiny swept through our ranks. We began to realize that we were now on the stormy Atlantic, graveyard of ships of two World Wars, set forth on the greatest sea-borne invasion in recorded history up to that time—an invasion which would cover thousands of miles and then one dawn strike out at strange beaches on a continent little known to any of us. This adventure was compounded by the sea; for many this was their first sight of the sea; for all, the first time to land on an enemy-held shore; for most, the first battle. All knew that some would never see America again; but there was a cheerful atmosphere; a feeling of elation that the training was over and that we were actually embarked on the task for which we had prepared and worked so diligently.

The convoy covered the whole horizon. Only ships and water could be seen in all directions. Columns of gray ships, lifting and falling with the swell of the gray sea, proceeded in orderly file spread wide across the surface of the Atlantic. The battleship *Texas,* preceded by darting destroyers, led the array, the long procession of ships playing follow the leader behind. Within each column were cargo ships, transports, tankers, and aircraft carriers. The might and power of this armada gave us the strength of a mobilized America, brought together not for profit or gain but for the defense of *freedom.*

This landing was made before the LST (Landing Ship Tank) was finally developed. Combat Command B, 1st Armored Division, was to use the prototype LST with great success in the capture of Oran. The seatrain was improvised. It was a ship that had formerly carried trains of railways cars in short journeys near our eastern coast. It carried the medium tanks of the 67th Armored Regiment and other vehicles from the 2d Armored Division all destined for the Safi landing. The selection of this ship was one of Patton's gambles for neither he nor anyone else knew whether it would be seaworthy on a trip across the Atlantic in November. If the ship had sunk, the success of his entire expedition might well have been jeopardized.

The light tanks used in the Armored Landing teams for the Fedala and Lyautey landings were carried in the hold of transports and destined to be launched in LCMs (Landing Craft Medium) which could carry one light tank. Light tanks, combat loaded, weighed about 16 tons each. The LCMs could not carry a medium tank which weighed about twice as much.

In addition to the medium tank battalion carried by the seatrain to be used on the Safi landing, there was also a 2d Armored Landing Team of light tanks for that landing.

To the landlubbers many interesting things were to take

place. Probably most interesting, the size of the flotilla, which, when under way on the open seas, stretched as far as the eye could see. Almost every type of naval vessel then afloat was in sight; the mighty battleships, cruisers, aircraft carriers, (which many had heard about but never seen), destroyers, tankers, and that one type so vital to the Safi operation, the seatrain with its precious cargo, medium tanks!

Here were a hundred vessels, all in perfect formation, all under perfect control, laying straight courses in the daytime, with airplane cover, to zig and zag during the hours of darkness, constantly alert to the menace of the submarine known to be lurking in their vicinity, and which were plotted on occasion, directly in line with the projected course.

Strict security prevailed. "Smoking lamp is out on all weather decks," it was soon discovered, meant no smoking. Doors leading to the decks, it had been found the first night out, were so wired as to automatically shut off all passage of lights in the gangways when opened.

The armored landing team for the Lyautey landing was on board two vessels of the convey that was carrying the Western Task Force to Morocco.

I was imbued with the importance of discipline from service with Patton in World War I. Thus, there was laid down a strict program aboard the two ships that carried the armor for Lyautey on the trip over. A landing operation, new to everyone, we knew would be confusing, and discipline must be kept high up to the time that the troops jumped off the landing boats onto the beaches. One of the best ways to lose discipline would be to have the soldiers on board ship in confined quarters for many days without the officers keeping control of the men. Close order drill, a good way to keep discipline high, was impossible in the lack of over-all space available on deck.

Therefore, from past experience, having learned the Patton lesson well, orders were given that the men above deck could relax only at noon hour. At all other times, when the men were out of their quarters and on deck, they would be held to the strictest possible application of the rules laid down for wearing the uniform: they would be required to wear helmets at all times when manning the antiaircraft weapons, which as previously stated, were always manned, day and night. The officers were given orders to police the ship continually above deck to be sure that all orders as to the wearing of the uniform were enforced.

It was a painful thing for officers to do the policing for the two weeks of the trip, and it took some of the joy out of life for the enlisted men, but the hold that the officers had on their men turned in fine dividends during the confusion of the landing.

By the 30th of October General Patton realized that the Western Task Force might get ashore without a fight. However, looking into the future, he felt we should fight now. The troops needed blooding and it would enhance our future prospects. He realized his destiny more fully, as we see from his diary on the third of November, 1942:

Every once in a while the tremendous responsibility of this job lands on me like a ton of bricks, but mostly I am not in the least worried. I can't decide logically if I am a man of destiny or a lucky fool, but I think I am destined. Five more days will show. I really do very little, and have done very little, about this show. I feel that my claim to greatness hangs on an ability to lead and inspire. Perhaps when Napoleon said, "Je m'engage et puis je vois," he was right.[8] It is the only thing I can do in this case as I see it. I have no personal fear of death or failure. This may sound like junk, or prophecy, within a week.

We had a Command Post Exercise this morning, which was very dull. I can't see how people can be so dull and lacking in imagination. Compared to them I am a genius.

The last communion service on board the *Augusta* which transported Patton and his staff was a solemn occasion. Patton attended communion with all his staff. At that time neither he nor the officers with him believed they had a one in ten chance of survival, and to many of them this communion service was felt to be their last.

There were many messages from those in command to the troops on the convoy vessels as they neared D-day. The message to the 3d Armored Landing Team, which I was fortunate to command, follows. A copy of this message was given to each soldier.

---

[8] Roughly: "I start fighting and then I look."

Soldiers—take pride that you have been especially selected as the spearhead in the greatest landing in the face of the enemy ever undertaken by United States troops. Pride in your arms, and your will to win, will write a page in history which Americans will always remember and read with quickened pulse.

All the world of free men are watching you. You cannot turn back, and you cannot fail them. You have put your hands to your weapons, do not loosen that hold until the job is done, no matter what the price you must pay in pain and hardship.

At this moment I am honored beyond anything in my life to command you.

Generations of our forefathers, cradled in liberty, are watching you. You are trained; you are fit; you have God and right with you, As true fighting men, I wish you many shows, many victories.

LT. COLONEL HARRY H. SEMMES, 3RD
Armored Landing Team Commanding

The weather was of paramount importance, for bad weather at the time of landing could spell disaster.

The *Contessa* joined the convoy on the seventh of November, 1942—a modern saga of the sea. This little vessel that carried ammunition and started late, came all the way without protection, and rendezvoused at the proper time and place.

Early in October our weather man, who was called to duty for this operation, definitely predicted, after hours and hours of careful study, that weather and tidal conditions would be good off the coast of Casablanca on the morning of November 8, 1942. The morning of November 5th, when the weather was threatening, General Patton stated that he still had faith in this meteorologist. Later, on November 8th when the weather was excellent and the tidal waves were the lowest they had been in many months, General Patton dubbed this man Houdini.

If one can say that such a precedent-shattering, history-making voyage was uneventful, it was. It was in the sense that everything went according to well-conceived, well-executed plans. There were many worries about probable omissions, but it was too late for those. Never before in history had such an armada set sail. Combat loading was in its infancy. Many items later to become common in the form of equipage, such as the LST, were in that early time still unavailable in their finally developed form. There were many "firsts" either to be adopted on larger scale, or to be abandoned if they proved unsuitable or inefficient.

The following message was sent to all ships before landing:

SOLDIERS: We are to be congratulated because we have been chosen as the units of the U.S. Army best fitted to take part in this great American effort. We are now on our way to force a landing on the coast of North Africa. Our mission is threefold; to capture a beachhead and secure an airport; to capture the city of Casablanca and secure its harbor for our use; to move against the enemy wherever he may be and destroy him.

It is not known whether the French Army, composed of French and Moroccan troops, will contest our landing. It is regrettable to contemplate the necessity of fighting the gallant French who are at heart sympathetic, but all resistance by whomever offered must be destroyed. However, when any of the soldiers seek to surrender, you will accept it and treat them with the respect due a brave opponent and a future ally.

In our landing, we will be supported by the full might of the U.S. Navy and our own Air Force, both from carriers and from air, who have been carefully trained in landing operations in conjunction with the Navy. When the great day of battle comes, remember your training, and remember, above all, that speed and vigor of attack are the sure roads to success. And you must succeed, for to retreat is as cowardly as it is fatal. Americans do not surrender.

During the first days and nights after you get ashore, you must work unceasingly, regardless of sleep, regardless of food.

A pint of sweat will save a gallon of blood. The eyes of the world are watching us. The heart of America beats for us. God is with us. On our victory depends the freedom or slavery of the human race. We shall surely win.

(signed) G. S. PATTON, JR.

The Moroccan troops referred to in Patton's message

97

are the famous Goumiers. The Moroccan Goumier of the French Army has always been led in the main by French officers. The soldiers and noncoms are of hardy Berber stock recruited from the Moroccan tribes of Berber people, many of whom are nomads or live in little villages high in the Atlas mountains.

Squads are largely recruited from the same tribe, or village, and are often related. When a vacancy occurs in a squad, Ali will be sent back to his people and may return with Uncle Mohammed to fill the vacancy.

They are hardy, fearless, have great endurance, and make superlative foot soldiers. Particularly, they excel in mountain fighting, and in night operations, where their gray burnooses with broad vertical brown stripes blend in with the rocks on a hillside. Many an enemy sentry has been found in the morning with his throat silently cut, for the Goumiers take pride in their stealth. In the squads may be specialists: one will be a skillful strangler, another will excel in throat slitting. They wear an unsheathed dagger in their belts and look like the tough fighting men they are. The French rate them high, and so do all who have fought with, or against them.

6. Landing in Morocco

Fedala—Casablanca Is Taken

LANDINGS are special operations. Principles and procedures governing this type of action were developed jointly by the Army and Navy before World War II. Experiences drawn from military history were tested in maneuvers and the results found their way into regulations and instructions. But the African landings on the coast of French Morocco and on the north coast of Africa in the Mediterranean were on a scale never before attempted and the lessons learned there had a material influence on subsequent landings.

The landings would be in the face of the French forces located there, but we were not sure what resistance we might encounter. The French have always been friendly to Americans but they were under the orders of the Vichy

French, whose leader was Pétain. The Vichy French were pledged to the Germans, who were then occupying France, to resist any landings by the Allied powers.

Patton and the other high commanders agreed that if these African landings were unsuccessful the whole Allied cause would be set back two years. It was a big gamble with high stakes. Little can be salvaged from a landing that is unsuccessful, for those not killed on the beaches will be thrown back into the sea.

In order to gain some practical experience in such operations, a comparatively small landing was made prior to the African landings at Dieppe on the coast of France. This was experimental and served its purpose as a proving ground for future landing tactics.

One of the rules learned at Dieppe was that always there should be several beaches, if the main concept is to get a toe-hold and hang on. It is hoped that at least on one beach success will be achieved. Another rule of landings is to reinforce success, not try to bolster failure. This is a hard rule, though sound. It is cruel for those on the unsuccessful beaches.

Patton's promise to the Chief of Staff, General George C. Marshall, on leaving for his Western Task Force Landing on the coast of Morocco, "I will leave the beaches either a conqueror or a corpse," is a realistic rule.

On the morning of the eighth of November, D-day for the TORCH landings, General Patton awoke at 0200. The lights at Fedala and Casablanca were burning brightly. The sea was calm and Patton, remembering his deity, said, "God is with us." H-hour was set for 0400, although it was delayed 45 minutes.

Three French merchant ships escorted by a French corvette moved into the transport area, which was completely darkened. Admiral Hewitt questioned one of his destroyer commanders why he didn't stop them and make them put out their lights. The commander replied, "I have signaled them three times to stop and put out their lights, but they pay no attention to me." Upon receiving the command "Stop them," the destroyer immediately opened fire, sinking the corvette. The three merchant ships headed north and beached themselves.

Patton was preparing to go ashore at 0800. His landing boat was on the davits, swung out with all the personal equipment of those to go ashore loaded on it. His orderly was sent to get the General's white pearl-handled pistols. At that moment a light French cruiser and two destroyers came out of Casablanca, tearing up the coast line to try to get the U.S. transports. At once the *Augusta* speeded up to 20 knots and opened fire. The first blast from the rear turret of the *Augusta* blew Patton's landing boat from the davits onto the deck. All personal belongings were lost overboard except Patton's pistols. There was a brisk naval battle between the French warships and the cruiser *Augusta* which lasted until about noon. Patton, to his amazement, found himself engaged in naval warfare in a critical period when his troops were establishing a beachhead, and it was not until 1320 hours that Patton and his party finally hit the beach.

Twenty minutes after they landed, Major General J. W. Anderson, who commanded the 3d Infantry Division, met Patton with a French Colonel who suggested that he (Patton) send a demand to Casablanca to surrender. Patton sent Colonels Wilbur and Gay. Although the French Army did not desire to continue the fight, the senior man was Admiral Michelier who commanded the French Navy. He refused to see Gay and Wilbur. However, they returned with advice obtained from the Admiral's staff on the easiest routes of approach to seize Casablanca. When they returned they directed a light tank and infantry attack which completed the capture of the last battery on point Fedala. General Patton concluded this memorable eighth of November with this diary notation: *God was very good to me today.*

The Germans had sent a so-called "Armistice Commission" to French Morocco, ostensibly to supervise the armistice following the fall of France. Actually, it was discovered after the American landing that the Germans planned to put key men in positions of power and gradually take over the country. This technique is not unknown to tyrannies of modern times. The Germans were good at it, but the Russians have developed this sinister procedure to a point beyond ordinary plotting. It has been raised by them to the status of an art.

Our landing spoiled the game of the German Armistice Commission in Morocco.

The capture of the German Armistice Commission was prearranged and carefully worked out in the initial planning. Colonel Percy G. Black, Patton's G-2 for the landing, suggested that a group of counterintelligence personnel be landed with the first wave with the task of seizing the Hotel Miramar at Fedala where the Armistice Commission was located. His plan was adopted and although they did not capture all the commission at this time, two of our Counterintelligence Corps members took over the records and remained half a day guarding them under both the fire from our own fleet and from the French shore battery. The last member of the commission was finally captured a month later in a French hospital. His reaction upon being told that he would be shipped back to the U.S. was typical of the German indoctrination. He begged to be shot rather than transported across an ocean where he fully believed an Allied ship could not survive. An indirect result of the capture of the German Armistice Commission was the internment of our embassy staff in Vichy by the Germans.

Patton got his entire staff ashore by 1500 hours on the ninth of November. Hap Gay, Patton's Chief of Staff for the African landing, reports that when Patton heard that there was a hard tank fight at Mehedya on the 9th of November in the vicinity of Lyautey, Patton said to him, "Semmes is having a good time."

On the tenth of November communication from his two other task force commanders, Generals Truscott and Harmon, was limited to "Truscott needs help" of which Patton had none to give. He decided to capture Casablanca with the 3d Infantry Division and Major Richard Nelson's Armored Battalion. Despite the fact that he was outnumbered he felt, and rightly so, that he should hold the initiative. At 2200 hours Admiral Hall arrived to arrange Naval support. He brought good news. Harmon at Safi had defeated an enemy column and was marching on Casablanca. This proved Patton's earlier theory to hold the initiative.

He was awakened by his staff at 0420 hours the morning of the eleventh and told that the French had ceased firing at Rabat and Lyautey. His staff recommended that the attack be called off but Patton felt it was still premature. General Anderson wanted to commence the attack at dawn but he had chosen 0730 in order to give the troops time to form up by daylight. We were not experienced battle-hardened troops at this time, hence Patton's decision to jump off at daylight appeared sound. Actually the

French quit at 0640. Patton had fulfilled his boast that he would take Casablanca by D plus 3.

"The God of Fair Beginnings / Hath prospered here my hand . . . I dared extreme occasion / Nor ever one betrayed." [1]

By coincidence, Patton's birthday was November 11th, and the Armistice was concluded on that day—his second armistice birthday present. The manner in which Patton handled the negotiations at Fedala for the Armistice indicated his comprehension of the feelings of the French. He, as was customary, had one purpose in mind—to defeat the Germans—and his skillful handling of this tense situation was designed to that end. Here were good troops, from a nation of free men. Here was the present opportunity to bind to us an important ally.

Representing the American Forces at the armistice meeting were General G. S. Patton, Jr.; Admiral Hewitt, U.S. Naval Forces; General Keyes, U.S. Army; Admiral Hall, Chief of Staff to Admiral Hewitt; Colonel Gay, Chief of Staff to General Patton; Colonel Wilbur, who acted as interpreter; and Colonel Harkins, Deputy Chief of Staff, and Colonel Lambert. Representing the French were General Noguès, French Army; Admiral Michelier, French Navy; General LaHoulle, French Air Force; and General Desré, French ground forces.

There had been two papers prepared by the American high command. The first armistice document was prepared for a situation in which the French did not resist. This contained liberal terms to the French. A second paper was prepared with harsh armistice terms to be used in case the French resisted bitterly. The situation lay in between these extremes, and Patton had asked Keyes, Wilbur and Culbert to prepare a document whose terms were neither extremely generous nor harsh.

Patton opened the meeting by praising the valiant defense of the French and the spirit of devotion that they had exhibited. The recently prepared document with the terms for the Armistice was then produced. Noguès said that they were more harsh than those of the Vichy agreement between the French and the Germans. Michelier wrote a

[1] "Song of Diego Valdez," by Rudyard Kipling, copyright, 1902, by Rudyard Kipling. Reprinted by permission of Mrs. George Bainbridge, Macmillan of Canada, Ltd., and Doubleday and Company, Inc.

single word on a piece of paper and passed it to Noguès. The word was *Inacceptable*.

At this point the meeting was very stiff and strained. Since the terms of the agreement that were being made at the armistice negotiations in Algiers and in Tunisia were not available, Patton seized on the device of concluding a gentleman's agreement between soldiers. No written document was ever prepared. Having determined that none of the terms of the surrender as written would be acceptable, he said: "I have known most of you French officers before when I was a student in your Army schools in France, as also has General Keyes. We all belong to the same profession, that of arms. Your word is as good as your written signature. Such has always been true of men of our profession. I propose, until final terms are arranged by higher headquarters, that you return all your men with arms to your proper stations; that you take your sick and wounded with you and your dead. I propose the prisoners of yours which we have we will turn over to you; that you will give me your word that you will not bear arms against these forces, that you will turn over to us without delay any prisoners of war which you have and any of our dead which are within your lines; but you will make every effort to maintain good order and discipline in Morocco to include the guarding of the railroad bridges and the railroad through Taza Gap."

To this proposal all readily agreed. The French in particular seemed to be very happy and pleased. Then General Patton stood up and said, "Gentlemen, I have forgotten one other thing which I must ask you to do." The French faces grew long and apprehensive. Then he said, "I must ask you to drink to the good health of the United States and France and to their union forever." Both General Noguès and Admiral Michelier, with their faces wreathed in smiles, threw their arms around him and kissed him on both cheeks. This was a most dramatic moment.

The French themselves have characterized the cooperation from the Armistice date, 11th November, 1942, as "complete, sincere and friendly." Patton fitted his actions to the situation as it developed. This instantaneous adjustment to the unexpected was characteristic and of incalculable value to his country in time of war.

The mission assigned by Patton to the Army portion of Task Force Blackstone, under command of Major General Ernest N. Harmon, was to capture and secure the port of Safi, located about one hundred and fifty miles southwest of Casablanca. First a beachhead at Safi was to be established. Then troops were to be dispatched to secure crossings over Oued Oum Er Rbid to the north, and prevent enemy forces at Marrakech from reinforcing Casablanca. The armored troops were then to continue northeastward to assist in the capture of Casablanca.

In order to perform this operation, Task Force Blackstone had Army troops consisting of a headquarters staff from the 2d Armored Division, which General Harmon commanded. General Harmon, an outstanding combat soldier, was later to command a corps in the campaigns in Europe. After V-E Day, he created the United States Constabulary which brought discipline back to the American Army in Europe. This organization, launched and trained by him, raised the prestige and esprit de corps of our army to a high mark in the confused period after World War II. General Harmon, now retired, is President of Norwich University, a military college of top standing which has produced career officers of the caliber of Lieutenant General I. D. White and Brigadier General Paul Disney, who both fought with the 2d Armored Division in World War II. Not least to be mentioned of the alumni of that illustrious school is Jim Burt, now a civilian, but formerly a lieutenant in the 3d Armored Landing Team of the 2d Armored Division, when they made the Moroccan landing, and who later was awarded the Congressional Medal of Honor. The Deputy Commander was Brigadier General Hugh J. Gaffey, who also normally commanded a combat command in the 2d Armored Division. Colonel Oscar W. Koch,[2] G-2 of the 2d Armored Division, was General Harmon's Chief of Staff in Blackstone. He was later to be the dependable and keen intelligence officer of Patton's Seventh Army in Sicily and again in the historic campaigns of Patton's fabulous Third Army in Europe in 1944 and 1945.

All were under the command of Patton, Blackstone

---

[2] Later promoted to Brigadier General.

being part of Patton's Western Task Force. There was a battalion of medium tanks (the 3d Battalion of the 67th Armored Regiment, 2d Armored Division) carried in the seatrain, the ship that had been used to carry railroad cars in ferry service and could carry the medium tanks, but needed a dock to unload them. The 47th Infantry Regiment, 9th Infantry Division, comprised the infantry portion of Blackstone. There was a small armored task force of troops from the 2d Armored Division, called the 2d Armored Landing Team, which included, among other supporting troops, a battalion of light tanks.

On the Navy side, under the command of Rear Admiral L. A. Davidson, there was a fire support group consisting of a battleship, a light cruiser, and three destroyers. These were accompanied by a formidable naval force including screening destroyers, minesweepers, oil tankers, an aircraft carrier, a reconnaissance submarine, a tug and a mine layer.

Every inch of space aboard the transport was to be used for fighting troops and their equipment. Staffs were held to an absolute minimum, with a total of 11 officers for Headquarters, Blackstone, with about one enlisted assistant each. Most remarkable of the limitations imposed were the duties assigned a young doctor (Captain M. T. Fliegelman) of the 2d Armored Division, whose versatility made him the Task Force Surgeon, the Task Force Chemical Officer and the Task Force Adjutant General. During combat he did successful brain surgery aboard ship, and later prepared the numerous citations and records which would have been the normal duties of G-1.

The town of Safi was the first place south of Casablanca which had the necessary port facilities to land the seatrain, with its cargo of a battalion of medium tanks aboard. It had a series of quays, one of which, known as the Jetée Transversale or Phosphate Pier, was approximately 500 feet long with alongside depth of 29 feet.

The hour for the attack was under cover of darkness. Secrecy and rapid success were essential to permit the tanks to land "with dry feet." To achieve surprise, the hour of attack was set for 0430, this being the time set for the first waves to hit the beach. The date was 8 November, 1942, the same as the landing dates at Fedala and Lyautey.

The actual landing operation was broken into three phases: the landing proper on hostile shores which embraced control of the beaches to a radial depth of 5,000 yards from the harbor installations; the beachhead phase which extended the landing phase to a radial depth of 10,000 yards; the third phase which provided for the securing of the port of Safi, while the armored components moved north to assist in the capture of Casablanca.

RED Beach, the northernmost one, was about 500 yards long and 200 yards wide, with exits only via steep paths to the top of the cliff above. Separated by about 700 yards of cliff, BLUE Beach lay to the south of RED Beach and was some 500 yards long and 200 yards wide at the center. RED Beach, if surf was running, was generally under heavy surf, and with high tide might not be usable even for the dismounted troops which it could accommodate only at its best. BLUE had generally a light surf. November, the month of the landings, was the beginning of the season of high surf on the Moroccan coast.

Inside the port area proper was GREEN Beach, which was about 200 yards square. It was generally used by fishing craft, there was no surf, it had a steep gradient, being adjacent to a dredged area. Its greatest advantage was that it provided a direct exit to the town itself.

If for any reason, by action of the sea, or by enemy action, these beaches could not be used by tanks, poor exits considered, another beach was necessary to meet this eventuality. One was found, almost incredibly, by a picture postcard, available at Jorf el Yahudi, about 9 miles south of the town of Safi, immediately contiguous to, and directly south of, a 285-foot cliff. The beach, coded YELLOW, was about 700 yards long and 200 yards wide. The north central part of YELLOW Beach looked most favorable, with exits to sparsely settled country to the east. Little was known of the surf conditions there, but if it was necessary to unload the light tanks from the 2d Armored Landing team across the beaches, this would be the place (with fingers crossed).

Accommodations for the seatrain with the medium tanks to unload still required a dock in the port of Safi.

Many questions were unanswered before leaving the United States. To determine the suitability of YELLOW Beach, Patton had a reconnaissance submarine reconnoiter it during the period D minus 2 to D minus 1 and reported its findings to Blackstone headquarters afloat.

Immediately upon entering the transport area, marking

106

parties were dispatched to mark beaches RED, BLUE and YELLOW.

Preceding the landing of any substantial number of troops, assault destroyers (the USS *Cole* and USS *Bernadou*) landed detachments of Companies K and L, 47th Infantry. Transfer of these men from the transport that carried them across the Atlantic to these destroyers took place about a day out at sea. In addition to these important missions of the Navy component, the accompanying Navy Air Force had support missions, and had naval gunfire observer missions as well.

The assault forces on the port proper, under command of then Colonel Edwin H. Randle, whose normal command was the 47th Infantry, were divided into three infantry battalion teams, of which two landed on the beaches in Safi, and another made landings at YELLOW Beach.

The unloading of Task Force Blackstone at night was magnificent. The ship's booms were lowered to dig down into the holds, bring a light tank up, put it over the side, and place it in an LCM landing boat not much larger in inside dimensions than the tank itself. All this was done quietly without use of lights, and in a rolling sea in pitch blackness. Many soldiers witnessed that operation on the night of 7-8 November with awe at the trained skill of the Navy. Men in rows along the rail, about four deep, with full equipment were awaiting their turn to get into the small boats at the bottom of the rope nets. There was tension among the troops, in this, their first landing on hostile shores.

Some consolation was derived from the fact that the lighthouse in the Port of Safi was still lit in the earlier hours, indicating secrecy had been achieved; moreover, there were no misgivings as to the ability of the boat commanders of the landing craft to hit their beaches on the nose.

The expression "everything went according to plan," wherever its origin, applied to Safi. For in about 12 hours after dropping anchor in the transport area some 4 miles at sea, and transferring to landing craft the tanks, artillery, jeeps, and previously untested radio equipment, the Safi resistance had been overcome, and the town with its port had been captured!

If that seems to oversimplify the operation, such was not the case. It means that everything worked as planned, and that all the painstaking details worked out 4,000 miles distant met the situation as it was found to exist.

Our plan called for the ship *Bernadou* with Rangers aboard to attack directly into Safi by beaching. The entry of the *Bernadou* into the harbor brought immediate fire at 3:30 A.M., as a result of an alert received by the French, according to reports later obtained. The dark and quiet night was interrupted by the clatter of machine guns, the cannonading of the 75s and the opening of fire by coast defense guns on Point de la Tour. The *Bernadou* was grounded according to plan, and promptly at 4:30 A.M., the infantry aboard went over her side and started shooting.

The Reconnaissance Platoon located the hostile positions south of the 130-millimeter gun positions and the hostile positions along the top of RED and BLUE Beaches and neutralized them at H-hour. As soon as the Commanding Officer, 1st Infantry Battalion team, was ashore, control of the Reconnaissance Platoon passed to him. He then established the northern arc of the beachhead radius.

Some light tanks attached to the infantry were put ashore on GREEN Beach about an hour later, and by 1000 hours the initial beachhead had been established. This was rapidly pushed out, so that early in the afternoon, the seatrain was brought into dock and unloaded its medium tanks. In the meantime, following naval gunfire and the dropping of some bombs by naval air, the heavy battery 3 miles south was neutralized. The coastal battery had been taken out by Navy fire earlier in the morning.

The 1st Infantry Battalion Team landed at RED and BLUE at H-hour, proceeded inland to form a beachhead 10,000 yards deep, including the 130-millimeter coast defense positions north of the town.

The landing of the 2d Battalion Infantry Team at YELLOW Beach had been postponed until after daylight because of a delay caused by an explosion near one of the transports, which was immediately, but erroneously, interpreted as a submarine attack. It was fortunate, for at that time, high surf was reported running on YELLOW, and later in daylight the surf was not high enough to hinder the landing operation. The landing continued on YELLOW until it was certain that the fall of Safi was assured. There were some boat losses on YELLOW Beach, but no personnel losses. It is interesting to note that those who did land over that beach, again according to plan, actually reached Safi at 2:00 P.M.

Since the Phosphate Dock was available, due to the success of the operation, the light tanks and other supporting armored vehicles that composed the 2d Armored Landing Team unloaded also at the Phosphate Dock while the medium tanks on the seatrain were being unloaded. It had been contemplated that the 2d Armored Landing Team might have to unload at YELLOW Beach, if the port had not been secured.

Unloading continued at a rapid pace. Those not fighting became stevedores because the next mission was to secure the port, and get moving on the River Rbia, then to Casablanca 150 miles to the north. Tanks as unloaded were assembled into a combat command under Brig. General Gaffey, which in turn was dispatched to the east, whence word was received that units of the Marrakech garrison were marching in motor columns. This column from the Marrakech garrison was attacked by our Navy air support and artillery. During the day of the ninth of November following a brisk artillery duel, General Gaffey reported that force effectively dispersed. He was ordered to an outpost position astride the Safi-Marrakech highway crossroads near El Tleta (about 15 miles east of Safi), in the vicinity of his victory.

Sniping continued throughout the day in the town, until one of the huts overlooking BLUE Beach was taken under fire by mechanized weapons, which put an end to the sniping.

Unloading continued, and on the 10th, final plans were made to have the tank forces destined for Casablanca depart for a night march on the second objective, the securing of the crossing over the River Rbia, about 10 miles east of Mazagan. Enemy troops were known to garrison Mazagan, so that city, one of the minor ports, had to be taken and secured en route. The rest of the Tank Force had to start its drive for Casablanca, its final objective. The 47th Infantry, which was to hold the port of Safi, remained in place.

The departure from Safi of this column was so timed as to reach the Tleta (also shown on some maps as Bou Gedra)—Mazagan highway at dark. If our column had been observed and reported during daylight, Marrakech could well have been considered its destination, and the march to Casablanca would then have been halted until any resistance from Marrakech had been subdued.

Every time the column was halted during the night of the advance from Safi to Mazagan, there was a most anxious moment and Harmon was continually going to the front to get it moved forward. One time he found that the leading vehicle had halted and the men had gone to sleep during a halt period and hadn't received the word to move out. Finally, about two o'clock, there was quite a lengthy halt and Harmon went up to the head of the column to see what was the trouble. Here he found a circle of soldiers gathered about something in the center of the road with a light. He made his way through the crowd and there found an old Frenchman, with a huge moustache, whose chest was covered with ribbons, standing beside a large rock. On the rock there was a placard with the words: *Egalité-Fraternité-République Française*.

Harmon realized at once that this was a special situation. Our men couldn't understand a word of French but were looking at the old man wondering what to do next. He asked the old man what he was there for, and he told Harmon that he had been ordered to put up a barricade and stop our advance; that this was a *barricade symbolique*. He further asked him what the lantern was for, and he replied that that was to keep us from injuring ourselves on the barricade. Right away Harmon sensed this Frenchman was one of the old school who in trying to carry out his orders was also a friend of America, so he asked him how close his home was. The old Frenchman pointed to a little house nearby with a light in the window. Harmon told him that he had done very well for his country, that he couldn't hope to stop our column of armor and that he must now go home to his wife as he had done a very fine thing. The Frenchman asked Harmon if he didn't want him to help roll the stone off the road, but was told that we would take care of that because we were in a hurry, and he must run along now and go home and let us get on about our business. The old man left the road and went toward the house with his little lantern and the soldiers got into their vehicles and the column moved forward. It was a dramatic incident, and it made Harmon feel proud and sympathetic for the gallant French soldiers with whom we had fought so well as comrades during World War I.

Ingeniously, to make up for the shortage of organic overland transportation for the hauling of ammunition, and the life blood of tanks—gasoline—Patton had the Navy arrange to haul both of those commodities by sea to the town of Mazagan, and to be in position to assist the land effort by naval action. After the reduction of Mazagan, gas and ammunition would be transferred to shore from our vessels, and the tank column could again proceed with full loads to its final objective, Casablanca.

Other threats failed to materialize, and at daybreak the tanks were in position to take Mazagan.

General Harmon was on personal reconnaissance the morning of November the eleventh, when the orders came at 0830 hours that an armistice had been declared. Bombers were already aloft ready to drop their loads at the appointed time, and great apprehension arose as to how to inform all concerned that, for the time being at least, the war was over. Resorting to anything white available, all waved frantically, attracting the attention of the aircraft, flying in formation, above. Finally, by a recognition signal, acknowledgment was received, and they departed.

General Harmon arranged for the local armistice terms, and placed his command in bivouac along the beach east of the city. A camaraderie was immediately established with the French. Proceeding over the River Rbia, which was found heavily defended, he arranged that the French troops would march back to their barracks with colors flying and under arms.

Our tanks, as previously indicated, had already deployed for combat against French infantry in position near Mazagan, astride the road to Casablanca. After receiving the radiogram, General Harmon decided to report to General Patton at Casablanca and ordered Colonel Leonard H. "Steamer" Nason to go with him. They stopped at the French positions and paid a friendly call on the French Commander, Major Signard.

"Steamer" Nason acted as General Harmon's interpreter and during the conversation learned that this French infantry unit was the third battalion of the RICM. Nason remembered them well, for this gallant soldier, between wars an author, had served with this regiment during the first World War on July 17, 18 and 19, 1918, in the counterattack north of Château Thierry.

The RICM has no regimental number. The letters by which it is designated are the initials in French meaning the Moroccan Regiment of Colonial Infantry. It was organized in 1914 from separate colonial battalions stationed in Morocco, and was then composed entirely of white French volunteers. During the first World War, the regiment won ten army citations, one more than the Foreign Legion, and is particularly celebrated for having recaptured Douaumont, north of Verdun, in 1916. The soldiers were easily identified by Nason that November morning, because they all wear the double *fourragère* on their left shoulder, one with the colors of the Croix de Guerre, and the other the Legion of Honor. After General Harmon had given the French permission to return to their barracks at Mazagan, he and Nason proceeded to Casablanca.

General Patton invited General Harmon and some of his staff to dinner in Casablanca. While at dinner several terrific explosions were heard. Immediate reports received indicated that several of the vessels in the transport area off shore had been torpedoed by German submarines. All immediately visited the beach, a few blocks away, and could see the vessels in distress. Survivors came in. Equipment losses were primarily of vital, and later difficult-to-get, communications equipment.

General Harmon returned to his bivouac at Mazagan after his visit with General Patton and that evening had another good meal with his aide, in a small restaurant by the sea, in which the main course was an omelet made of a dozen eggs. After the diet of "C" rations, the omelet was such a welcome change that he conceived the notion of trying to get enough eggs to feed the 1,500 men of the advance force with him at Mazagan; the remainder of his troops having been used on other missions. He told the French proprietor of the restaurant to deliver without fail to the American bivouac 5,000 eggs by the next morning. With French gesticulations of despair and after deep consultation with some Arab merchants, the restaurateur reported that he would do his best but, *"C'est impossible, mon Général."* Harmon never expected that this order would be filled.

About two o'clock the next morning he was awakened by a tremendous noise in the bivouac punctuated by guttural Arab cries and rushed out of his tent to repel the attack from the Arabs. The place was full of small donkey carts with Arab drivers and crate after crate of eggs in the carts. Everyone had fresh eggs that morning. It is strange how small incidents like that are retained in soldiers' memories. Two years later in Belgium, Harmon, who again commanded his old division, having given up command of a corps in the United States to return to the fight, was pointed out to a new arrival in the 2d Armored Division. He heard above the roar of the passing tanks, "That's Ernie Harmon, the general that gave us the eggs at Mazagan."

On the twelfth of November, Task Force Blackstone was ordered by Patton into bivouac in the Mamora Cork Forest, about twelve miles east of Rabat-Salé.

Lyautey—Northernmost of the Patton Landings

The mission assigned by Patton to the army portion of Task Force Goalpost, under the command of Brigadier General Lucian K. Truscott, Jr., was to secure Port Lyautey and its airfield; then move to the south towards Casablanca preventing French reinforcements; next move to reinforce Casablanca and secure the airfield at Rabat, 25 miles south of Port Lyautey.

It turned out that Goalpost produced hard fighting which continued for three days in the vicinity of Port Lyautey until finally the Portuguese Kasbah (fort) at Mehedya and the Lyautey airfield were taken by our infantry. Casualties of the defending forces of French Moroccan Goumiers were heavy. Taking the fort at Mehedya was a military operation of great difficulty. The fort was taken and lost several times before our infantry finally captured and held it.

In the last successful attack, all available Americans, including cooks and clerks, and sailors from the landing craft, fought forward, crawling on their bellies for over two hundred yards.

The infantry fighting was bloody, and in commanding the Goalpost Task Force, Brigadier General Lucian Truscott proved his leadership qualities in this first battle; qualities that were to find him in command of the Fifth Army as a lieutenant general by 1944. Now retired, he was recently promoted to four star rank.

Too much cannot be said in praise of the devoted fighting of the U.S. troops from the 9th Infantry Division under the command of Colonel de Rohan in this landing. This was the type of effort that Patton demanded, and which his troops willingly gave.

Trying to follow his teachings, on the trip over I had spent half of each day in a lifeboat on the top deck of the *John Penn* studying general information about Morocco, particularly the coast, including the orders for Goalpost Task Force, and the SOI (Signal Operation Instructions). The over-all plans of the battle were clearly expressed in the orders. We knew that we should have the general plan very thoroughly in mind, since in the landing it would be certain that very little would go smoothly. Because of the uncertainty and inevitable confusion, it would be good to know the whole plan so that anything that happened could be fitted into the general picture.

We were pleased with the orders, which for armor were very short and concise, placing the responsibility for details on the man on the ground. Nothing was stated in the order except a series of objectives in the order of importance.

The 3d Armored Landing Team, which was my command, was to land on order of the Sub Task Force Commander on beaches to be designated. This small task force was to reconnoiter without delay to the south in the vicinity of Rabat-Salé and to protect Goalpost against hostile forces advancing from the south and southwest and to participate in the attack to capture the airdrome at Port Lyautey. The next mission of the 3d Armored Landing Team was to capture the airdrome in the vicinity of Rabat-Salé and Sidi-Yahia. The last mission was to seize the radio station at Rabat-Salé.

The 3d Armored Landing Team was an armored task force; a miniature armored division. There were approximately 900 men and 160 vehicles. Included in the team were a battalion of 54 light tanks, the First Battalion of the 66th Armored Regiment, each tank armed with a 37 mm. cannon and a machine gun, with a four-man crew; a company of armored infantry; a battery of armored field artillery; some engineers, and signal and headquarters troops. All these troops were from the 2d Armored Division, in which I had commanded and trained the First Battalion of the 66th Armored Regiment.

Daily all officers on the *John Penn* had conferred about the possibilities of what might be done under various circumstances on the beach. Everyone had a chance to imagine what might happen, and put forth his ideas as to what should be done. Despite all this conversation and thought, no one pictured that the waves would become so high that only seven tanks would land, and that these seven would have to go into battle without radio communication, and without having a chance to adjust the sights on their guns. The daily skull practice, however, was excellent because it had everyone thinking about the problems. As a result, no one in the engagement was appalled by the situation that did develop when we had to go into battle with only seven tanks out of the 54 in the command, and no other armored vehicles.

The 3d Armored Landing Team was transported by the *John Penn,* which carried most of the troops and the officers, and the *Electra,* which carried a lesser number of troops and officers, but all of the vehicles. The convoy that was going to Port Lyautey steamed by the town of Rabat, the capital of French Morocco, at a distance of about five miles from shore. That night of 7–8 November, the town was ablaze with lights and the inhabitants were having their usual Saturday night big time, while the blacked-out, Lyautey-bound convoy crept silently along the coast.

Off Lyautey, the vessels carrying the armor ran into some vessels upon whose hulls the French flag had been painted to indicate their nationality. The Americans withheld their fire, knowing that by the time the French ships landed at Port Lyautey and spread the news, the attack would have begun and, therefore, to sink them would serve no useful purpose.

The attack commenced in the early hours of the next morning with the landing of a detachment of infantry from the 9th U.S. Infantry Division on the beaches at Mehedya, just south of the jetty-guarded inlet to Lyautey harbor. Port Lyautey itself lay about five miles up the Oued Sebou, a river that flowed into the Atlantic between the jetties.

The troops, on the vessels carrying the 3d Armored Landing Team and its vehicles, heard some firing but it was scattered and not concentrated. Evidently the opposing troops had not grasped the situation immediately. The personnel from the *John Penn* were to be transferred to the vehicle-carrying transport *Electra.* The latter was commanded by Captain J. J. Hughes, U.S. Navy. He had commanded the gunboat *Panay,* in China waters, the first

American vessel to receive a hostile shot before Pearl Harbor. He had been severely wounded in that engagement.

About noon of the eighth, batteries at the old Portuguese fort at Mehedya started to bracket the *Electra* located offshore not more than a mile or two. Captain Hughes, knowing what was in store for his ship, started full speed ahead and pulled out beyond range of the French guns. The *Electra* went many miles out to sea, and there received the first LCM landing craft which had been dispatched to the armor after landing the infantry. There were seven LCMs in the group that the infantry commander sent to the *Electra*, after they had completed their first task of getting the infantry on the beach.

The first wave of seven LCMs were loaded with light tanks and their crews, and went on their way to the landing beach, Mehedya Plage, which was a bathing beach adjacent to the ancient town of Mehedya.

Mehedya had been founded by the Carthaginians, on a periplus from Carthage many centuries ago. Three hundred Carthaginians, including wives, were put ashore at that time. Strangely enough, no more than three hundred people were in Mehedya when the Americans landed.

When the first wave of seven LCMs was launched the sea was calm. The seven tanks were in line, nearly abreast of each other, and had the strain of our first amphibious landing been absent we could have called to the crews of adjacent tanks. All were silent, however, for there is nothing like a landing on hostile shores to dampen the flow of useless conversation. As we approached the beach, the tension mounted, for our recollection was vivid that that morning the *Electra* had been driven out to sea by the shore batteries lying to the northeast. As each minute passed and we neared the land, we expected to hear the scream of shells around us. The shore battery which had caused the *Electra* to move out to sea failed to shoot at the landing boats, and the beach where the tanks landed was being held by our infantry, who had landed earlier.

The tanks rolled off the LCMs into the shallow water and onto the beach. The LCMs turned around and returned to the *Electra* to get the next wave of tanks. The crews of the group of seven LCMs noticed how many small landing craft had been beached and were unable to extricate themselves from the sand. These LCM crews were

116

careful not to share the same fate, for the shore was littered with landing craft that had been stuck on previous trips.

It was near dusk and there was no chance to bore-sight the guns on the seven tanks. Two weeks at sea without this opportunity caused the guns carried by the tanks to be very inaccurate because their sights were not properly adjusted for firing. Also, it was found on landing that there was no radio communication between the tanks. Because of complete radio silence for security reasons while the tanks were on board it was impossible to discover that the radios were inoperative. Immediately work was started to rectify this.

We could not get them working for about twenty-four hours so the seven tanks had to go into battle without communication. For this first battle, the Americans had to resort to the communication system of the first World War. Communications between the tanks in that war took place during lulls in the enemy fire. The officers would dismount and go on foot to yell their instructions to the various tank crews. In some cases in the engagements on the ninth of November, enemy fire was resumed before the American officers got back to their tanks. They all became surprisingly agile in remounting.

Night soon came and the tankers patrolled the beach hoping that another wave of tanks would arrive from the *Electra*. Later it was found that the seas had become high and that no more tanks would be received for twenty-four hours, the Navy being unable to launch them into the LCMs. Military commentators had predicted that no force could land on the coast of Morocco in the fall or winter months. Frequent storms, called "la Houle," kick up high waves in a few hours, often without any accompanying wind. These waves are formed by distant storms in the Atlantic. The waves on that coast sometimes measure sixty feet from crest to trough and start to break more than a mile from shore in sixty feet of water. From there into the Moroccan beach there can be successive rows of waves of lesser height, as the gradually sloping beach produces shallower water.

By good fortune the dread "la Houle" was not in operation early in the afternoon on the eighth, as the tankers were to start to land, so the first wave of LCMs with their tanks from the *Electra* safely made the beach at Mehedya. The seven LCMs returned from the beach to the ship, many miles out at sea, and by that time tanks could not successfully be loaded on the landing craft. Two LCMs and two tanks were lost in an attempt to load the tanks on the boats during the heavy seas.

Our tank crews searched up and down the beach to find the tanks of the second wave that were supposed to land that evening. I was under considerable apprehension for I knew we would be engaged in battle shortly, and wanted to augment our little force of tanks. We expected a tank fight to protect our infantry, while they fought north to the Lyautey airfield from our beachhead.

Just before midnight of the eighth, one of the officers of General Truscott's staff located me while we were searching the beaches and told me to report to him. While he was giving me his orders, a dark-complexioned sinister figure, bizarrely dressed, came and stood nearby, overhearing the orders. The man had on a helmet, a navy blouse, and army pants. It was probable that he was an Arab spy for the French. Truscott said, "George" (the challenge for the landing operation). The reply should have been "Patton." No response came from the man of mystery. Truscott seized the man by his blouse and shook him, yelling "George" again. The figure spoke, "Me no George, me Sergeant Lee, best damn cook in Army." He was thereupon enlisted on Truscott's staff. His Thanksgiving turkey and the fixin's in November 1942 proved that he was not boasting, as those who ate with the commander of Goalpost on Thanksgiving Day, 1942, can testify. Later Sergeant Phue P. Lee became General Patton's cook.

General Truscott gave instructions to take our seven tanks and proceed east before daybreak beyond the lagoon that lay inland from the beach, and take a position astride the Lyautey-Rabat road at the junction with the lagoon road to engage enemy tanks that were coming north from Rabat. First, however, I was instructed to proceed immediately to the lagoon with the seven tanks to act as guard to prevent infiltration of enemy troops. The tanks went to the lagoon and the crews and officers rested. There was no possibility of sleep because of the seriousness of the situation. The crews were dismounted and a guard on foot for each tank was established in addition to one of the crew left in each tank. The others lay on the ground awake.

This was our first night on a hostile shore. Our crews had been living and sleeping on the ground for many months and could not forget the characteristic smells of the earth. In the part of the United States where the 2d Armored Division had trained often there were overtones of the chicken yard, though in the pine woods it was sweet and pungent from the fallen needles. The ground near this pestilential lagoon had a sour, acrid, penetrating smell entirely unfamiliar and foreign. This strange African smell, compounded of 5,000 years of sheep and nomads living on the land, constantly reminded the tankers that they were on a strange continent.

There were ominous and chilling sounds; a sepulchral croaking, suggestive of Poe's raven. It seemed a bad omen and they hoped the expedition was not ill-fated. Later they learned that it was only the mating call of the great African tree toad.

Before first light, our tanks left the evil-smelling lagoon, coming to the top of the ridge which lay a half mile east of the sea. Looking down from the ridge in the dim light onto the grassy plain that lay at the foot of the inland slope of the ridge, we saw below us, less than half a mile away, a white farmhouse just east of the junction of the Lyautey-Rabat and lagoon roads. It seemed peaceful in the semi-light. We did not know the house was bulging with French infantry who were withholding their fire until their own tanks arrived on the scene from the south.

The American tanks proceeded down the eastern slope of the ridge to the road junction in the plain below. Two of the tanks were placed under Lieutenant John Mauney, from South Carolina, on the east side of the Lyautey-Rabat road within a hundred yards of the French-filled farmhouse; five of the tanks remaining on the west side of the road. The tanks were led into position, on foot, because radioing was impossible. The French infantry in the farmhouse withheld their fire although the officers on foot were lying in the rifle sights of that infantry at a range of about 100 yards. All was peaceful and quiet while the tanks were led into position. It was the time of morning (on the ninth) when the first streaks of dawn appear. No sooner were the U.S. tanks in place than true first light came, and with it a number of French tanks to do battle.

The fact that the French tanks, coming up from Rabat to the south, were not as far advanced as this road junction from their march of the day before has an unusual explanation.

On the eighth General Truscott sent two infantry platoons as outposts down the Lyautey–Rabat road. One platoon was sent to Sidi Bou Knadle several miles south of the landing beaches. The men in this platoon were either killed or wounded by the French tanks from Rabat early in the afternoon of the 8th of November. The other platoon was entrenched about a mile north of Sidi Bou Knadle along the Lyautey–Rabat road facing south toward Rabat. In a small trench at the side of the road a bazooka crew was located—a gunner and a loader.

The French tanks proceeding up the road from Rabat in the afternoon of the eighth, after passing through Sidi Bou Knadle, came within fifty yards of this slit trench and the gunner fired the bazooka at the first tank. The bazooka missed the tank and mowed down a eucalyptus tree about ten feet off the road. The tree was over a foot in diameter at the point where it was severed. The French saw this and fired a 37 round from one of their tanks at the Bazooka crew. The shell killed the loader and knocked the gunner unconscious.

The bazooka, however, was truly a surprise weapon and the French tankers did not realize that the strange contraption they found in the slit trench fired a rocket charge which could mow down a sturdy eucalyptus tree. Therefore, because they did not understand the operation of this new weapon, they started a reconnaissance to see if they could locate the U.S. heavy artillery that could cut off a tree of such size. This took several hours, and night fell before they had decided that they could not locate the U.S. heavy artillery.

Patton had always emphasized the surprise value of new weapons when first employed against the enemy; our bazooka produced surprisingly excellent effects on the enemy.

The French then went into bivouac for the night without advancing and did not start to move until just before daylight the next morning. It was only at first light the next day that the French tanks arrived at the junction of the lagoon road with the Lyautey–Rabat road to engage our tanks.

As a consquence, the 3d Armored Landing Team was able to place its seven available tanks astride the road leading to Rabat, preventing the French coming through onto the backs of our infantry, who were fighting north to take the airport at Lyautey. Our mission was to buy time for the infantry to capture that airfield.

The action of the new bazooka had unusual and unexpectedly good results. Without it the French might have gotten through with their tanks and thus killed many of the U.S. infantry and the remaining Americans might have been thrown back into the sea.

Scarcely had the American tanks been placed in position when the enemy tanks appeared in the half-light and we knew that we must turn them back. It flashed through each man's mind that this was what we had been trained for during the many strenuous months in the States. It was the survival of the fittest, for both tank forces could not remain on the same battlefield. Our five tanks on the east of the road were hotly engaged; sometimes the French and American tanks were within one hundred yards of each other. We met the enemy tanks head on, for "Heaven never helps the man who will not act" [3] and it was from that direction that unexpected help eventually came. Lieutenant John Mauney, with his two tanks on the west of the road, stopped the attack of two battalions of infantry and almost annihilated their leading company so that they never again tried to get through his position.

In accordance with our training, each American tank during battle that morning, by backing and then running forward, and never turning sideways, maneuvered to keep the thick front armor plate of each tank pointed always toward the French. In the lead tank I noticed there would be a shower of sparks when the front armor plate was hit. I thought the French were using high explosive instead of armor-piercing shells. I learned afterwards that the sparks were caused by the impact of the hard armor-piercing core of the French shells with the armor plate of the tank. The white-hot hard steel core of the French shell ricocheted off the thick frontal armor of the American tank high into the air. It was found a little later, however, that the American side armor would not turn these shells. Two U.S. tanks from C Company, 70th Tank Battalion, for a short time under my command, and which I had ordered to an outpost position, were ambushed by French tanks hiding in a clump of cactus and received hits from the side. They were

[3] Sophocles.

121

pierced and the American crews were either killed or wounded.

Tank tactics, as constantly expounded by Patton, follow the rule of using part of your force to "hold the enemy by the nose" and sending the remainder of the tanks around the flank "to kick him in the ass." But I had no communications and our flanking force, if used, would be completely out of touch with our holding force. Further, to permit any gap in our inadequately held line of tanks might permit one or two enemy tanks, which greatly outnumbered us, to get through and onto the backs of our infantry. The only thing to do was to hit the French tanks head on, so as I stood in the turret, I waved my arm forward as a signal, ducked into the turret, and went to work with our 37 mm. gun.

Despite the inaccuracy of American fire, our lead tank made some lucky hits on the French tanks. By 0830 hours our situation was desperate; the superior number of French tanks were delivering extremely accurate fire. Because the weather was chilly, the mechanisms of the breeches of our American tanks guns did not properly eject the empty shells when the guns were fired. All the loaders, who were also the tank commanders, lost their fingernails clawing out the shells after the guns had been fired. If my throat had been cut I would not have bled a drop. What surely turned the tide, however, was the unexpected supporting fires of the U.S. Cruiser *Savannah*. It was manna from Heaven! It was part of Patton's plan to have a spotter plane from the *Savannah* flying over the battlefield ready for any emergency.

The *Savannah* had been steaming along the coast several miles from shore while the spotter plane, in radio communication with the ship, watched the battle. Since the American tanks' radios were not working, it took the plane crew considerable time to sense the desperate predicament of the little American tank force. When they fully appreciated the difficulties below, they ordered eight-inch naval gunfire over the ridge of hills which lay between the battlefield and the sea. The plane crew adjusted this indirect gunfire up from the rear of the French tank forces to within one hundred yards of the American lead tank. The duel between the American and French tanks took place at distances between three hundred and one hundred yards. This highly accurate and unexpected naval gunfire was the

122

deciding factor in the fight. The eight-inch naval shell made giant craters almost big enough to hold a tank and they really discouraged the French.

It is believed to have been the first time naval gunfire was used in support of a tank duel. We will always have a warm spot in our hearts for the *Savannah* and her crew. She was later badly disabled with a high number of casualties and the tankers of this little tank force sent a letter of appreciation and condolence to the survivors of this brave ship.

The French withdrew to the south towards Rabat. The tank guns had scarcely stopped smoking when General Truscott and his aide appeared. He asked me what tactics I had been using and laughed when I replied, "Nothing fancy—we just kept pecking away at 'em, General."

The French tanks attacked again that same day, and once more fell back under our tank fire and the assistance of naval gunfire from the *Savannah*.

The valorous Lieutenant Mauney received the DSC for his work in this, his first engagement. He went on to similar deeds in Sicily and in Europe, until on the day of the St. Lô break-through, he was killed leading his tank platoon.

The second day of the tank fighting, which was the tenth of November and the third day of the operation, a still larger force of French tanks appeared from Rabat about noon and another tank duel was under way. By that time, however, more American tanks and other fighting vehicles had been landed from the *Electra*. Our landing team communications half-track equipped with radio, and its crew, had landed and could communicate with the spotter plane from the *Savannah*. So, on the second day of the tank fighting, our half-track radioed the spotter plane and called for supporting naval gunfire, which again turned the trick, and the French tanks once more retreated to the south.

That evening General Truscott told the tankers that on the following morning they were to leave enough tanks to hold the position, and take the remaining tanks south to capture the airfield at Salé, an adjacent town on the north bank of the Oued Bou Regreg, a river dividing the towns Salé and Rabat. (It was at Salé that Daniel Defoe reputedly wrote *Robinson Crusoe* while in prison.)

In these battles for the strategically important airfields the Navy played an important and daring part. Lieutenant Commander Robert Brodie, Jr., was in command of an old teakettle of a destroyer, the *Dallas*, DD 199, that was supposed to be a burnt offering in the battle for the Lyautey airport. On the tenth he charged up the Oued-Sebou between the jetties at the river's mouth, ran aground three times, but doggedly ploughed ahead through mud and silt to land the Army Rangers at the airport. On his way past the old Portuguese Kasbah lying high on the cliff on the south bank of the river, he engaged an enemy battery nearby and succeeded in silencing it. Seventy-five Rangers were landed by the *Dallas* at the Lyautey airport and materially helped in the capture of this strategic installation.

That evening of the tenth, before we were to attack the Salé airport, a good portion of the landing team tanks were on shore and I established armored headquarters on the ridge between the junction of the lagoon and the Lyautey-Rabat roads and the Atlantic Ocean. There I hoisted the 3d Armored Landing Team flag that had been made for us by a little seamstress near Fort Bragg just before we left the States.

The line that night was outposted with armored vehicles, and the order was given for all available U.S. guns to fire on any vehicles approaching on the Lyautey–Rabat road from the south. The firepower that could be concentrated on this road was tremendous. About 2200 hours a strange formation appeared. A small car, the French equivalent of a U.S. jeep, came down the road toward the American lines. Flying at the front of the radiator was the Tricolor upon which was turned a flashlight so that all could see it. In addition to the driver, there was a bugler, blowing vigorously, and a French officer holding the flashlight trained on the flag.

This car had not gone far when the American armor cut loose. The occupants of the car hit the ditch on the side of the road and nobody was hurt. But there wasn't a piece of the car left "as big as your hand." Afterwards the French major in charge of the group was questioned as to why he took this risky method of delivering a message to the American forces. He replied, "Why, I knew everything would be all right, because our bugler was blowing 'Cease fire'!" The Good Lord was with those French that night.

This unofficial French cease fire was later confirmed about two in the morning of the eleventh, when our tanks were preparing to go on their mission to take the airfield at

124

Salé. Our command half-track which was high on the ridge between the ocean and the Lyautey–Rabat road received a welcome message, "General Pétain asks that we cease this useless bloodshed. Please relay this message to General Truscott in command of the task force 'Goalpost.' "

This was spoken in English by one of our Air Force officers, Major P. Morgan Hamilton, in Patton's G-2 Section. He was speaking from the radio carried by his jeep. He and Colonel Craw at great risk had driven a jeep into the French lines and the French had told him that Pétain wanted an armistice negotiated immediately. Colonel Craw, who was in the jeep with Hamilton, was killed on this mission. The airfield now at Port Lyautey is named Craw Field in his honor. Both Major Hamilton and Colonel Craw were awarded the Congressional Medal of Honor. To have gone to the French as they did under the circumstances was almost certain death. The French Goumier troops would be sure to fire on them, and that one of the two survived is miraculous.

The over-all plan of the Armistice was dictated by Patton. The Lyautey armistice was merely a local and a formal matter.

The description of the battles at Lyautey are given largely from the point of view of armor because of my intimate knowledge of the details. It is nevertheless true that the role of our infantry was bloodier and more difficult. An observation is in order. One ingredient of Patton's success in war was highlighted by the Goalpost action. The fine discipline of the troops under Patton, and their performance in this, their first show, were characteristic of all Patton operations.

The Béthouard Conspiracy

After the Armistice we learned of an abortive attempt, known as the Béthouard Conspiracy, by some of the French Army to assist the Americans.

Colonel Magnan, of the French Army, gave Lieutenant Colonel Leonard H. "Steamer" Nason the following account of this plot, as he knew it. On the Saturday morning prior to the landings, that is, November 7th, at 10:00 A.M., Colonel Magnan who commanded the French Regiment, RICM, was summoned to Casablanca by General Béthouard, who told him that American forces were landing at Morocco the next day and asked if he would co-operate to assist the landing. Having agreed, Colonel Magnan was ordered to issue ammunition to his regiment, to seize the communication centers in Rabat, and to accompany General Béthouard to place the Governor General of Morocco, General Noguès, in arrest if Noguès planned to order resistance.

General Béthouard arrived in Rabat Sunday morning about 1:30 A.M. and he and Colonel Magnan proceeded to the Residence. They asked to see Noguès on a matter of extreme urgency. Noguès appeared in his dressing gown. General Béthouard then asked what Noguès' attitude would be in the face of an invasion of Morocco by the United States within the next few hours. Instead of replying definitely, Noguès asked to be excused to put on his clothes. Noguès telephoned to Admiral Michelier, commanding the French naval forces in Morocco, and asked him if he had any knowledge of a hostile fleet close enough to the Moroccan coast to launch an invasion before dawn. Michelier replied that he had no such information, nor anything that might faintly indicate any hostile naval concentration offshore. More than that, he asserted that if any such naval concentration existed, his security services, which consisted of air, surface and submarine patrols, would certainly have discovered it. Noguès ordered Michelier to direct vessels under his command to fire on any suspicious vessels they encountered.

While Noguès was still dressing, he received a telephone call from the German Armistice Commission of Casablanca informing him that they had intercepted a radio broadcast, presumably by the President of the United States, informing the French population of North Africa that an invasion was taking place and urging the civil population to receive the American troops with friendliness.

The time of this telephone call is easy to estimate. The commander of the forces at Safi, in his official report to his French superiors, stated that he was alerted at 3:00 A.M. Sunday morning by the local members of the German and Italian Armistice Commission who had been notified from Casablanca. Noguès must have received his alert at about the same time.

A lieutenant from the Signal Company of the RICM told "Steamer" Nason that these telephone calls could pass between Noguès and Casablanca even though the RICM had seized the telephone exchange. Noguès had a direct wire to Admiral Michelier through the German Armistice Commission switchboard.

General Béthouard and Colonel Magnan remained with General Noguès until about ten o'clock Sunday morning. Naturally there was no sign of an American landing at Rabat. The only report received by the French from Safi was that a destroyer of unknown nationality had tried to enter the harbor and was sunk. Shortly after 10:00 A.M. on Sunday, Noguès remarked to General Béthouard and Colonel Magnan that there appeared to be no sign of an American landing and suggested that they submit to arrest. He promised that if they would do so they would get a fair trial. If they refused to surrender and order the RICM to leave the strategic points it had seized, he would have the two officers shot immediately for disobedience to orders. The two officers were then sent to Casablanca and confined in the military prison where they remained until released by General Patton's personal intercession.

Apparently this intervention by French troops had been arranged between Mr. Murphy, our Ambassador in Algiers, and General Béthouard in the early fall of 1942. The plan for the American landings then contemplated a landing at Rabat.

7. Occupying Morocco and Fighting in Tunisia

THE Armistice between the French and ourselves was in effect, and shortly after November 11th Patton ordered his troops into the Mamora Cork Forest. Patton met with some of Eisenhower's staff who immediately chastised him for not disarming the French. Assuming the offensive, Patton proved to them that to disarm or discredit the French meant an Arab war which would immobilize 60,000 men as a starter. He finally persuaded them he was right. Moving to Casablanca, he established his headquarters in the Shell Building which was very modern and first class even by American standards. Extracts of the diary show how his men shared their comforts with the Navy, and how the Navy felt about him when he left the *Augusta*.

November 12, 1942

We had over 2,000 Navy ashore from sunken boats and clothed all, but hope to get clothes back as we have no reserves. My men gave blankets to the wounded and slept cold. . . .

When I left the *Augusta* for keeps today, the entire crew lined the side of the ship and cheered. I was later told that this was spontaneous and seldom, if ever, accorded a non-naval person.

For the 3d Armored Landing Team, the tension of these times was broken in an amusing way the day following the Armistice. Our armor had gone into bivouac on the ridge separating the Atlantic Ocean from the Rabat–Lyautey road that paralleled the sea. The small armored staff of two officers were riding along the road near the Mamora Cork Forest a few miles south of Lyautey. Their jeep flushed a covey of chukker quail. The staff (Major Shorty Parker and Captain John Werts) automatically leaped out of their vehicle and pursued the birds on foot, firing at them with their tommy guns. The quail flew in a series of short flights, as they do the world over. The staff were bird shooters from the South, and their reaction at sight of the quail was that of any good hunting dog—they could not resist the urge to hunt.

The net results were immediate. First—no quail. Second—the adjacent commands, who were on edge from the recent fighting, started radioing each headquarters to find out the direction of the attack. These two bird shooters had to spend the rest of the day visiting and mollifying the outfits nearby.

Patton placed his troops in the best strategic and physical locations available. Bivouac areas were organized in the surrounding countryside and were occupied primarily by units of the 9th Infantry and 2d Armored Divisions. These areas were in the vicinity of the Mamora Cork Forest. This forest had been planted by the French about twenty-five years before our landing. The cork bark is removed from the trees periodically, and about the third skinning, when the tree is twenty years old, the cork is thick and dense and suitable for corks for wine bottles.

The Mamora Cork Forest extends from Lyautey at the north to Rabat twenty-five miles south and for many miles inland. The bivouac of the 2d Armored Division was located in the vicinity of the little town of Monod about ten miles east of Rabat. When "la Houle" was operating, the roar of the surf on the Moroccan beaches could be heard that far inland.

Patton and the immediate staff of his command, the 1st Armored Corps, moved from the Grand Hotel in Casablanca to the Villa Maas. The staff consisted of Major General Keyes; Brigadier General Wilbur; Colonel Gay; Lieutenant Colonel Harkins; Major Jenson and Captain Stiller, Aides-de-Camp.

The villa, a magnificent one, was located in the suburbs of Casablanca near the Anfa Hotel where the famous conferences between President Roosevelt and Prime Minister Churchill, and Generals de Gaulle and Giraud of the French Army were later to take place in January and early February, 1943. The villa had been occupied for some time by the German Armistice Commission which fled Casablanca precipitately on November 11, 1942. They had left the villa in beautiful condition. It was here that General Patton later conferred with President Roosevelt and Prime Minister Churchill.

He also issued a short order on November 15th predated to November 11th, announcing the victory and warning his troops that there must be no letdown for there was a long, hard road ahead.

HEADQUARTERS WESTERN TASK FORCE
Fedala, French Morocco

November 11, 1942

1. Soldiers of the Western Task Force aided by the Navy, you have accomplished the impossible and on the anniversary of Armistice Day have added another Armistice which too, will live in history—at 0700 the enemy ceased firing.

Do not let your joy in the present victory slacken your efforts to achieve greater fame in the glorious battles which are to come.

In solemn loyalty to our country and our heroic dead, we must bend every effort to perfect ourselves, not only in tactics, but also in deportment and soldierly appearance.

With complete confidence for our continued success, I congratulate you on what you have already achieved.

s/ G. S. PATTON, JR.
Major General, U.S. Army
Commanding

Even in his message of congratulations the troops were told that he was still running a "tight ship." It was this conviction that was at the bottom of the alleged "feud" (at least a strong difference of opinion) between Patton and Bill Mauldin, the cartoonist of *Stars and Stripes*. Mauldin, by the glorification of his unkempt characters Willie and Joe, encouraged many to imitate them and Patton believed this lowered discipline and cost lives. This celebrated argument between Patton and Mauldin resulted in both remaining unconvinced and the matter ended there.

Operating from his headquarters at first in Casablanca and later in Rabat, Patton found himself in the role of conquering hero, military commander and senior American representative in Morocco. His position was unique. He had invaded and liberated a country, which almost instantly became friendly. For a while he was, under Eisenhower's direction, the American representative in a complex country larger than California with a population of over 7,000,000.

Having to deal with the slippery resident French High Commissioner, Noguès (later executed by the French), the French Army and Navy, the Sultan of Morocco, and later the spiritual leader of the Berbers, El Glaoui of Marrakech, General Patton was an impressive and forceful representative. Both as a diplomat and a military commander he showed his worth in the following letter to General Eisenhower. He illustrated his knowledge of history and diplomacy in his impromptu address to the Sultan. Many subjects of interest were covered in this letter: international statemanship; French cooperation; new weapons; and excess equipment.

November 19, 1942

When Nogues had finished his speech and been answered by the Sultan, it occurred to me that as a representative of the dominant power in Morocco, I should say something. Therefore, without asking anyone's permission, I stepped up in front of the throne and made the following statement in English, which the Sultan clearly understood but which was translated into French and then into Arabic in order to comply with the formality of the occasion.

I said, "Your Majesty, as a representative of the great President of the United States, whom I have the honor to represent, as the commander of huge military forces in Morocco, I wish to present the compliments of the United States on this occasion, the 15th anniversary of your ascension to the throne of your ancestors, and I wish to assure you that so long as Your Majesty's country, in cooperation with the French government of Morocco, cooperates with us and facilitates our efforts, we are sure, with the help of God to achieve certain victory against our common enemy, the Nazis.

"I am convinced that Your Majesty and the French Government of Morocco share this opinion. So long as we are in accord on this point, we have only the brightest future to look forward to. I am impelled to the belief in this mutual accord when I remember that one of Your Majesty's great predecessors presented to our famous President, George Washington, the buildings now occupied by the American Mission at Tangier, and when I also remember that since the days of the great Washington, the accord and friendship with the French has been equally profound.

"I wish to take this occasion of complimenting Your Majesty on the intelligent cooperation which his subjects have accorded the Americans and also to express again my profound appreciation of the excellent bearing and splendid discipline of Your Majesty's soldiers."

These remarks seem to have had a very satisfactory effect on both the Arabs and the French. In fact the Sultan told me that my presence and my remarks would have a profound effect on the whole Moslem world of which he was the spiritual head, because, since the Turks had unveiled their women, they had lost face with Allah. I am not sure my influence with Allah is very profound, but it is nice to have him think so. I trust that I did not overstep the bounds of propriety in doing what I did, but as I have already said, I felt that the prestige of the United States must be upheld.

So far as I am able to learn, both from reports of others and from personal observation, the French cooperation with us has been complete on the part of the Army, Navy, and civilian affairs. Yesterday, the French Navy performed a truly masterful feat in bringing in practically all of our Number 2 convoy into the harbor, rapidly and efficiently. It is only fair to say that the work of the American Navy, particularly that of Admiral Hall, was of the highest order.

In the attack on the old Moorish fort at Lyautey, we had a real movie war. Truscott moved his 101 self-propelled guns to within 200 yards of the wall, blew holes in it, and the garrison was finally overcome by bayonets and hand grenades, many men being actually killed by both weapons. The French defending this fort belonged to the Foreign Legion and fought magnificently.

NEW WEAPONS

One point of interest is that while we were holding the lighthouse, the French counterattack at dusk was made with more than a battalion. At that time we had one platoon at the lighthouse. An infantry 2nd Lieutenant S. W. Sprindis, 60th Infantry, armed with a rocket launcher, moved from place to place behind the wall, firing on the French and giving them the impression that a battery of 75's were present. This impression was so strong that the French fell back and the lighthouse was held.

I believe that this fact will be of interest to you as demonstrating the effectiveness of the rocket launcher. On the other hand, steps should be taken which will protect the firer of the rocket launcher from the back blast of the rocket. At the present time, the firer is considerably burned each time he discharges the weapon. While these burns are not serious, they are disconcerting. I promoted the man to a First Lieutenant, and shall recommend him for a decoration.

EXCESS EQUIPMENT

I desire to point out that in future landing operations

we must dispense with gas masks, extra ammunition, and even packs. Our men were too heavily loaded. The leading waves should have only rifles and 100 rounds of ammunition.

General Patton was a great admirer of the French and believed they were doing fine work in Morocco. He knew that America would be intimately associated with the problems of the defense of French Morocco. Including the French and other Europeans who number about 400,000, it has a population of roughly eight million, of whom over half are Berber. There are also 200,000 Jews. The avowed aim of the French in Morocco is to make the Moroccan capable of self-government.

Mindful of the importance of military pageantry to bind the Americans and the French together, Patton shortly after the Armistice held three combined United States and French troop reviews at Rabat, Casablanca and Lyautey. Rabat is a town of many thousands, part Arab and Berber, and part French. The original walled Kasbah at one time comprised the whole town, but as with many fast-growing Moroccan communities, it has spilled outside of the old Kasbah, like vines overflowing a garden wall.

Patton planned to knit the French and American nations into amicable partnership for war against the common German enemy. As a soldier, dealing with soldiers, he used his natural characteristics to do the gracious and the useful thing. These reviews were part of his long-term planning that resulted in later victories of French troops fighting with the American Army. The entry of the French 2ème Division Blindée (2d Armored Division) into Paris under French General Le Clerc was one product of his long-range planning.

A joint review and the party at the Sultan's palace afterwards are described in a letter to his wife:

December 21, 1943

DARLING BEA:

Since writing you yesterday morning, I have been to two more functions. At noon yesterday, we flew to Rabat, had a lunch at the Residency, and then went to an American-French parade. Nogues and I went in my jeep, with the flags and the handrail. Nogues was much impressed and the people thought it wonderful.

133

Opposite the reviewing stand was a regiment of Moroccan Chasseurs-à-Chaval—red uniforms, white capes and white turbans. A band of about 100 pieces from the same regiment was in front with their sheep mascot and the umbrella with the bells.

First a battalion of our Seventh came by, very impressive as to size of men and strength of companies. The heavy weapons company with the machine guns and antitank guns, all motorized, made a big hit. Then a battalion of French territorial infantry, white. This regiment stormed Fort Douaumont in the old war. Then, a battalion of Moroccan infantry, very famous, with the red Fourragère. Then, a dismounted French air squadron who held the record for the number of Boche planes downed in 1914–1918. Next, a company of new Renault tanks the French had hidden in the hills for two years while the Germans were there.

The French all march better than we do and their bands are much better, but their weapons are not as good as ours. Then we brought a battery of 105's and one of 75's, self-propelled; then, a company of our M-5 light tanks, and finally a platoon of our mediums.

The Grand Vizier and his retinue were in the stand, and were very pleased when I went out of my way to speak to them.

Driving back from the review, I had a regular ovation. It is quite thrilling to have about 100,000 people cheering, yelling and clapping and shouting: *"Vive l'Amérique."* I kissed my hands to them, which had the effect of rousing them still more. Even some of the veiled women waved at me, which is quite unusual.

Today at noon we went to a Diffa given by the Pasha of Casa. We were seated at round tables for six. We sat on divans and cushions. My table was of cypress wood, inlaid in ebony, lemonwood and pearl. It had silver vases of hospitality inlaid around the edge.

The Pasha of Safi and the Pasha of Casa are sons of the Grand Vizier. They were both educated in England and Switzerland, and spoke perfect French and good English. Here is what we had to eat:

1. Pigeon pie, with meat, eggs and other things; very fine pastry.
2. A sheep.

3. A turkey.
4. Brasia, which is a stew of meat, vegetables, honey and almonds, and which is very nice.
5. Chickens—one each.
6. Kouskous—which is barley molded in a circle and full of lamb stew and vegetables. It is hard to eat with only one hand—thumb and first and middle fingers.

Then we had cigars and coffee; then mint tea and cakes. Then they brought washbowls with soap; then incense, and finally silver perfume bottles. The Arabs went to town with this—squirting it on their heads and up their sleeves.

The tea-making is quite a ceremony and two old gentlemen were much honored to have the right to do it. They were very clean about it. Geoff Keyes said one was a five-goal tea maker, the other a one-goal man. The five-goaler made two separate pots, then mixed them so as to be sure both were exactly alike.

Today I saw a set of very fine pictures of the actual landing. Surles probably can get you a set. We have no extras here.

G.

General Patton wisely decided not to disturb the internal affairs of Morocco. He established cordial relations with the Residence at Rabat and while keeping careful watch on Noguès, made no attempt to have him removed. The same relations were established with all other civil government officials under Noguès. Thus, there were no internal difficulties, or emergencies, which could have distracted us from our primary mission of furnishing troops and supplies to Tunisia.

This policy definitely displeased some of the public in the United States. There were articles written against retention of the Vichy crowd in power. Patton took a long chance of political disfavor at home, for had Noguès double-crossed him, it would have gone hard.

On the other hand, French cooperation in protecting the hundreds of miles of railroad to Oran was essential. Many Army leaders were still strongly attached to Pétain and thus to Vichy. Internal trouble in Morocco might have spelled defeat in Tunisia; and the policy of cooperation with the existing French authorities, though involving risk, turned out to be successful.

The American dead were buried a few days after the Armistice at a little cemetery near the old Portuguese Kasbah at Mehedya. The ceremony was touching at this far, strange place, accompanied by the Atlantic rollers booming on the shore. A number of French widows dressed in black attended. Their husbands had just fallen fighting against us. Now we were Allies united and fighting for the freedom of man. In no better way could the French have shown their desire to join with us.

General Patton was deeply impressed by the presence of the French widows at the burial ceremony of the American dead. When he saw them, tears came in his eyes. Two days later he and his staff attended a similar ceremony for the dead French soldiers and sailors.

A few days after the Armistice, November 11, 1942, General Patton sent word to me that my old friend of World War I, Prince Charles Murat, wanted to see me. He was a French first lieutenant in the Somme counter-offensive of the spring of 1918, a great-great-grandson of Napoleon's Marshal Murat, Prince of Piedmont.

Lieutenant Colonel Murat was assigned to the 2d Armored Division and bunked in the Mamora Cork Forest in my tent. Murat, twenty-four years after the Somme battles of 1918, in another World War, on another continent, studied American tanks and tank tactics, but the enemy was the same.

Murat acted as liaison between the United States 2d Armored Division and the French tank group based in Rabat, and the French were furnished American tanks and were trained by us. There was created the French 2ème Division Blindée, which took that name in honor of our 2d Armored Division. General Le Clerc commanded this division which was to enter Paris in triumph later in 1944, for the honor and glory of the taking of Paris was given to French troops. The joy of the Parisians on the appearance of their French armored division in their beloved capital was unbounded.

During the lull in activity, after the Armistice in Morocco, Patton found time to enjoy the sport afforded by the country. That country is famous for its wild boar, which feed on berries and nuts in the forests and attain great size and ferocity. He went on many boar hunts and killed a great number of boar. There is a continual open season for shooting them, because of their danger to the population and also because they are great destroyers of crops.

December the 19th was a great day of celebration and Moroccan political festivities. The activities centered around the Sultan's palace in Rabat. The palace buildings are grouped around a grass-covered square. That day many Caids came to pay homage to the Sultan, who received them under a large umbrella carried by retainers. Each Caid presented the Sultan with a symbolic small bag of salt in token of fealty, bowing deeply in reverence. There was more bowing that day than an American is likely to see in a lifetime, for individuals not only bowed but there was bowing by the squad and by the platoon.

The platoons of cavalry that formed the palace guard put on a lively show of charging toward the Sultan firing blanks from their long-barreled rifles, which are shot from horseback and handled with one hand like a pistol. One platoon was mounted on black horses, one on bay mounts and one on pure white horses, all of pure Arabian stock and of great beauty and well trained. The coal-black troopers were dressed in baggy pants with much red in the uniform. They must have been Senegalese stock.

There were street performers who put on gymnastics and other shows. The hat was passed after each act was finished. One act consisted of a man and his donkey. The man would lean over to pick up his hat and the donkey would kick him in the pants. The head of the act would feign sleep and the donkey would lie down beside him. These actions brought wild applause. Then the donkey would lie down and the man would take off his sandals and take a running jump, landing with his bare feet on the donkey's stomach. There was a loud report. This had the audience rolling in the aisles.

All American troops during this stay in French Morocco trained strenuously and at least one day a week went on maneuvers, where they went without sleep for twenty-four hours. We knew there was much hard fighting ahead. There were many rumors that the Spanish were going to attack south from Spanish Morocco, so a company of tanks, from my battalion, was sent to outpost the border between Spanish and French Morocco and was located at Souk el Arba (translated, "Market on Wednesday") on the French side of the border. It was commanded by Captain Ray Gerritty, who later made the supreme sacrifice in Tunisia. Often I would go to Souk el Arba to inspect, though we were in constant and clear radio communication through our battalion communications half-track, even though the distance from our battalion headquarters in the Mamora Cork Forest to Gerritty's "A" Company headquarters was 90 miles.

Always I would try to go on Wednesdays, the market day, for then the town was full of bustle and life. Merchants would come into town to bring honey, eggs, fowl, and woven grass rugs. There would be on sale camel's butter and camel's milk, and the storytellers would be plying their trade. The young girls, often riding behind their fathers on donkeys, would flirt with the young camel drivers and the salesmen of oranges. Not all the Arab and Berber women in Morocco are veiled and some were very pretty. There was an atmosphere of cheerful confusion which was a tonic and a change from the regimented life of soldering.

In January General Patton arranged to meet General Orgaz who commanded the Spanish troops. For accuracy the diary is quoted here.

January 4, 1943

Met General Orgaz at the border at 12:05. He looked so much like (our Mrs. Shorb) Aunt Lubby, moustache and all, that I almost kissed him. We had a very pleasant talk and a nice laugh. The Spanish infantry in the Guard of Honor at Larache were the best looking and the best drilled troops I have ever seen. Their weapons were out of date. In passing in review they are at left shoulder and swing the right hand as high as the face. The field music and band both executed an exaggerated eyes right while playing which is every effective. Gave General Orgaz my dagger whip.

Orgaz returned the favor with a case of very fine sherry. This meeting created uneasiness in General Noguès' headquarters, as it was directed by Allied Force Headquarters in Algiers and excluded the French. General Eisenhower agreed to permit Noguès to send a representative to accompany Patton. Noguès' point was that the absence of French representation would be misinterpreted by the Arabs and the Berbers.

Roosevelt and Churchill came to Morocco for the Casa-

138

blanca conference. Sergeant Meeks was in charge of a dinner at Villa Maas, Patton's quarters in Casablanca when the President visited there. Meeks remembers that special table water was served to the President from a spring in Maryland. At the meal were President Roosevelt, Churchill, General Marshall, General Patton, General Keyes, General Gay, Harry Hopkins, General de Gaulle, and others. Roosevelt and Hopkins and Generals George Patton and Mark Clark had lunch in the field with the troops just north of Rabat, between the Rabat–Lyautey road and the sea. I happened to command the honor guard on this occasion. President Roosevelt's jeep stopped in front of the guard, composed of those who had been decorated from the landing operation. The President, who had never seen any of these men before, said to Lieutenant Colonel Stokes: "Fancy meeting you here."

The troops who had made the landing on the Moroccan shores a few weeks before were lined up on either side of the road for miles, proud to be reviewed by their President and eager to see him. By this time all units had been spruced up from their battle days and presented a magnificent appearance. President Roosevelt dismounted from a staff car and tranferred to a jeep.

It was the first time since the Civil War that a President of the United States had ever looked into the faces of over 40,000 men who had just come from combat. It was said that the President expressed himself as being very deeply moved. Imagine the disappointment of the troops, however, to find as the President's jeep approached that the Secret Service bodyguards so flanked him as to make him almost invisible beyond fifty yards. The American troops, to a man, were amazed at the diligence of the Secret Service men who each held a drawn pistol to protect the Commander-in-Chief from being assassinated by his own loyal troops. Every officer and man present shared General Patton's feelings of utter disgust.

During Mr. Churchill's attendance at the Casablanca conference, an amusing incident took place. He had dinner with General Patton in the Villa Maas, staying up very late telling stories, at which he is a master. Finally at about 3:00 A.M. he decided to go back to his quarters near the Anfa Hotel. He was positive in insisting that nobody accompany him, as he wished to walk. When he approached the wire enclosure around the Anfa Hotel he was halted by an American sentry, a farm boy from North Carolina, who challenged the Prime Minister and then called, "Corporal of the Guard, I have a feller down here who claims he is the Prime Minister of Great Britain. I think he is a goddamn liar." When the Corporal of the Guard arrived he recognized Mr. Churchill. This incident apparently pleased Mr. Churchill greatly, for he told it afterwards on many occasions.

Patton visited the Tunisian front in December, 1942. Helmeted and carrying two revolvers, he arrived in his armored scout car with machine guns mounted and manned fore and aft, shouting, "Where are the bastards? I want to get shot at!" But he hardly had time to get shot at before Allied Forces Headquarters ordered him back. Somewhat surprised, he remarked, "Those damned Spaniards must be acting up." Nevertheless, he remained in the news that came from the U.S. as the leader of American Armor at the front. Much had happened on that front before he finally did arrive to take command of the U.S. II Corps in March 1943.

Following the successful Allied landings in the vicinity of Oran and Algiers, the British First Army, under Lieutenant General Kenneth Anderson, was activated and initiated the drive on Tunis. The Germans entered Tunisia shortly after the Allied landings and the French Commander, General Barré, began the withdrawal of his poorly equipped and relatively immobile troops toward the west.

American tank units of CCB (Combat Command B), 1st Armored Division, were attached to the British and largely used up before that command itself entered the battle. There resulted a scrambling of inadequately supported units of three nationalities at the front with a lack of maintenance and communication facilities. This situation, together with mud and stubborn German resistance, stalled the Allies and eventually threw them back on the defensive.

Reinforcements were pushed to a front that soon spread out along the Eastern Dorsal, covering all too thinly the whole width of Tunisia. American troops were widely scattered along the front under British or French commands until January 1943, when the U.S. II Corps took over a sector. But before this occurred the Germans were prepared to disrupt the menace forming in the rear of Rommel's forces which were withdrawing westward before the British Eighth Army along the northern portion of Libya and Tripolitania near the Mediterranean Sea.

After the Germans had defeated a number of American counterattacks at Lessouda and Sidi-bou-Sid, whose object was to restore Allied positions in the vicinity of Faid Pass, Rommel drove forward and quickly secured Kasserine Pass, only to be fought to a standstill on Foussana Plain and at Thala and Sbiba passes. He was then forced to retreat back from whence his attack had been launched.

The account of the tank fighting northwest of Kasserine Pass is of historic interest. About the 20th of February, 1943 Rommel broke through elements of our troops at Kasserine Pass. Brigadier General P. M. Robinett commanding Combat Command B of the 1st Armored Division was ordered by Major General Harmon to stop Rommel. He went into position with his American tanks in front of Djebel el Hamra. A pitched battle between Rommel's tanks and ours took place there on February 21st. Robinett's tanks held. On the 22nd, Rommel re-formed and attacked again, and this time he was thrown back for a loss. Robinett had the distinction of turning Rommel at his point of greatest penetration into the Allied lines. Never again in Africa did the German armor have the success that they had achieved before this. Robinett's victory marked the turn of the tide, though there was much hard fighting still to be done.

But the German offensive had inflicted serious losses and heads had to fall. One vacancy made an opening for a corps commander which Patton filled in March 1943. The troops had been criticized by the High Command and Patton himself believed them undisciplined. Some claimed that he gave them discipline in a miraculously short time, and that they fought well thereafter. However, many of his friends among the troops contend that no disciplinary miracle occurred but that the bringing together of American troops and a real American leader, willing to be seen and felt at the very front, was the true story of the transformation that accompanied the arrival of General Patton in Tunisia.

German forces were later, in June, to be completely defeated and captured, caught in a nutcracker between the Allied troops driving to the east and the Eighth British Army driving north.

On arriving at the front, one of Patton's early activities was to insist that his orders for the proper wearing of the uniform be carried out. Both officers and men were disciplined for failing to obey his orders. Our newspaper correspondents were hostile to his enforcement of orders which they considered trivia. To their minds at this early stage of the war, this insistence on making the men fight and also wear what they were told seemed unduly harsh and oppressive. They had not seen the results that Patton could achieve by his formula for saving lives and winning a war so effectively demonstrated by his Third Army later in Europe in 1944 and 1945. Therefore, the press was less than enthusiastic.

Sergeant George Meeks states that in Tunisia Patton gathered up enlisted men and officers who were not wearing their helmets, and told them that he would fine them $25 or give them a court martial. The court martial would show on their records; all took the fine and their records were not harmed.

Among the front line troops, there was a fable that Patton caught one of his staff officers on the latrine without his helmet and fined him $25.

If possible, Patton gave punishment in such a way that it would bring the lesson home without injuring the official record of the officer or enlisted man. Because of fines imposed for not wearing the steel helmet, when and as prescribed, this item of wear became known as "the $25 derby."

He boosted the fighting spirit of troops happy to return to the command of a fighting American and made them a winning team in less than thirty days. His peculiar and, perhaps, undemocratic methods helped. To win wars and hold down casualties, some of the teachings of personal liberty must be abandoned in the cause of fighting efficiency.

Patton was well under way and entrenched as II Corps Commander by the 23rd of March. Diary entries depicting his humility are worthy of note:

The Lord helped a lot today. I visited the surgical hospital—it was pretty gruesome, but it was strange how the men followed me with their eyes, fearing I would not speak to each one. I talked to all who were conscious. One little boy, said, "Are you General Patton?" I said, "Yes," and he said, "Oh, God." Another one said, "You know *me*. You made a talk to my battalion at Casablanca." I told him I remembered him well.

I hate fighting from the rear, but today it was too complicated to leave the telephone.

The fighting in Tunisia was looked upon as a chance to train both American troops and American officers, therefore the operations were "under wraps"; objectives were restricted.

On March 25th, General Alexander gave the U.S. II Corps under Patton a series of three missions. All these missions were accomplished. This directive from Alexander stated that the firm base initially held along the line Abiod-Sbiba should be moved forward to the line Gafsa-Sbeitla. That the 9th Division and the 34th Division were released to II Corps, the 9th to attack in conjunction with the 1st Division along the Gafsa-Gabes axis, with a view to opening the pass north of Hill 369 to permit passage of the First Armored Division. That this attack was to secure the road junction north of Hill 369 and the hills north and south thereof.

By capturing this hill, the II Corps would control the pass between Djebel Chemsi and Djebel Berda. When this second phase had been achieved, the pass would be open so that our troops could harass and destroy the enemy's line of communications to the north and inflict all possible damage on him without bringing on a major tank battle. The words "To create a tank-infested area similar to what we used in Egypt" were used by Alexander in describing the mission of the 1st Armored Division.

To insure the integrity of Maknassy, Patton was directed to leave one medium tank battalion, the 60th Regimental Combat Team, and two additional artillery battalions in that vicinity. The 34th Division was to move to Sbeitla, and leaving a combat team there, to advance rapidly on Fondouk.

The creation of a "tank-infested area similar to that we used in Egypt" is an unusual way of phrasing an order. The British are skilled and graphic users of the English language. Other phrases used by them on other occasions come to mind. In one situation where there had been a small break-through the British Major General commanding the 9th Indian Infantry Division was given the task of stopping the Germans. This he did most effectively. In reporting the success of his mission, he remarked that the assigned job had been done but that he "would like another twenty-four hours to tidy up the battlefield."

Major Jenson, an aide-de-camp of Patton, was killed on April 1, 1943, while Patton was visiting the forward CP of Task Force Benson. The diary describes the death and the burial.

Twelve Junker 88's bombed them with 500 pound bombs with instantaneous fuses. They fell right in the command post. All jumped into slit trenches, of which there were plenty. One bomb hit right at the edge of the trench Jenson was in, killing him instantly. His watch stopped at 10:12. I am terribly sorry as he was a fine boy, loyal, unselfish and efficient. As soon as he was brought in, I went to the cemetery with Gaffey. He was on a stretcher rolled up in a shelter half. We uncovered his face and I got on my knees to say a prayer, and all the men did the same. There was some blood from his mouth, but he was not mangled and I doubt if he was hit. There was a small stone bruise on his forehead. I kissed him on the brow and covered him up.

At 1600 Stiller, Sergeant Meeks, Sergeant Mims and I went to the cemetery. Dick was on a stretcher wrapped in a white mattress cover. We had a squad and a trumpeter, but did not fire the volleys, as it would make people think an air raid was on. The Corps Chaplain read the Episcopal Service and he was lowered in. There are no coffins here, as there is no wood. Captain Stiller, Lieutenant Craig, Sergeant Meeks and Sergeant Mims carried the stretcher. They were all his friends.

I enclosed a lock of his hair in a letter to his mother. I radioed to Bea, through Beedle Smith, to notify the Jenson family. He was a fine man and officer. He had no vices. I can't see the reason that such fine young men get killed. I shall miss him a lot. *C'est la guerre.*

Patton never permitted personal grief to interfere with the demanding duties of combat. A battle leader must develop the ability to throw off bereavement. To get on with the battle is the price of leadership.

144

On April 13th, he wrote his wife the following letter which gives our remarkable nurses well-deserved praise.

DARLING BEA:

The time you mail letters has not the least connection with the time they get here. Your 12 page diary, which was most interesting, arrived some days after another letter written on March 20th.

We finished the fighting here on the 7th, and on the 10th, the First Armored forced the pass at Faid against practically no opposition. However, they did it in a reasonably short time, for which I was personally responsible.

I left here at 0830 and at 12 got to their C.P. to find that, in the meantime, they had been ordered to attack. Everyone was eating lunch, and there was no push, so I started to work.

First, they told me that one could not go through Sidi Bu Zid, as it was mined. I saw some fresh tracks, so went on through. Then, we came to the road leading to the pass, and I was assured that it was mined and that the engineers were demining while everyone sat and waited. So I drove up to the minefield and walked through it; this seemed to restore confidence.

I could see no reason why we had to stick to the road anyhow, so I told McQuillin [Brigadier General Raymond E.], who had come up, to turn off and parallel the road at a thousand yards. We blew up a couple of half-tracks, but killed no one, and got through. General Alexander was quite complimentary at the speed of the move.

I have been lucky in happening to be at the right place at the right time on several occasions. I think I wrote you that I was third vehicle in column when Benson broke through on the 7th.

The nurses are doing a swell job. I saw one yesterday soothing a man, most of whose brains were shot out, and she was fine. He was a crazy as a coot. They have given as many as twelve blood transfusions to one patient and saved him. The bad cases they transfuse before they operate.

I saw one poor devil yesterday, missing a leg. I asked him how he felt, and he said, "Fine since you came to see me." I suppose I do some good, but it always makes

145

me choke up. I have no personal feeling of responsibility for getting them hit as I took the same chances, but I hate to look at them.

Thanks for your letter of March 20th. Very inspiring.

G.

In the middle of April Patton left the fighting in Tunisia. General Bradley, as planned, was taking over the Tunisian operation and Patton was about to return to his headquarters in Rabat to continue with his plans for "Husky," the Sicilian landing and campaign, that was to be launched in July.

The Tunisian campaign was successfully finished by Bradley; little of the Axis forces in Africa escaped capture.

Patton believed he had developed in command, as he stated in his diary.

April 15, 1943

As I gain experience, I do not think more of myself, but less of others. Men, even so-called great men, are wonderfully weak and timid. They are too damned polite. War is very simple, direct and ruthless. It takes a simple, direct and ruthless man to wage war. Sometimes I wonder if I will laugh at myself for writing things like the above, but I think not. I have developed a lot and my never small self-onfidence has vastly grown. I am sure that with God's help I will succeed at "Husky" and so on to the end, which is far distant.

Before leaving Gafsa I picked some nasturtiums in the yard and Gay, Sergeant Meeks and I went to the cemetery to tell Dick [Major Jenson] good-by. There are more than 700 graves there now.

General Patton and his little party spent the night of the 15–16th of April in Constantine, Tunisia. The next morning, they boarded a C-47 airplane at a little airstrip near Constantine. Aboard the plane besides General Patton was General Spaatz, Commanding General of the U.S. Air Force. The pilot of the plane was so excited on seeing General Spaatz aboard that he had trouble starting the plane. Finally the plane took off and the pilot asked General Spaatz if he wanted a parachute. General Spaatz replied that he did, and he wanted it now. The pilot immediately brought him the parachute and asked if he could help him adjust it. General Spaatz replied that he could do what he wanted to do with it himself. He then put the parachute on the floor of the plane, lay down with his head on it, and went to sleep. Sergeant Meeks said he was sure traveling in high-priced company. The trip from Constantine to Algiers was made without incident.

Patton's last entry about the Tunisian campaign is that of April 17, 1943.

Left at 14:00 in a C-47, loaned by Spaatz, and got in to Rabat at 18:00. Keyes and Harkins met me. I have been gone 43 days, fought several successful battles, commanded 95,800 men, lost about ten pounds, gained a third star, and a hell of a lot of praise and confidence, and am otherwise the same.

To recapitulate, the higher command had planned that Patton was to gain experience on the battlefield in Tunisia, but not finish the campaign there. Bradley, as agreed, took over the command in Tunisia and finished the campaign while Patton planned the United States Army invasion of Sicily, and commanded our troops in the conquest of that island.

Tunisia was a battlefield upon which to train the American and British commanders. Rommel is quoted in *The Rommel Papers,* edited by B. H. Liddell Hart, as follows:

In Tunisia the Americans had to pay a stiff price for their experience, but it brought rich dividends. Even at that time, the American generals showed themselves to be very advanced in the tactical handling of their forces, although we had to wait until the Patton Army in France to see the most astonishing achievements in mobile warfare. The Americans, it is fair to say, profited far more than the British from their experience in Africa, thus confirming the axiom that education is easier than re-education.[1]

---

[1] *The Rommel Papers,* edited by B. H. Liddell Hart, Harcourt, Brace and Company, 1950.

8. Sicily

ONE concept Patton had regarding the invasion of Sicily was to land on the north coast of Palermo and fight east to Messina, thus cutting off the Axis troops trying to escape across the Straits of Messina. From World War II history we know this was not adopted. Instead there was a final plan named Operation "Husky" in which the British Eighth Army under Montgomery would land on the southeast tip of Sicily and fight north along the east coast past Mount Etna and take Messina. The U.S. Seventh Army, in the "Husky" plan as finally adopted, would land on the southeastern coast at Gela and Licata, and act as flank protection for the British Eighth Army.

The Eighth Army met stern resistance and its progress was slow. The Axis defenses near Mount Etna were particularly strong. In the actual operation, the western half of Sicily was taken by the U.S. Seventh Army under Patton. After the Seventh Army had fought across the island and captured Palermo on the northern coast of Sicily, it turned and fought to the east, arriving at Messina just before the Eight Army, ending the campaign.

As in all operations, there were some last-minute changes in the disposition of the Seventh Army in the landings at Gela and Licata. A reserve force was provided for, which was an unusual arrangement for the Americans. Up to this time, a reserve in a landing operation, though much to be desired, had been impossible.

At a staff meeting General Keyes recommended that one infantry combat team plus one combat command of the 2d Armored Division be held in reserve. General Patton accepted the idea and his diary reference is worthy of note, for he again stresses leadership.

May 5, 1943

No one present had any objection, so that plan was accepted. It all took about one hour. Someday bemused students will try to see how we came to this decision and credit us with profound thought we never had. The thing as I see it is to get a definite, simple plan quickly,

148

and win by execution and careful detailed study of the tactical operation of the lesser units. Execution is the thing, that and LEADERSHIP.

When Eisenhower pulled Patton out of the Tunisian campaign and put him into the planning for the Sicilian operation, it was realized that this would probably cause some unfavorable newspaper comments.

Bradley and Patton always worked well together, not only at this time, but later when Bradley had the Twelfth Army Group, and Patton, in command of the Third U.S. Army, served under him in Europe.

Patton considered Bradley a very sound and extremely loyal soldier. They both felt that the U.S. chances of surviving "Husky" were approximately 50-50. Both felt that God and lady luck would favor them, however. A diary entry on the 20th of June emphasizes Patton's appreciation of having the Deity on his side.

Went to church with Gay. We had a new preacher, at my insistence, who was good. He preached on the willingness to accept responsibility, even to your own hurt. I pray daily to do my duty, retain my self-confidence and accomplish my destiny. No one can live under the awful responsibility I have without Divine help. Frequently I feel that I don't rate it.

Just prior to D-day for "Husky," General Alexander, now Minister of Defense of Great Britain, paid a visit to General Patton's headquarters in Mostaganem, Algeria. General Alexander was most pleasant during his conversation at lunch. He stated that much to his chagrin he had to go back to England for a few days and then added, "You know, George, men in our positions have to mend our political fences occasionally however distasteful such may be."

Patton felt that his luck had not run out. He honestly believed that his destiny was to perform many more missions. His lifetime preoccupation with luck and destiny and the help of the Almighty has been emphasized repeatedly.

He always encouraged new ideas. If the testing of those ideas involved some danger, he welcomed the opportunity to participate.

When I was with the 2d Armored Division in Africa, I suggested, shortly after the landings in Morocco, that our tanks could go forward under our own covering time fire. Time fire is artillery fire timed to explode in the air over a target. Our air bursts over the target would keep the enemy infantry in their foxholes and artillery gun crews in their trenches, or shelters. Thus it would minimize the return fire of their guns at our tanks. Our tanks, buttoned up —that is with the turret doors closed—could, it was believed, withstand the shell fragments of the concentrated time fire of our artillery, and could advance directly on to the enemy target while the target was covered by that fire. When our own time fire was raised, the tanks would be in place and we would have already captured the enemy positions.

A little experimentation had been done, but it was not certain how badly the tanks might be injured in a full-scale demonstration of concentrated time fire, such as would be necessary in battle.

Such a full-scale demonstration, using a battalion of our 2d Armored Division artillery, was put on at Arzeu, Algeria, shortly before the jump-off for the Sicilian landing. I was in command of the tanks from the 2d Armored that went in buttoned up. Patton and Bradley were there to witness the show. Though I had officially reported my plan to Patton, through military channels, shortly after our landing in Morocco, this was to be the first real test. To our consternation, Patton demanded that he be a gunner in the leading wave of our tanks. Fortunately all went well and no one was injured. The tanks took quite a beating from the time fire of our artillery, and required much repair and replacement, particularly the antennas and gun sights, to get into fully operative condition again. However, as a battle operation, it was proved to be feasible. Patton had a wonderful time shooting the tank cannon of the tank he rode at the "enemy" 88 battery and having the antenna and gun sights of his tank shot away. He was enthusiastic about the new tactic.

The use of time fire was mentioned in Patton's plans for his Third U.S. Army break-through at Avranches, France. Development of new Armored Personnel Carriers and our new family of tanks allows the armor now to go deep into the enemy territory under protection of our own overhead artillery. When on the position the artillery is lifted and the tanks and infantry are able to protect each other. We have truly come a long way since this demonstration in Africa some eleven years ago.

The 45th Division were to go into their first fight in the "Husky" operation. Patton's message to green troops points up his character.

June 27, 1943

To Officers and Warrant Officers of the 45th Division:

Clearly all of you must know that combat is imminent. However, it is probably not so near as many of you imagine.

You men of the 45th Division must face the fact that you are competing with veterans, but don't let that worry you. All of them, too, fought their first battle, and all of them won their first battle just as you will win yours.

Battle is far less frightening than those who have never been in it are apt to think. All this bull about thinking of your mother, and your sweetheart, and your wives (who should also be your sweethearts) is emphasized by writers who describe battles, not as they are, but as the writers who have never heard a hostile shot or missed a meal think they are.

Battle is the most magnificent competition in which a human being can indulge. It brings out all that is best; it removes all that is base.

All men are afraid in battle. The coward is the one who lets his fear overcome his sense of duty. Duty is the essence of manhood. Americans pride themselves on being he-men and they *are* he-men.

Remember that the enemy is just as frightened as you are, probably more so. They are not supermen. We have licked the best of them, and those whom we shall face in the next fight are not the cream of the crop. Further, remember that in fist fights or in battle the attacker wins. You cannot win by parrying. Yet the enemy, being uncertain of our intentions, must parry.

General C. L. Scott, who is a very small man, said, "By God, I could lick Joe Louis if he wasn't permitted to attack me!" The way to prevent the enemy from attacking you is to attack him and keep right on attacking him. This prevents him from getting set, and it also in-

151

duces in his mind the idea that you are far more numerous than you are; though, as a matter of fact, we will be more numerous when we meet our next opponent.

Death in battle is a function of time and effective hostile fire. You reduce the hostile fire by your fire. You reduce the time by rapid movement. When you come into a fire-swept zone, it is foolish and contrary to orders to dig in. Move forward out of it. It is difficult, if not impossible, for the enemy to shorten his range, and remember to shoot.

If you don't see the enemy, figure out where he would be and shoot at that, but keep shooting and aim your shots. In case of doubt, shoot in front of where you think he is. The whistle of a ricochet or the effect of being hit by one is very alarming, while an over is hardly ever heard.

The enemy is afraid of the bayonet. He is also physically inferior to us. Therefore go after him with the bayonet, and see that the bayonet is sharp. When you land, land with your bayonets fixed.

You have heard a lot about mines. They are dangerous but far less dangerous than artillery or machine gun fire. The purpose of mines is to delay you. Don't help the enemy by being delayed. You can move forward through a mine field. All you have to do is to look at the grounds. If you see a place where it has been recently moved by a shovel, don't step on it. If you see wires, step over them. Furthermore, there are not enough mines in the universe to cover everything, therefore, they are placed in positions where foolish soldiers are apt to walk; namely along the edges of roads, at the foot of telegraph poles, and in the bottoms of sandy washes where the going is easier. If you move where the going is hard or over rocky ground, you will not meet mines.

Air bombardment and strafing from the air are both very alarming but not particularly dangerous. Here again your fire against airplanes is your surest protection, but be careful not to fire at our own planes. If they are so high that you cannot recognize the plane, it will do you no harm. Only fire at planes you can recognize as enemy planes by the markings, or on planes which have loosed their bombs. If you see a plane, watch it. You can see the bomb bays open. You can see the bombs starting down, and after that you have plenty of time to get clear. The bombs will fall along a line parallel to the direction of flight of the plane. Therefore, after the bombs are released run at right angles to the line of flight of the plane. Just before the bombs drop, lie down, and instantly after they explode again fire at the plane. It is surprising how many planes we have shot down in this manner.

Booby traps are what the name implies—boobies get trapped. Here again the newspaper correspondent has overplayed them. Personally I have been in quite a few fights in this war and have never seen a booby trap.

Owing to the bad teachings of maneuvers, some of our troops have been foolish enough to surrender. Any man who still has a weapon in his hand and who surrenders is a coward. But he is worse than a coward, he is foolish. It is far better to fight it out and probably win than it is to surrender and surely starve, for that is what happens to prisoners captured by the Axis. They haven't enough food for their own people. Certainly they will not waste it on you.

In the use of antitank guns, be sure to place them where they can neither see nor be seen beyond the limit of their killing range against tanks; that is, for the 37—400 yards; for the 57—600 yards. Your artillery can fire on tanks at any range, and if they use white phosphorus will probably almost surely stop them.

It is unnecessary at this point to talk about discipline because what I have seen of you makes me know that you possess it. There is another thing which an officer must possess which he alone knows. That is the feeling of obligation. You have a sacred trust in your men and to your country, and you are lower than the lowest thing that lives if you are false to this trust. An officer, no matter what his rank, must always be willing and anxious to take the chances his men must take. He must lead, not push, and he must assert himself. He must not whisper his commands. He must give them as per the drill book. This business of saying, "Come on fellows, let's go" is not a command. It is the talk of the mob leader. Use the word "Forward." Use the words, "Follow me." The men will go forward and follow you, and will be proud of you, and you will be proud of yourself.

Pride is the greatest thing a man can have. Not foolish

pride as in the man who says, "I have on gold bars, therefore I am a great man," but the pride which says, "I have on gold bars and therefore I have done my duty. I have led my men. I have seen that they were fed. I have seen that they were cared for. I have seen that we have destroyed the enemy together."

We Americans are a competitive race. We bet on anything. We love to win. In this next fight, you are entering the greatest sporting competition of all times. You are competing with Americans and with Allies for the greatest prize of all—victory; and the one who wins this prize is the one who first attains victory—captures his objective. Never forget that. And remember also that the Deity, in whatever form you think of Him, is with us.

Patton noted that his soldiers were no longer amateurs, as expressed in a letter to his wife dated July 2, 1943:

Within the last few months, there has been a great improvement in the soldiers. They are at last the coming professionals and look and act the part. Yesterday, a lot of them saluted me when I was in my bathing suit. This is truly remarkable and shows that they wanted to as they could have easily pretended not to recognize me.

Patton's headquarters had moved from Mostaganem to the harbor at Algiers where headquarters were established aboard the U.S.S. *Monrovia*.

He delivered a message, written on June 27th, to the Seventh Army troops he commanded, which was to be read at sea. The message follows:

HEADQUARTERS SEVENTH UNITED STATES
ARMY
APO NO. 758, U.S. ARMY

By Auth. of CG 7' Army
Initials   CW
Date   27/6/43

At sea.
Soldiers of the Seventh American Army:
We are indeed honored in having been selected by General Eisenhower as the American component of this

154

new and greater attack against the Axis. We are teamed with the justly famous British 8th Army, which attacks on our right, and we have for the Army Group Commander that veteran and distinguished soldier, Sir Harold Alexander.

In addition to the two armies, our attack will be supported by the annihilating might of the Allied Navies and Air Forces.

Owing to the necessity for secrecy, I am unable to put in writing the location of our impending battle. However, I hereby direct the officers who will read you this after you are at sea to tell where you are going and why.

When we land we will meet German and Italian soldiers whom it is our honor and privilege to attack and destroy.

Many of you have in your veins German and Italian blood, but remember that these ancestors of yours so loved freedom that they gave up home and country to cross the ocean in search of liberty. The ancestors of the people we shall kill lacked the courage to make such a sacrifice and remained as slaves.

During the last year we Americans have met and defeated the best troops Germany, Italy and Japan possess. Many of us have shared in these glorious victories. Those of you who have not been so fortunate, now have your opportunity to gain equal fame.

In landing operations, retreat is impossible. To surrender is as ignoble as it is foolish. Due to our Air Force and our Navy the enemy is unable to evacuate prisoners. Therefore, our soldiers who are taken prisoners will remain to starve and run the risk of being bombed or shelled by their own comrades who will be unable to tell prisoners from the enemy.

Above all else remember that we as the attackers have the initiative. We know exactly what we are going to do, while the enemy is ignorant of our intentions and can only parry our blows. We must retain this tremendous advantage by always attacking; rapidly, ruthlessly, viciously and without rest. However tired and hungry you may be, the enemy will be more tired and more hungry—keep punching! No man is beaten until he thinks he is. Our enemy knows that his cause is hopeless.

The fact that we are operating in enemy country does

not permit us to forget our American tradition of respect for private property, noncombatants, and women. Civilians who have the stupidity to fight us we will kill. Those who remain passive will not be harmed but will be required to rigidly conform to such rules as we shall publish for their control and guidance.

The glory of American arms, the honor of our country, the future of the whole world rests in your individual hands. See to it that you are worthy of this great trust.

God is with us. We shall win.

s/ G. S. PATTON, JR.
Lieut. General, U.S. Army
Commanding

Patton's Sicilian campaign was to be fought in choking dust and intense heat. One of Patton's subordinates, Lucian Truscott, then a major general, for the Sicilian landing commanded the 3d U.S. Infantry Division. Attached to the 3d Infantry for the campaign was Combat Command "A" of the 2d Armored Division, which was then commanded by Brigadier General Maurice Rose. Truscott called all officers together for instructions in an open field near Bizerte a few days before the jump-off, and the first sirocco of the season came. We thought it might be a good omen for the approaching landing. The sirocco is a wind that comes from the oven of the Sahara to the south. We had heard it would be hot but we had not pictured this blast from hell.

The searing winds of the sirocco were so parching that the windows of staff cars on the roads were closed—in July under a blazing African sky. The whole countryside shook in a very ague of heat.

Patton wrote to his brother-in-law, Frederick Ayer, on July 5, 1943 as follows:

As you will read in the papers, I am now commanding the Seventh Army. It is actually not a great deal bigger than what I commanded in Tunisia, but will continue to grow until it is quite sizable.

If you read in the papers that I have been killed wait till you get a War Department confirmation, because I have a great many lives, and at the moment do not feel at all dead; in fact, I am looking forward with a lot of pleasure to some very good excitement.

However, in the event that the War Department does announce that I have passed on, you can give the letter for Bea, which I wrote you last October, to her. Otherwise keep it for future eventualities.

If we should not meet again until we get to the other side, I am assured on credible authority that the heavenly foxes are fast, the heavenly hounds keen, the fog-bank fences high and soft, and the landings firm. The horses of the sun have always been celebrated, "Whoop Ho! for a kill in the open!" [1]

The convoy embarked for Sicily on the eighth of July. On that day Patton was on board a warship just off of Cape Bon at about 0830. He remarked to his staff that many officers look forward to fishing, farming, etc., but "I don't—I look forward to fighting, here, in Japan, or at home, for the rest of my days." He also said that he had the usual shortness of breath he always had before a polo game, but that "I would not change places with anyone I know right now."

He told Colonel Maddox that if he had to make a maneuver, it would possibly be necessary to attack with the maneuvering unit for about four hours before dark and then pull out. He remarked that at this time he could not plan further ahead, for the motto of Napoleon "Attack and then look" is true.

After the Sicilian beachheads were established, Patton asked permission to advance and take Agrigento. This was beyond the line specified for the front of the Seventh Army. General Alexander replied he had no objection provided only limited forces were employed. Patton realized the value of holding the initiative and continuing the attack. By taking Agrigento a new port would be available which could supply most of the Seventh Army troops. The detailed constructive efforts for defense of Sicily amazed Patton. Also, the lack of heart to defend these positions was almost unbelievable to him who moved forward continually. This further spurred him on to continue the attack.

He appreciated American troops more and more as they gained battle experience, as he stated in his diary entry of the 19th of July, 1943.

[1] Quoted from *Atlantic Monthly*, November, 1947. Copyright, 1947, by Atlantic Monthly Co.

I think that the British have the bear by the tail in the Messina Peninsula and we may have to go in and help. Had they let us use Road 117 and take Caltagirone and Enna ourselves, instead of waiting for them, we would have saved two days and been on the north coast now. Alexander has no idea of either the power or speed of American armies. They attacked Catania with a whole division yesterday and only made 400 yards. Keyes has patrols in Sciacco now, and we may be able to turn the armor loose on the 23rd. Our method of attacking all the time is better than the British system to stop, build up, and start, but we must judge by the enemy reaction.

In the late afternoon of July 21, 1943, as Headquarters Seventh Army was settling in its new command post in Agrigento, Sicily, a corps commander from the adjoining army appeared in camp and asked to see the General. Upon being presented to the Army Commander by the Chief of Staff, he said, "Although my Corps is seventy-five miles from here, I have my radio with me and I can command as well from here as I could if I were there."

General Patton looked him squarely in the eye and said, "General, in your case I think that is evident."

Patton felt that his employment of armor to capture Palermo, thus sealing off the escape route into Italy for Axis forces, would be a classic example and be studied by the service schools for years to come. He was probably right but his Third Army exploits which were soon to follow will make military history for time immemorial.

Patton on the way to the front on July 22nd noted that the road discipline of the 2d Armored Division was superior. Whenever he passed any of the troops of that division, the men first saluted him and then waved—very cheering to a commander.

In addition to speaking about his armor tactics, he again shows his disdain toward defensive tactics in an excerpt from his diary entry of the 22nd of July.

On the way up we passed some very fine tank traps. There was a pit on the right ten feet square and about ten deep covered with matting and dust so it looked like the land. Then some thirty yards further a similar pit on the left. Each had wire in front of it so that traffic had to stop and make an "S" to get through. The hope is that in battle tanks will disregard the wire and go straight in. They did not. "Love's labor lost." They also had antitank ditches ten feet deep and twenty wide, as long as a mile. We went around them. Only killing stops good troops—*defenses sap the vitality of those who make them*. I feel that future students of the Command and General Staff School will study the campaign of Palermo as a classic example of the use of tanks. I held them back far enough so that the enemy could not tell where they were to be used; then when the infantry had found the hole, the tanks went through and in large numbers and fast. Such methods assure victory and reduce losses, but it takes fine leadership to insure the execution. General Keyes provided perfect leadership and great drive. The praises should be his.

He arrived at the Command Post of the 2d Armored Division and was told by Colonel Redding F. (Speed) Perry that Palermo had fallen and that Generals Keyes and Gaffey had entered it. Perry guided Patton into Palermo through the pass in the hills southwest of that town and high above the cathedral town of Monreale. In the pass there had been brisk fighting that day and the night was translucent with light from the burning hills on each side of the pass. Elements of the 3d Infantry and Combat Command A of the 2d Armored Division had the town under control.

Alexander radioed Patton: *This is a great triumph. Personal for General Patton from General Alexander. Well done. Heartiest congratulations to you and all your splendid soldiers.*

Americans try to hide their emotions. The Sicilians take pride in exhibiting theirs. The 1st Battalion, 66th Armored Regiment, 2d Armored Division, went into bivouac in an orchard of young lemon trees in the suburbs of Palermo. The orchard was surrounded by a high stone wall which the tanks drove through, breaking the wall. Then they were parked under the lemon trees to camouflage them from air reconnaissance of the Boche.

The owner of the orchard, a prosperous man of about thirty-eight, well dressed, who looked like the vice president of one of the good Palermo banks, came to see me and asked us to be careful of the young lemon trees. This was promised, but I later told the battalion sergeant major, Sergeant Murphy, to tell the owner that we could be careful of the lemon trees only if we were not attacked. In case of attack, by the Germans and Italians, we would have to do whatever was necessary to survive and we might not be able to preserve the lemon trees.

Sergeant Murphy told this to the owner after I had left on other business. Sergeant Murphy reported that on hearing this explanation the orchard owner fell on the ground and cried and tore his silk shirt. "I almost took his little pants down and spanked him," said the sergeant.

Patton moved into sumptuous quarters in Palermo, as described in the July 27th letter to his wife:

DARLING B,

Green Meadows and even Avalon are going to look pretty measly to me after this. To get to the Royal Apartment [Palermo] in which I sleep, you have to traverse seven anterooms and a small dining room, about 40 x 60. Keyes lives at the other end, but he has only three anterooms—a piker.

The palace was built in 1600, but is modernized, though not cleaned. I got quite a kick about using a toilet previously made malodorous by constipated royalty.

The bed has a spring mattress and then three other down ones on top, like the story of the princess and the pea, only unfortunately, you are not here.

The State Drawing Room is huge—I imagine over a hundred feet long and forty wide. We eat K-rations on china marked with the cross of Saxony.

Stiller [Captain A. C., A.D.C.], who has no soul, took one look at the place and said: "General, if you let me look, I can find a nice modern house much better than this old dump!"

The "old dump" is some two blocks long. One end has offices, the middle a church, and the other end, living quarters. The living part has two courtyards and also a grand staircase. You can either go up the stairs, or else drive on a sort of circular street and get off where you like.

Mrs. Patton, after the close of World War II, said, "General Keyes told me that he went to see Georgie the night before he was to enter Palermo, and that Georgie said, 'You took it. You enter and I will enter it after you.' Keyes said that this was the proudest day of his life."

Shortly after Palermo was taken General Patton started his fight across the northern coast toward Messina. Armor was used to land from the sea behind the lines, but the great bulk of the armor of the 2d Armored Division was used to outpost the northern coast of Sicily to prevent landings by the Germans and Italians.

The slapping incident which was the source of much criticism by the press is referred to in the August 3rd entry in the diary:

On the way I stopped at an evacuation hospital and talked to 350 newly wounded. One poor fellow who had lost his right arm cried; another had lost a leg. All were brave and cheerful. The 1st Sergeant of "C" Company, 39th Infantry, was in for his second wound. He laughed and said that after he got his third wound he was going to ask to go home. I had told General Marshall some months ago that an enlisted man hit three times should be sent home. In the hospital, there also was a man trying to look as if he had been wounded. I asked him what was the matter, and he said he just couldn't take it. I gave him the devil, slapped his face with my gloves and kicked him out of the hospital. Companies should deal with such men and if they shirk their duty they should be tried for cowardice and shot. I will issue an order on this subject tomorrow.

His longhand diary said: *One sometimes slaps a baby to bring it to.*[2]

Patton was under much pressure at this time as shown in his diary entry of the sixth of August:

One man had the top of his head blown off and they were just waiting for him to die. He was a horrid bloody mess and not good to look at. I should not dwell on this or I might develop personal feelings about sending men to battle. That would be fatal for a General.

---

[2] This incident is treated more fully in the diary entries of August 20 and 22, 1943, found later in this chapter.

On August 9th Patton wrote a letter to Mrs. Patton setting forth his thoughts on the current operations in Sicily.

DARLING BEA,

We moved our Command Post up the coast to a place named after Ellen's husband [Ellen, the cook in Alhambra].

The camp is in an ancient olive grove where Hannibal may have wandered if he ever came this way. It was full of mines, but Hap had it deloused and it is very nice. I have flown over it twice in a cub and can't see it. Besides George [Meeks] has dug me a slit trench as large and deep as a grave in which I can retire.

The first afternoon they shelled us, but all were Overs. Then about seven they began getting Shorts. They had hit the ridge to our east and exploded and some of the fragments would howl overhead. I was disgusted to find that my pulse went up—I timed it—but soon I got myself in hand. Mostly I can have a shell hit or a mine go off quite close without winking or ducking. This is a great asset and besides, if they are going to get you, they hit you before you hear them. One must be an actor.

I had a unique experience two days ago. I went to an observation post not over three thousand yards from a place we were attacking. You could see the sixty millimeter mortars and hear the machine guns and rifles, yet it took seven hours for our troops to march from where I was to the battle I saw. It is the God Damnedest country I have ever seen. Indio looks like foothills.

We pulled a landing operation the other night—no opposition. When we got in an orchard, there were 400 Germans asleep. It was butt and bayonet for a while. It was too dark to shoot. We won. Then, one of our soldiers with a sub-machine gun, got up to the road. At four A.M., very dark, he saw what he thought was one man and challenged. The man did not know the reply, so he pulled the trigger and was too excited to quit till he emptied his clip. When the sun rose, there were eighteen dead Germans in column of two's.

I tried to put on another landing tonight, but no soap. We are trying to win a horse race to the last big town (Messina). I hope we do, but if we lose, it will be destroyed roads more than enemy who stop us.

I saw a letter taken off a German corpse the other day in which he said that this was worse than Stalingrad. He wrote to his parents, telling them good-by—he was right. We have what is left of two and one-half German divisions against us. The other one and a half are against the cousins.

I am really very proud of the Seventh Army. We have fought without a day's rest since the 10th of July and have killed or captured over one hundred ten thousand enemy, besides numberless guns, tanks, and trucks. Some day Leavenworth will study this campaign.

"Men live in deeds, not years," and I have lived a long time in the last thirty days, but I feel very humble. It was the superior fighting ability of the American soldiery, the wonderful efficiency of our mechanical transport, the work of Bradley, Keyes, and the Army Staff that did the trick. I just came along for the ride, except on the 11th, when I think that I personally changed a possible defeat into a positive victory. I certainly love war.

I had seven letters from you today dated July 10-24. I will answer them more in detail when I get a chance.

This is the longest day I have ever spent. I have been at the extreme front every day for three days and decided I was being a nuisance, so stayed in camp all day. It was hell. I can hear the guns and they have the damnedest effect on me. I am scared but want to get up.

Give my love to the children and Fred.

LOVE, GEORGE

Patton's changing a possible defeat into a victory occurred when he insisted upon making a landing despite recommendations from Generals Bradley and Truscott to call it off because the 3d Infantry Division was not in position to support it. The landing was successfully made, forcing the enemy to withdraw. This audacious attack practically ended the campaign.

There is an entertaining story of a small maneuver against the British earlier in the campaign before the Seventh Army took Palermo.

On the 18th of July when General Patton was planning a quick thrust to Palermo, his staff received a coded radiogram from Alexander directing that no advance be made beyond a line running generally northeast and southeast through Caltagirone, Agrigento. The staff, knowing that such a restriction would definitely foil the General's plan, took a great deal of time getting the message decoded and then some twelve hours later radioed back in code that the original message was garbled and could not be decoded, asking for a repeat. By the time the repeat was received and decoded, it was too late: Patton's U.S. Seventh Army troops were on the outskirts of Palermo. Actually General Patton did not know this until days afterward. His Chief of Staff, Hap Gay, has said he himself was entirely to blame.

Patton's depression at the end of the campaign is typical of any combat officer worth his salt, when the shooting has stopped, hence his diary reflections are worthy of note.

August 17, 1943

Well, I feel let down. The reaction from intense mental and physical activity to a status of inertia is very difficult.

I got a second DSC yesterday and ended a war. I feel that the Lord has been most generous. If I had to fight the campaign over, I would make no change in anything I did. Few generals in history have ever been able to say as much. So far in this war I have been a chip floating on the river of destiny. I think I had best keep on floating—I will surely be used some more, though at the worst things look gloomy. For the moment the future of the Seventh Army does not look bright, but I trust that the same fortune which has helped me before will continue to assist me. I have been very lucky.

George Patton was talking to a scholarly native of Sicily after our campaign there, and said that he was sorry that the country had suffered so much damage. The Sicilian said that there had not been anywhere near the destruction that the country suffered in the last war. Patton said, "What do you mean by the last war?" "I am referring, of course, to the First Punic War," replied the native.

Paddy Flint, a colonel commanding an infantry regiment in the Seventh Army, and a close family friend, had been congratulated for his valor by Patton and cautioned to be more careful—an unusual thing for Patton to do. The following is a letter dated August 16th from Paddy.

DEAR GEORGIE,

Thank you. I was grateful and shall always be to you —I laughed once, right out loud, thinking of what you said about trying to remember that I did not have armor around me. Bless your heart, and more power to you! You are a Commander and we are proud to be on your ranch. Triple A bar zero, ~~AAA0~~ is our brand. Stands for Anyhow, Anywhere, Anytime, Bar-Nuthin. Bless your heart.

Always your gunman,

PADDY

This letter was written from Paddy's headquarters, which he named "Suicide Ranch."

Patton in his August 20 diary entry admitted his slapping was wrong and regrets it and makes what amends he can:

After lunch General Blesse, Chief Surgeon AFHQ, brought me a very nasty letter from Ike with reference to the two soldiers I cussed out for what I considered cowardice. Evidently I acted precipitately and on insufficient knowledge. My motive was correct because one cannot permit skulking to exist. It is just like any communicable disease. I admit freely that my method was wrong and I shall make what amends I can. I regret the incident as I hate to make Ike mad when it is my earnest desire to please him. General Lucas arrived at 1800 to further explain Ike's attitude. I feel very low.

Again he took action with respect to the slapping.

August 22, 1943

Went to church in Royal chapel at 1000. At 1100 I had in all the doctors and nurses and enlisted men who witnessed the affairs with the skulkers. I told them about my friend in the last war who shirked, was let get by with it, and eventually killed himself. I told them that I had taken the action I had to correct such a future tragedy.

The mistake that Patton made he freely admitted. He apologized to the soldiers involved. Eisenhower, realizing the great value of Patton as a leader, though not condoning the slapping, planned to use him in further battles. A friend of Patton's, Colonel A. N. Slocum, Jr., was in the United States and went to see Secretary Stimson about the slapping incident. The Secretary of War said that he and General Marshall had great confidence in Patton, and that they had much more important work for him than ever before. The War Department made no comment on the slapping incident, because they were using Patton as a decoy to keep a German Army away from the Salerno area in Italy, where the United States Army had made a landing. By not making any statements about Patton at this time the War Department kept the Germans in a quandary. It would have been a great relief to them if Patton had been shelved; that was well known by our top planners and by making no statements they kept the Germans on the anxious seat.

Patton made a series of addresses to the divisions of his Seventh Army, after the successful conclusion of the Sicilian campaign. The following are excerpts from the notes he used for these speeches:

Our success was primarily due to continued offensive —day and night, relentless and unceasing—and to the fact that we used maneuver. We held the enemy by the nose and kicked him in the pants. We never, except in the initial landing, attacked head on.

However, nothing is ever perfect, and it behooves us to examine out tactics with a view to improving them.

The points I would stress are: the vital necessity of reconnaissance—before, during and after battle. We also have a defect, inherent in our ardent natures, of attack piecemeal because we are in too much of a hurry. Due to the efficiency of our weapons, the superior nature of our equipment, and the valor of our troops we have succeeded in piecemeal attacks, but we would have succeeded better had we developed coordinated attacks and used maneuver and firepower in just proportion.

Again, possibly as a result of peacetime scarcity in ammunition, we do not fire enough, neither with rifles, mortars, or artillery. It is true that when we fire we hit, but it is also true that by firing more we would produce the psychosis of fear in our enemy. No man likes to hear bullets whistling around.

When we meet the German in continental Europe, we will find that initially, true to his principles of the offensive, he will attack us. We will not sit still and receive these attacks. We will attack him. The result will be so-called meeting engagements.

After we have stopped him in his initial attacks, he will have recourse to large formed counterattacks, participated in by several divisions. He will attempt in these attacks to make salients into our line and then operate laterally.

The answer to such attacks is to attack him on the flank of his salient. For such operations armor and guns are the surest answer. To make such attacks against large counterattacks, we must know where we are going, and we must attack with violence, speed and precision.

It is needless to point out to men like you the pre-eminent value of disciplined valor. Discipline, as you know it and practice it, comes from meticulous attention to the small details of dress, deportment, and bearing; but discipline is a failure unless it produces alert, prideful soldiers. You are such soldiers. You have demonstrated your courage and have, I am sure, realized the safety which results from courageous actions. The fixed determination to close with the enemy reacts both on you and on him. In you it develops the superiority complex; you are certain of victory. In him it produces the certitude of defeat.

In my dealings with you, I have been guilty on too many occasions, perhaps, of criticizing and of loud talking. I am sorry for this and wish to assure you that when I criticize and censure I am wholly impersonal. I do it because I know that if you are permitted to drive head-and-tail, to fail to take cover, to fail to keep the roads clear, you are exposing yourself to needless death and wounds. For every man I have criticized in this Army, I have probably stopped, talked to, and complimented a thousand, but people are more prone to remember ill usage than to recall compliments; therefore, I want you officers and men who are here to explain to the other soldiers, who think perhaps that I am too hard, my motives and to express to them my sincere regret.

You know that I have never asked one of you to go where I feared to tread. I have been criticized for this, but there are many General Pattons and there is only one

Seventh Army. I can be expended, but the Seventh Army must and will be victorious.

I am very proud of you. Your Country is proud of you. You are magnificent fighting men. Your deeds in Sicily will fill the pages of history for a thousand years.

When Patton was at his lowest, after Messina, and the Seventh Army units were being transferred away from him, he called in the Staff and told them that if they wanted to leave him he would find them the best jobs he could. "They stuck like limpets," he wrote to his wife.

9. Postlude to Sicily and Prelude to the Third Army

WHILE visiting the various Divisions who had served under him in Sicily, in addition to complimenting them on their superb fighting abilities, Patton also interviewed certain officers on their battle experiences. He was aware that there was no better way to get accurate comment on fighting than to hear what is to be said by those who have been at close grips with the enemy in combat operations. This was his invariable practice in two world wars.

He also was aware of the fact that officers who lack battle experience fail to realize that divisions and armies are not animated tables of organization but have a soul just as human beings have, and that in order to get the best results, they must be maintained at strength with men who have been in them long enough to acquire the unit soul. Until this point is made clear, full efficiency will not be attained.

Patton was also "loyal down" to a fanatical degree. It was one of his most outstanding characteristics and paid dividends in performance. Consequently his staff idolized him and at times would perform the impossible.

In this loyalty he continually was in quest of something by which he could better understand and appreciate the enlisted men. He always wanted to better their conditions. In return he always demanded more when in combat and he usually received more.

In a letter to Mrs. George Marshall, wife of General

Marshall, quoted in part, Patton comments on the difference in appearance of those who have been in combat and those who have not. He also speaks of the value of decorations.

I really appreciate very much what you said about the men. They are wonderful soldiers and we are mutually crazy about each other.

One very interesting thing has taken place and that is in the facial expression of the men who have been in battle. I first noticed it inspecting guards of honor and then recently I had to pin on quite a number of decorations, and I have been even more struck with it. The eyes and mouths have changed. The eyes are more penetrating and have crow's-feet around the corners, and the mouths are much firmer.

When old General [Winfield L.] Scott told the soldiers of the Mexican War that they had been through fire and blood and had come out steel, he told the truth. That is what has happened to these men, and they certainly are magnificent-looking people now.

The medals which General Marshall has insisted on have had a wonderful effect, and I am sure that when we get the Bronze Battle Stars this effect will be even further enhanced.

The result of decorations works two ways. It makes the men who get them proud and determined to get more, and it makes the men who have not received them jealous and determined to get some in order to even up. It is the greatest thing we have for building a fighting heart.

Not only did Patton study U.S. troops, leadership, and techniques, but he was a keen observer of the Allies as well. He once made the remark that he did not feel that his boisterous method of command would work with the British. Despite this, General Alexander noted the outstanding success obtained by Patton and made a study of the "Patton prescription." Patton made a visit to General Alexander, at General Eisenhower's request, for the specific purpose of explaining his (Patton's) method of command. He commented upon these differences between the Americans and the British in a letter to his wife.

The more I deal with the British, the more I marvel at how different we of the same blood are, at least in language. The French and Italians always say that they speak American or that they speak English and consider them as things apart. Certainly the British are much more polite than we are. Sometime ago at a meeting, one of them absolutely disagreed with the rest. We would have said—"I won't have a thing to do with that proposition—to hell with it." But not my friend. In dulcet tones, he said, "Really, I hate to be difficult, but what you say moves me profoundly, indeed I am shocked." That was all. Yet he was quite as positive as we would have been."

Patton and Alexander had a great deal of mutual respect for each other. When Seventh Army was relieved from General Alexander's command, Patton sent a wire to him expressing his pleasure to have served under him. The return wire from Alexander to Patton is quoted.

Personal from General Alexander to General Patton. Thank you so much for your exceedingly nice message, which I greatly appreciate. I can assure you and your grand soldiers that I consider myself fortunate to have had the privilege, honor and may I say pleasure to have had under my command such a famous commander and his army. My dearest hope is that we will be associated together again. The best of luck to you all.

Patton's reply by letter emphasizes the high esteem he held of General Alexander.

MY DEAR GENERAL ALEXANDER,

Please accept my most sincere thanks for your splendid telegram.

I should like to express, in more detail than my wire permitted, the deep appreciation of all of us of your splendid leadership and the considerate treatment of this force while under your command. Personally, I trust you will believe me when I say that I have never, in all my military career served under an officer who combined in his person so many attributes of greatness as you possess and at the same time was so warmhearted and unassuming.

Should the fortunes of war again permit me to serve

under you, I should consider it my crowning piece of good fortune.

With warm personal regards, I am,

Most Sincerely,

G. S. PATTON, JR.

Lieut. General, U.S. Army,

Commanding

After he was relieved from General Alexander's command, Patton, with a limited number of his staff, was sent to Corsica with General Alphonso Juin of the French Army, and corresponding members of the Juin staff. The plan was to have Patton appear in various locales so that the Germans, and Italians, could do their own speculating as to what might be happening in the Mediterranean. While at Napoleon's birthplace at Ajaccio on Corsica, he and members of his staff touched and rubbed the bed in which Napoleon had been born. This was considered to be a lucky omen. Later Patton was sent to Cairo to visit the Polish Division under Anders. He was bobbing up in many places, with some cover of security and publicity later. At Ajaccio Patton and his staff landed about 10 to 15 minutes earlier than planned. Promptly at the appointed hour, the Germans bombed the airfield. Fortunately, he had already departed.

At a memorial service which Patton attended on the eleventh of November the Chaplain preached a sermon on sacrifice. The service was held at an Allied cemetery, predominately American, located near Palermo. As Patton put the wreath at the foot of the flagpole, he said. "I consider it no sacrifice to die for my country. In my mind we came here to thank God that men like these have lived rather than to regret that they have died."

Despite his seriousness he realized that there was a lighter side of battle. Lack of it in World War II concerned him. He felt, as did many World War I veterans, that all the fun and gaiety had gone out of war. The only song that is a reminder of World War II is the German song "Lilli Marlene," whereas one still associates "Pack Up Your Troubles in Your Old Kit Bag," "Over There," and "Tipperary" with World War I. His diary entry of November 14, 1943 points out the reason for this feeling.

Hodges noted the same thing which I have remarked that, due to bad psychology at home, our troops have no

171

zest for battles. In World War I this was not true. We wanted to fight and did. In this war the men, who are much better trained and in every way much better soldiers, go in considering themselves martyrs. They fight magnificently but do not fight with any pleasure. We both think this is due to too much security and lack of ballyhoo at home. It is bad!

Prior to his departure for England, he attended an Italian dinner described in this quotation from a letter to Mrs. Patton dated November 20, 1943.

DARLING B:

We went to a very heavy Italian dinner about a week ago. So far I have not come down with any bad symptoms, but I may yet. First they had a cordial made of laurel—I always thought that was poison, but I may have confused it with hemlock. In any case, it is as strong as brandy, but sweet. Then we had soup, quite good, the sort you sprinkle cheese on. Then we had a sort of pie about four inches thick: it had potatoes, cauliflower, cheese, fish, beans, and other ingredients I could not determine in it. Not only was it powerful, but it was copious. The hostess—I sent you her picture, the fat one with the good features next to whom I sat had made it so I had to eat two helpings. Then we had a dish that would have been a great boon to a geologist; it was stratified; on the top was lobster, then shellfish, then green assorted vegetables, then cheese, and God knows what else, all smothered in thick mayonnaise. No one near me had made it so I got by with one small helping. For dessert we had an Italian creme which had been made by the lady on my right, so I had to eat all of it, but the eating ability of the Italians is wonderful. I have never seen such helpings as they took and they all had at least two. One little girl of thirteen had enough to founder a horse. After dinner I examined her contour to see if she bulged and there was no sign.

His letter to his wife on Christmas Eve again shows his sense of humor.

DARLING B:

As you have seen in the papers, I have been to Egypt.

I will write you a good account when I have time. The enclosed picture is of my Polish loot. The eagle on the collar is their insignia for a Lt. General. The mermaid on the shoulder is the badge of the 2nd Polish Corps. I sent them to you in the purse I sent George. I also sent a Legion of Merit. The red ribbon with the silver bow and self-starter is the Legion of Honor (Commander), and the yellow and white one with the gold bow and self-starter is the Grand Cross of Morocco. They are rather dirty, as I had them in the Sicilian Campaign.

I got some fine pictures of my trip which I will send as soon as I get them censored and the titles on them. I sent Ruth Ellen a couple of pictures of Jim.

The Cardinal (La-Vitrana) sent me a blessing which clears me to date and also a fruit cake, which if I eat, will make me need the blessing.

Lots of love and Merry Christmas.

GEORGE

When Patton was low in spirits he was noticeably depressed and was unable to hide his emotions. At the end of 1943 he expected to lose his Seventh Army staff. This belief was unfounded as the key personnel later joined him in England to assist him with the Third Army. Because of the uncertainty of the situation he was not sure of his own future. Diary entries of December 31st and the first of January point up these traits.

December 31, 1943

Another year ended. I hope I do bigger and better fighting in 1944. Harkins got back yesterday and I can't make head or tail of the mess. The Seventh Army Staff is going to Algiers to plan "Anvil" but Hughes writes that I won't command "Anvil." He thinks I am going to UK. I hope not. I would hate to play too far down in the team, also if I get to England, as it seems to be set up, it means I go alone to pick up a new staff. I prefer my present one to any I have seen. They have stuck by me and I propose to stick by them.

January 1, 1944

I feel very badly for myself but particularly for the staff and headquarters soldiers who have stood by me all the time in good weather and bad. I suppose that I am going to England to command another army but if I am sent there to simply train troops which I am not to command I shall resign. There is no appreciation of the fact that a staff is a living thing; not simply an animated table of organization. I cannot conceive of anything more stupid than to change staffs on a General, nor can I conceive of anything more inconsiderate than not to notify him where he is going. A Hell of a "Happy New Year."

Never forgetting his Deity despite personal reverses and success, on January 1, 1944 Patton wrote:

A SOLDIER'S PRAYER

God of our Father, who by land and sea has ever led us on to victory, please continue Your inspiring guidance in this greatest of our conflicts.

Strengthen my soul so that the weakening instinct of self-preservation, which besets all of us in battle, shall not blind me to my duty to my own manhood, to the glory of my calling, and to my responsibility to my fellow shoulders.

Grant to our armed forces that disciplined valor and mutual confidence which insures success in war.

Let me not mourn for the men who have died fighting, but rather let me be glad that such heroes have lived.

If it be my lot to die, let me do so with courage and honor in a manner which will bring the greatest harm to the enemy, and please, oh, Lord, protect and guide those I shall leave behind.

Give us the victory, Lord.

On the sixth of January, 1944, Patton called his Seventh Army senior staff members into his office in the palace that was his headquarters. He told them of his pending departure, and that he felt sorry for them because they had apparently hitched their wagons to the wrong star. He said he was going to take as many of them along with him as possible when he went to England; however, he believed he was going to be limited in the number he could take. He promised that he would do everything in his power to help those he could not take with him. Patton asked if any of them wanted him to seek a job for them right away, or if they wanted to wait a bit, take a chance, and cast their lot with him. Not one wanted to leave him.

Upon his arrival in the United Kingdom Patton called on Ike and found he was to command the Third Army. As far as he can remember this was his twenty-seventh start from scratch since being commissioned in the U.S. Army. He had always been successful and he felt this oportunity would be his biggest challenge. As history proved, he was right and he was also successful.

He met the advanced party of the Third Army aboard the *Queen Mary*. Here he told them that he was still a secret and should not be mentioned.

The Third Army was not destined to go into France until D plus 10. However, Patton knew that he would make a name for himself. He still felt destined for bigger things. In early February he was forced to go to the hospital for a sore lip which resulted from too much sunlight on his blond complexion. His diary entry of the second of March states, *After all the ass kissing I have to do, no wonder I have a sore lip.*

Briefings and discussion for "Overlord" (the code name for the French Invasion) were under way. Patton attended a briefing in early April with some of his key staff personnel. Extracts from the diary reflect his feelings about overstrengths in personnel. This is a vital situation in combat and deserves considerable thought.

April 7 1944

I had quite a talk with them trying to justify an initial overstrength of 15%. I base this on the fact that the normal loss from disease and accidents runs around 8%, so that troops invariably enter battle short. The first day's casualties cannot be replaced for a few days or even a week. That is added to the first shortage so that at the crucial point of a battle, usually the third or fourth day, there is a serious shortage. If we started with the 15% overstrength, we would enter the battle the first day 7% overstrength, and if we assume that 5% casualties per day will occur, we would still be 1% understrength at the end of the third day.

It is further necessary to remember that the efficiency of a division is not measured by its shortage in personnel. A shortage of 10% in personnel reduces the effectiveness of a division about 20%, and as the losses increase, the efficiency decreases in almost geometrical ratio.

I can't get anyone to realize this. I expect I take chances because I do not have to earn my living in the Army, because of judicious selection of parents and besides I am a soldier—a simple soldier.

Patton felt that many who depended on pay and pensions had an inordinate fear of *they*. He was pre-eminent in his ability to influence troops. His audacious statements were part of his strength in creating the will to fight, and conversely they often boomeranged to hurt him personally.

Eisenhower, essentially discreet and diplomatic, was always disturbed and apprehensive because of Patton's free speech, as were Mr. McCloy and General McNarney. He was unquestionably so audacious in every way that it is doubtful if in wartime the lack of such independence, financial or otherwise, would have curbed his speech.

Patton was right in his thoughts and statements on replacements and overstrength as demonstrated later in Korea in 1950. The initial divisions going into combat in Korea in 1950 only had two battalions of infantry per regiment and two firing batteries of artillery per battalion, and, to make it worse, when the third battalions for the infantry regiments were sent out from the United States, they were sent badly under strength. In paper work Table of Organization & Equipment was abbreviated to TO&E. To take care of the situation described above someone had coined a neat phrase "TO&E reduced strength." This was satisfactory in the Pentagon but not on the battlefield.

Hospitalization of wounded patients was always a source of worry to Patton. He discusses this problem in his diary.

April 17, 1944

Colonel Elliott Cutler, of the Medical Corps, was here for breakfast. He has a very good idea which he acquired from visiting the Russians, namely, to put the slightly wounded in a hospital by themselves, and the badly wounded and badly diseased in another hospital by themselves. He says that doctors, particularly civilian doctors (and that is 99% of our Medical Corps), naturally spend most of their time on serious cases, whereas in war you should spend most of your time on the cases which can be got back to the front promptly. Furthermore, if the slightly wounded men associated with the badly wounded or diseased men, they learn a lot of symptoms which they then tell the doctors they themselves possess, and the doctors are big enough fools to leave them in the hospital when they should go back to the fighting. Cutler also pointed out that it has a great moral effect to get men back to their old unit, because in that case the soldiers see that getting wounded is not a very serious business.

The so-called "Knutsford Incident" occurred at this time, when General Patton's Third Army headquarters was located at Peover Hall near the small township of Knutsford in Northern England.

In the interests of local good will General Patton accepted an invitation to attend the opening on the afternoon of April 25, 1944, of the Knutsford Welcome Club, organized by local residents to provide entertainment for our service men stationed in the region.

The gathering, consisting of about fifty townspeople, mostly women, and a few local functionaries, was quite informal. It was understood by General Patton, also by Colonel Campanole and Major Stiller who accompanied him, that no members of the press were to be present. The chairman, a Mrs. Constantine Smith, spoke of the club's objectives, introduced a number of local personages, and finally asked General Patton to say a few words.

The General, emphasizing that he was there unofficially, made a short impromptu speech on Anglo-American amity in the course of which he made a jocular remark to the effect that since it was self-evident that after the war England and America, and of course the Russians too, would be called upon to guide the destinies of the world, the better they all got to know one another, the better it would be for all concerned.

The following day a number of British newspapers reported the General's speech. Some quoted the General as saying "America and England are destined to rule the world." Others claimed he had included Russia. Still others reproached him for having omitted Russia. SHAEF called up to inquire what General Patton actually had said. He told them.

On April 30 he received a telephone call from Beedle Smith ordering him to report the following morning to General Eisenhower at the latter's hearquarters near London, where General Eisenhower admonished him to be careful of any further statements. For accuracy his diary entries of this incident are important.

May, 1 1944

I feel like death, but I am not out yet. If they will let me fight, I will; but if not, I will resign so as to be able to talk, and then I will tell the truth, and possibly do my country more good. All the way home, 5 hours, I recited poetry to myself.

> "If you can make a heap of all your winnings
> And risk it on one turn of pitch-and-toss,
> And lose, and start again at your beginnings
> And never breathe a word about your loss." [1]

> "I dared extreme occasion,
> Nor ever one betrayed."

My final thought on the matter is that I am destined to achieve some great thing—what I don't know, but this last incident was so trivial in its nature, but so terrible in its effect, that it is not the result of an accident but the work of God. His will be done.

May 3, 1944

When I got back, Gay handed me an Eisenhower dispatch telegram which said in effect: "Since the War Department has placed the decision of relieving you on me, I have decided to keep you. My letter on this subject will be put in the Official file [cover plan]. Go ahead and train your army."

I felt much better and wrote Ike thanking him. He called me up in person and was very nice.

---

[1] Quoted from "If," *Rewards and Fairies,* by Rudyard Kipling, copyright, 1910, by Rudyard Kipling. The two lines following are from Kipling's "Song of Diego Valdez," copyright, 1902, by Rudyard Kipling. Reprinted by permission of Mrs. George Bainbridge, Macmillan of Canada, Ltd., and Doubleday and Company, Inc.

At the time of this controversy, Patton told his personal orderly, Sergeant George Meeks, "We are going to have to go to the United States this time." Later, after the matter was patched up, he told George Meeks not to worry, that it was going to be all right, to which Meeks replied, "You're the boss. You can say 'em but you *can't* say 'em," to which Patton replied, "You're like all the rest."

There has been a lot written about the animosity that existed between General Montgomery and General Patton. Most of it probably stretched the truth. They attended a dinner on the first of June. The diary quote, again for accuracy, is given.

June 1 1944

At dinner, General Montgomery produced a betting book and asked me whether or not England would be at war again in ten years after the close of the present war. He bet she would not, therefore, to be a sport, I had to bet she would. Also his Quartermaster offered to bet me $40.00 that an American horse would not win the next Grand National. In order to stick up for my country I had to risk the $40.00. The only chance is that, since England has bred no horses during the war, American horses may have a chance. When the port was passed, General Montgomery toasted the four Army Commanders. Nobody did anything about it, so I said, "As the oldest Army Commander present, I would like to propose a toast to the health of General Montgomery and express our satisfaction in serving under him." The lightning did not strike me. After dinner we gambled in a simple way. At first I won too much but finally succeeded in finishing a slight loser. I have a better impression of Monty than I had.

"Overlord" was under way. The Third Army was in reserve and not employed on D-day due to lack of shipping. They were to break through at Avranches later. Patton felt that he would not get in the war before it was over. On the contrary, he still considered himself a man of destiny and would succeed in getting in. He was so right! He even hoped that he would be called upon to replace a commander should he (the commander) be killed. Hence he was always ready in case of an emergency.

For the operations in Northern Europe, the participating

179

forces were organized into two Army groups. Supreme Commander over both of these was General Dwight D. Eisenhower. His headquarters was known as SHAEF (Supreme Headquarters, Allied Expeditionary Forces). Within SHAEF, Air Marshal Sir Trafford Leigh-Mallory was Commander of the Allied Expeditionary Air Forces, and Admiral Sir Bertram Ramsey was Commander of the Allied Expeditionary Naval Forces.

The U.S. 12th Army Group was commanded by General Omar Bradley. Within this Army were the U.S. First Army, commanded by Lieutenant General Courtney H. Hodges, and the U.S. Third Army commanded by General Patton.

The British 21st Army Group was commanded by General Sir Bernard L. Montgomery. Under Montgomery were the British Second Army commanded by Lieutenant General Sir Miles C. Dempsey, and the Canadian First Army commanded by General Henry D. G. Crerar.

For the early days of the invasion a slightly different organization was adopted. General Montgomery was made temporary Allied Ground Commander, and as such he controlled the U.S. First Army and the British Second Army during the invasion. General Bradley took direct command of the U.S. First Army for the invasion. As soon as the U.S. Forces ashore swelled to the size of two armies, Bradley turned First Army over to General Hodges, entered Patton's Third Army into the fighting, and reassumed his role of Army Group Commander. A week after this change-over was made on August 1, General Eisenhower landed in Europe and General Montgomery reassumed his status as an Army Group Commander, equal in status to Bradley.

The over-all plan for "Overlord," as the Normandy invasion was called, used the American First Army to capture Cherbourg and the British Second Army to capture Caen. Caen's geographical location, only 120 miles from Paris over open country ideal for tanks, made it the obvious choice for Allied concentration. Thus, the British were to draw the bulk of the enemy opposition in their area, while the U.S. forces were to break through along the western coast of Normandy, cut south through Brittany, isolating the Brittany peninsula, then pivot eastward toward Paris and the Seine. This strategy was successful, for the enemy concentrated against the British on the eastern flank, thus opening the way for the U.S. break-through so ably executed by General Patton in the operation called "Cobra" at Avranches.

Patton now felt that the staff of the Third Army was good. In fact, he had his loyal staff of the Seventh Army and some good additions. His fears, that he would lose his old staff and have to start over again to build his team, were unfounded. He complimented them whenever he felt it was due them. He felt that the Number Two men were better than he had in Seventh Army. His top men were the same.

He believed in giving an officer a fair chance to attain his stride. Those who have served with him know that there was never a commander who strived more to give credit where credit was due. If he knew that a subordinate did his best he would make allowance for the performance. In this way those who worked with him constantly did better than they knew how. It was inspiring to have served under him, something that his subordinates will never forget.

Patton was not yet in but he was thinking of a break-through. This is the dominant factor of armored offensive combat—"attacks in depth and on a narrow front." Armor, to achieve its greatest effectiveness, must achieve the break-through. To do this great pressure must be exerted in a restricted area. Once through, the armor can fan out and attack rear areas and communications.

While he was readying his plans to get into the fight he received the news that Colonel Paddy Flint was killed, in action. Harry Flint was a great personal friend. In fact, he was the godfather of George Patton's son. His diary entries concerning the loss of his friend again show his humility.

July 25, 1944

At about 1600, Colonel Odom called to say that Paddy Flint had just been killed, shot through the head. His body is to be sent to Ste. Mère Église and he will probably be buried this afternoon. I sent Stiller to wait at the cemetery and inform me when the funeral would take place. Paddy was a gallant soldier and a great friend. He died as he would like to, in battle. He was getting pretty worn out and would probably have been sent home. Probably his death was fortunate because he had been fired at too much and it had gotten to the

181

point where he was timid, not for himself, but for his men. I hope when it is my time to go I go as gallantly and as easily. I will write to Lady, his wife, after the funeral.

Paddy's death occurred when he was moving ahead of one his battalions. The battalion had not done too well and had stopped. He went up to get it moving accompanied by Major Mosely, his peep driver, and a radio operator. They found a tank which was not fighting, and Paddy told it to come along with him. The tank driver said that the turret was jammed and he could not rotate it, so Paddy told him that he would come anyway and should be very glad of the honor of having a Colonel of Infantry for a bodyguard. They went up the road towards a church from which they were receiving considerable fire. Paddy climbed on the tank to tell the driver which way to go and while so doing had two bullets go through his clothes, but refused to pay any attention, or get down, until Major Mosely pulled him down. About this time the radio operator was hit and Mosely took him under cover and then rejoined Paddy, whom he found firing at the Germans at a range of 40 yards. He was persuaded to stop and get down. At this time an infantry platoon came up and Paddy got out on the road with the Sergeant to show him where to lead the platoon. While doing this he was hit in the head. The bullet went through the left side of his helmet and came out near the top. It did not penetrate the brain, but it punched a sliver of bone into the brain, paralyzing the voice centers and also producing complete paralysis. Paddy was conscious for some time and smoked a cigarette, but eventually lost consciousness and never recovered. He was given the best medical care and one of the finest brain surgeons operated in an attempt to save him. The radio operator, who had been wounded, upon hearing about Paddy being hit, got in a peep, drove to the camp to get assistance and brought it back to him. God rest his soul.

The unsolicited remarks in a letter by Sallie Flint, Colonel Flint's widow, follow here. They serve well to pierce the outer shell of George Patton.

This is a very inadequate effort to express my regard

182

for the friend that George Patton was, my friend and more especially the friend of my husband Paddy Flint. Probably only his family and those closest to him really know this great soldier. Loyalty to them and to his profession were his outstanding qualities and I am sure had he been faced with the necessity of a decision he would, without hesitation, have held his integrity as a soldier above all else. Few people, outside of his family, knew the gentleness, the true courtesy, the almost puritanical uprightness and devotion to his religious convictions that were the real George Patton. Many of his friends had evidence of these traits. Underneath the seemingly rough and tough exterior was the thoughtful, sympathetic, almost boyish man.

I have always had the conviction that the "Blood and Guts" manner, the tough talking, was really a sort of "Whistling in the Dark" which he had from the very first contrived to serve as a kind of apparatus to build himself into the person he wanted to be as a soldier; that he thought a soldier *had* to be strong, physically, mentally, morally, (and he was all these); that he believed a soldier should be unmoved by fear, suffering, the sight of death, blood, any horrible or vile thing; *that he must endure*. This, it has always seemed to me, was the motivation back of all the rough, profane, and at times almost vulgar manner and speech.

My husband, were he here, could cite many instances of his thoughtfulness and consideration, many instances of his devotion as a friend. I would like to tell of some of these kindnesses in which I have been the beneficiary.

Colonel Flint died on July 25, 1944 in Normandy, France, of wounds received in action the preceding day. He was buried at Ste. Mère Église on July 26th. General Patton had personally arranged for this ceremony, notifying Paddy's friends and classmates, had a coffin made, which in a combat zone was not usual, had an Army Band there, and attended to other details that only he could have made possible, and was himself present at the burial. To this he gave his time and attention, the last rites for a friend, though on that day his Army was to start its great push across the Normandy plain.

At this time he made an inventory of my husband's personal belongings, listed them and directed that they

183

be sent to General Everett Hughes, then in England, with the request that they be dispatched with all possible speed to me in the States, rather than await the usual slow routine procedure, writing to me to that effect. He made this so very personal a matter that he wrote on the last page of his (Paddy's) diary, following the final entry, a wonderful testimony to him as a soldier and added en expression of his affection and friendship. On a sheet of paper which he found in the writing case, he made a notation calling my attention to an envelope which Paddy had addressed to me awaiting a letter to be written on his return that day. He also wrote on the holster that he found there, "I had this made for Paddy in Palermo. He wore it in his last fight." And on this day he wrote a personal letter to me in his own handwriting, in which he spoke of his great grief and sense of loss in Paddy's death and telling me as gently as he could the manner in which he died. He also had a transcript made of the statement of Major Mosely covering the circumstances. This was the officer who was with Colonel Flint when he was wounded. He sent this to me later together with a copy of a speech which Paddy made to his Regiment before they left England. He had photographs made at Ste. Mère Église of the grave, those who were there, the burial, etc. He wrote that they were being sent under separate cover, that I might not want to see them right away, perhaps never, but that they had been made for me and for the record, should I ever wish to refer to them. In closing this letter he expressed his profound sympathy and the sincere wish to be of service in any way, "financial or otherwise." Only a very understanding person could have thought of all these things and carried them out in such a way.

This is all part of a picture of a very different George Patton than is generally known to the public which heard only of the exploits of a great and successful General and a tough "Blood and Guts" fighter. One of the greatest, but also a loving and sensitive friend.

Sometime after his own death, a package came to me through Captain Charles Codman, who had been the General's aide. It contained the flag that had covered the coffin at Ste. Mère Église. In such ceremonies the flag is given into the hands of the nearest of kin to the deceased. Captain Codman wrote me that it had been General Patton's intention to bring this home with him and to place it in my hands himself—another example of the thoughtful and considerate person that this man really was. This he could not do, for he too met his death over there.

I wish the people for whom he fought, deeming it an honor and a privilege to do so, could know what manner of man George Patton really was, that underneath the rough-spoken, cold-blooded exterior he was a gentle and kindly person who had to make himself tough to do the job he had. He wasn't born that way.

About this time, on the eve of Third Army's commitment to battle, a young officer wrote to his father of his first meeting Patton. He was on the staff of the Third Army, who with others had been working on the plan of the break-through in the headquarters that were established in France in advance of General Patton's coming to the continent and during the period when it was desired to keep from the Germans knowledge as to whom the Army Commander was to be.

The letter told how one afternoon, about July 25th, the staff was assembled, by order, on the lawn in front of the château housing the headquarters, and how, while they were speculating as to what it was all about, the front doors were thrown open and a strange officer walked out and stood in a ray of sunlight, looking them over and at first saying nothing. Everyone stopped talking and looked at him and soon he began to speak, in a high and somewhat unpleasant voice. Their first impressions were of a powerful figure, immaculately and superbly uniformed, shining boots and insignia, looking every inch the soldier and leader. And before he had talked very long, they knew that he *was* a soldier and a leader. As the writer said, "I suppose the performance was carefully staged and that he came there to hook us all, but I'll say he did it! As for me, he not only hooked, but landed me, and I will go with him to the ends of the earth."

10. The Dash Across France

WHEN the Third Army entered the European campaign, General Patton was given initially the type of operation he had always believed in and in which he excelled—the break-through. No operation better suited General Patton's special qualifications than the break-through. In it his audacity, speed and tactical skill all became at once manifest, for an operation of this type was ideal for a bold armored leader.

Also, the knowledge Patton had gained of the Bocage country back in 1912, when he and his wife had driven through France, proved to be useful to him. Then he had traveled the back watershed roads used by William the Conqueror, hence he knew that these would be the routes which would be passable in any kind of weather.

Patton used a method of advance which resembled a game of leapfrog. He ordered the advance guards of each column to surround and contain the enemy groups that were met, cutting them off from supply and communication. While these troops remained to mop up the enemy, another advance guard was immediately formed to continue the forward sweep until another enemy force was encountered. Then the system was repeated. This method was typical of Patton for he believed that the enemy should be kept so busy retreating that he could not marshal his forces to counterattack.

Although the Third Army did not make the initial invasion of France, Third Army planners were confronted with the preparation of alternate plans, with combinations to be used, in case the Normandy invasion, as such, required alternate beaches to overcome containment of the Normandy beachhead.

The attack was actually commenced on July 26th by the VII Corps of the First Army and the VII Corps of which Patton's Third Army took control on July 28th. These two corps executed the initial break-through, which was named "Cobra." The line held by the Allies, when the attack was opened, ran roughly from Caen to Lessay. Everything possible was done to make the Germans believe our attack would come from the east. Instead these two corps struck southward along the west coast of Normandy to Avranches. By August 1 Avranches had been taken, and through this gap General Patton exploded his army onto the Brittany peninsula. Within a week most of Brittany was overrun.

When the Third Army went into full operation on August 1st, it was assigned approximately 325,000 troops, divided as follows:

The VIII Corps, commanded by Major General Troy H. Middleton, consisting of the 6th Armored and 8th and 83d Infantry Divisions.

The XII Corps consisting of the 4th Armored and 80th Infantry Divisions was initially commanded by Major General Gilbert R. Cook. However, General Cook became seriously ill on August 19th and was replaced by Major General Manton S. Eddy.

The XV Corps, commanded by Major General Wade H. Haislip, consisting of the 5th Armored and the 79th and 90th Infantry Divisions and the French 2d Armored Division.

The XX Corps, commanded by Major General Walton H. Walker, consisting of the 7th Armored and the 5th and the 35th Infantry Divisions.

Many supporting units were also assigned to the Army, such as Tank Destroyer, Engineer, Signal, Quartermaster, Medical and Ordnance Battalions, various artillery groups of all calibers, and the 2d, 15th and 106th mechanized cavalry groups.

The XIX Tactical Air Force, commanded by Brigadier General O. P. Weyland, was assigned to support the Third Army.

So great a force necessitated a large staff, with all the potential evils of size. General Patton, however, knew all the drawbacks of huge staffs and was unusually intelligent in minimizing them. One of his devices was a special briefing which only a few attended, which gave the day-to-day picture to him in open forum style, where thoughts were exchanged, and all were invited to present their views. These were held daily about 7:00 A.M. and lasted only 30 minutes. These special briefings resulted in Patton and his high staff thinking alike. Thus, they almost invariably arrived at the same conclusions.

The special briefing was followed by a general briefing,

which was attended by all staff sections. These were more formal affairs and were held about 8:00 A.M. Here the G-2 formally opened the briefings, followed by the G-3, and then the other appropriate staff sections. These briefings finished with a roundup of what was happening in other parts of the world.

General Weyland, Air, attended the early morning briefings, and was always planning in close liaison with Patton. A typical attendance for Third Army early briefings would be General Patton; General Gay, Chief of Staff; Colonel Harkins, Deputy Chief of Staff; Colonel Maddox, G-3 Operations; Colonels Koch and Allen, G-2, Air; General O. P. Weyland, and Colonel Roger Browne, Weyland's Chief of Staff. Sometimes dignitaries, such as Eisenhower and Bradley, would attend.

A Third Army air-ground team was established of a caliber that may have been equaled, but never surpassed, in World War II. General Weyland never said, "It can't be done." Because of the close interchange of thoughts between General Patton and all the staff and Weyland, most of the air missions suggested, or ordered, were already under consideration by the XIX Tactical Air Command. The slight shifts necessary for XIX Tactical Air Command to meet the final Army plans were generally made in a matter of minutes, and there was always the feeling that the missions could be accomplished.

On August 1, the day when the Third Army erupted through the gap, many of the Army's divisions were still unloading their troops on the coast of Normandy. As rapidly as possible, each corps was pushed through the gap at Avranches. The VIII Corps went first, and was ordered to turn west toward the port of Brest at the tip of the Brittany peninsula. Patton ordered a special tank force organized, headed by Brigadier General Herbert L. Earnest, 1st Tank Destroyer Brigade. This task force was sent along the northern coast road of Brittany to capture the small ports and towns along the way.

The XII followed and headed southwest towards Rennes and Vannes to cut the Brittany peninsula off from the rest of France.

The XV Corps was sent through next with orders to head east through Fougères and Mayenne.

Last of all, the XX Corps struck southeast through Laval, in a general direction southeast of Paris.

Regardless of Patton's decisions, he invariably compared them to practical theory as taught by our Service Schools. A portion of his diary entries on the first day that his Army was operational in France point out his feelings and emphasize his differences with known practice.

August 1, 1944
Gaffey, Harkins, Haislip and myself then visited the VIII Corps to coordinate the movement of the 90th Division through their rear area. This is an operation which, at Leavenworth, would certainly give you an unsatisfactory mark, as we are cutting the 90th Division through the same town and on the same street, being used by two armored and two other infantry divisions. However, there is no other way of doing it at this time. . . .
Of course, it is a little nerve-wracking to send troops straight into the middle of the enemy with front, flanks and rear open. I had to keep repeating to myself, "Do not take counsel of your fears."

According to Colonel Harkins, Deputy Chief of Staff for operations for the Third Army, General Patton, about this time, mentioned to him that there had been a slowdown once the Avranches bridge had been secured by an armored division. Patton related to Harkins, who is presently a Major General, that the Division Commander had been asked whether he remembered about Horatius at the Bridge. Pointing it out as an historical example, he emphasized that securing of the bridge was only part of the job; to get the troops across in force without delay was the important consideration. Patton directed that the division keep moving, and that the movement continue on a 24-hour basis. It did.
The 90th Infantry Division was green and inexperienced in combat, and therefore subject to all the usual troubles that a new division suffers. This division was later, when it found itself, one of the most aggressive and dependable divisions in the United States Army. It was commanded by the late Major General Ray McLain, a National Guardsman who was integrated in the Regular Army and retired as a three-star General. During the war he was elevated to command of a corps.

On arrival at General Middleton's headquarters, on the 2nd of August, Patton asked him the position of one of his divisions. Middleton replied, "It is on the bank of the Selune River."

Quick as a flash General Patton said, "What bank—the far one or the near one?"

"The near one," General Middleton replied.

General Patton answered, "Good God, man, history is full of examples of battles being lost because units stopped on the near side of a river."

On about the 4th of August, General Patton's Third Army was simultaneously committed in four cardinal directions—east, west, north and south. He remarked to his G-2 that this was the first time in history that an army on the *offensive* was actually attacking in four directions.

On the 6th of August, Patton visited one of his corps headquarters to ascertain why the capture of a certain town was being delayed. His answer points up his own self-confidence.

"Apparently it is simply the fact that people are so damn slow, mentally and physically, and lack self-confidence. [I] am disgusted with human frailty. However, the lambent flame of my own self-confidence burns ever brighter."

The reference to his own self-confidence is not a boastful remark. Since his early life Patton had schooled himself to have confidence in his own military decisions. It was part of his prescription for battle leadership.

The German attack on the 7th of August was not a bluff as Patton first believed. Instead it was a desperate attempt to cut off the Third Army from the rest of the Allied troops, by cutting across the narrow Avranches gap through which Patton had been pouring his army. Patton although aggressive was not foolhardy. He had three divisions ready for this attack. While the German attack was being repulsed, Patton's XV Corps made an end run and came up on the exposed southern flank of the German Seventh Army. Although this corps was halted at Alençon to wait the arrival of Montgomery's troops from the north, which did not arrive as planned, the major part of the German Seventh Army was captured or destroyed. This operation might aptly be described by one of Patton's often repeated favorite expressions, "Hold them by the nose, while you kick them in the pants."

While the XV Corps was catching the entire German Seventh Army in a vise, Patton continued to send his other Corps forward, and he shuffled his divisions into position for a drive to the Seine.

The following is the written order for the attack of the XV Corps. This was written personally by Patton. At the time many officers said that this was historic.

HEADQUARTERS THIRD ARMY
APO 403

8 August 1944

Subject: Letter of Instruction
To: Major General W. H. Haislip
           Commanding General XV Corps
           APO 436
           U.S. Army

The purpose of the ensuing operation along the axis of LeMans-Alençon-Sees is to drive the German Army heretofore confronting the First American Army and Second British and Canadian Armies along the channel coast, against the Seine between Paris and Rouen.

In consonance with this plan you will advance along the axis LeMans-Alençon-Sees with the purpose of initially securing the line Sees-Carrouges, both inclusive, prepared for further advance utilizing the 5th Armored Division, the 79th and 90th Infantry Divisions and the Second French Armored Division, which is hereby attached to your corps.

You will utilize all available transportation, including tanks to maintain one infantry combat team in the immediate rear of each armored division; the remaining combat teams of the two infantry divisions to proceed by marching.

In view of the shortage of trucks, it will be necessary to shuttle.

The 80th Division of the XX Corps will close on LeMans, and under orders from that corps will relieve you of the maintenance of the bridgehead. The 35th Division will close initially on Laval.

It is the present purpose of this Army to eventually operate with two corps abreast; decision on which of the two corps moves to be determined by subsequent circumstances.

This letter is for the purpose of giving you the plans

as now envisioned. Irrespective of anything in this letter your mission is and will continue to be to destroy Germans in your front.

Nothing herein inhibits you from using roads within the zone of action of the Third Army. The boundary between the 1st U.S. Army and the Third U.S. Army is Ernee-Mayenne-Lehorps-Charchigne-Couptrain-Carrouges-LaPelietrie-Argentan (all to Third Army). First Army troops south and east of this line to have running rights on roads until clear of Third Army area.

Signed/ G. S. Patton, Jr.
Lieutenant General
U.S. Army
Commanding

Typical of a good commander, regardless of rank, Patton followed through with a visit to XV Corps the very next day to be sure that they had jumped off on the attack.

A diary entry of the 11th of August notes the handling of German prisoners of war. Our potential present-day enemy could well take a lesson from such humane treatment.

The night before last the Germans strafed our prisoner of war camps on the Granville-Avranches road three times, getting seventeen of their own people. Our Provost Marshal very properly opened the gates and let the prisoners scatter. About fifty failed to return. Those who did come back were very grateful to us and loud in their condemnation of the Germans. They all opened up and talked much more freely. The officers said that in Germany, prisoners would not have been treated with equal humanity.

During the first two weeks of August, the Third Army advanced farther and faster than any army in the history of the war. The situation by the 14th of August was roughly as follows: The VIII Corps was besieging Brest and mopping up the Brittany peninsula, the XII Corps was south of LeMans, the XX Corps was just to the north of the XII, and the XV Corps was nearing Argentan but was halted and sent back to Alençon. Patton was in position for his drive to the Seine. The minute he received approval from General Bradley, Commander of the 12th Army

Group, he was ready to move. Patton, on this singular occasion, had Bradley believing that this attack was his (Bradley's) idea. Patton was never famed for his diplomacy, yet he knew that there were times when it was more rewarding than forthrightness. Of Bradley's diplomacy, as well as perception and tact, there is no room for doubt.

Though Patton handled many situations with diplomatic skill, as in the Armistice negotiations in French Morocco, when his temper got the best of him he was led to make statements that boomeranged to hurt him. He was a highly literate Bedford Forrest, the great cavalry leader of the South in the Civil War, whose prescription for victory was "Git thar fustest with the mostest." They both had hot tempers and a skill in profanity. Bedford Forrest refused the oral leave requested of a young captain, who then wrote a flowery letter, again requesting leave to see his wife. The longhand endorsement of Forrest at the bottom of the letter was, "I told you twict Goddamit—no."

Two divisions of the XV Corps, the French 2d Armored and the 90th Infantry Division, were left at Alençon to hold the Falaise Gap. These were later transferred to the V Corps of the First Army commanded by Major General Leonard T. Gerow. When this happened, Patton's diary entry of August 17 shows the loyalty he always felt for his junior officers. He tried to keep General Gaffey whom he had sent to Alençon in command of the division there.

August 17, 1944

This morning at 0730 Gerow called from Gaffey's headquarters north of Argentan, saying he was there with a small staff, ready to take command. I told him that since Gaffey had arranged the attack, which might come off at any moment, Gaffey should run it and he, Gerow, could take over as the opportunity afforded. I could not talk to General Bradley on the radio as it is too dangerous, so I decided to fly up and see him.

The weather was so bad that I could not take off until 1200, arriving at Headquarters 12 Army Group at 1250. General Hodges was there, also under the impression that Gerow was commanding. The temporary corps, consisting of the 90th, 80th and 2d French, is attacking in conjunction with the rest of the First Army, and for this reason it is sound that Gerow should run it.

Imagining that something like this would happen, I told General Gay before I left headquarters that I would call him on the radio, and that it Gerow was to take over at once, I would simply say, "Change horses." I therefore called Gay on the phone and gave this phrase, adding that the attack should take place at once on same objectives. I doubt whether in the history of the world an attack order was ever shorter.

The remaining divisions of XV Corps were sent to the east towards Mantes, on the Seine north of Paris, while the other two Corps, the XX and XII, struck the Seine south of Paris.

The Seine was reached by the 19th and successfully crossed on August 21. Patton was then sure that he could reach Germany in ten days if permitted to do so. He never changed this opinion.

On the 23rd Paris was entered by a Provisional Corps of the First Army, consisting of the French 2d Armored and the 4th U.S. Infantry Divisions. The Third Army had been ordered to bypass Paris to the north and south. Patton's troops could easily have entered Paris if it had been permitted. But the use of a French division was much more diplomatic. Thus the French had the honor of liberating their beloved capital.

Patton had been operating as an individual before August 1, 1944. His wife sensed this for she felt that Patton strategy was on the march. On July 28 she marked the map and mentally inserted Patton's name in the official communiqué. Actually the Third Army, as has been indicated before, became operational in early August, but Patton was not announced at that time as the commander, probably to prevent the Germans from anticipating the tactics of the Army. Apparently the primary reason for the delay was to give him an opportunity to prove himself in combat before the ravenous noncombatants, thirsting for his blood, woke up to the fact that he again had a command.

For future students of these campaigns, Patton believed that one of the two greatest mistakes made in the operations which directly involved his Third United States Army was the halting of his XV Corps. He felt, and so stated at the time, that if the Falaise Gap had been closed, the entire Seventh German Army would have been trapped.

194

As it was, the gap was not closed and part of that German Army escaped.

General Patton never failed to recognize the work of his subordinates. When General Cook was forced out of the war with bad arteries they both felt upset about it. On his visit on the 18th of August to the hospital his diary quotes his handling of this particular instance.

August 18, 1944

I visited General Cook at the hospital. His circulation is so bad that he has no feeling in his hands or legs below the elbows and knees and his toes are turning black. It is impossible for him to walk a hundred yards. After a long conversation, in which I was very frank and honest, I told him that in justice to himself and his men, I could not retain him in command. It was a great blow to us both. I telephoned General Eisenhower, asking him as a personal favor to give General Cook a DSM. I also wrote General Cook a letter of commendation, and wrote General Lear asking him to use Cook at home.

Recognition of Patton's prowess was not limited to the American public. The French, English and all the Allies respected his abilities. Contrariwise he was feared by the Germans. One of the leading instructors at the French Army General Staff School at Langres during World War I paid him a visit at this time. General Koechlin-Schwartz, the instructor, said, "Had I taught twenty-five years ago what you are doing, I should have been put in a madhouse, but when I heard that an armored division was heading for Brest, I knew it was you." Schwartz further said that the trouble with the French Army of 1940 was that for ten years they had taught, thought and practiced defense, never attack.

It must be remembered that Patton's dash across France was the culmination of a lifetime devoted to being ready for this supreme moment. His whole active manhood had been dedicated to equipping himself for the task in which he was then engaged. The soldiers of the Third Army were freeing the countryside from the German yoke. The soldiers were cheered and greeted with flowers in every town where they passed, for they were the saviors of France.

The 2d Cavalry Group, commanded by Colonel Charles Reed, reported to the Corps Commander, General Eddy, at his headquarters. Eddy asked Reed to give him the newest picture of the enemy situation. Reed explained that the two Panzer Grenadier Divisions, the 3d and the 15th, had moved up the east bank of the Seine and were preparing to prevent further American crossing between Troyes and Bar-sur-Seine and that his own troops had been driven back to the bridges. He believed, however, that he could hold until the arrival of the 35th Division. General Eddy then ordered Reed to hold the bridges, stating that on the next day he (Eddy) would launch a corps attack with two divisions across the river.

It was at this point that Patton interrupted: "No, Eddy, that is just what these German divisions want; to make you attack across the river there. Those two German divisions are good ones—just up from Italy; they will slaughter you in a river crossing, even if Reed can hold the bridges. Have Reed blow all the bridges between Troyes and Bar-sur-Seine and hold the river line, protecting your flank. Then cross all your troops at Troyes and attack up the east bank of the Seine. You'll catch them off guard and they'll pull out. Then we can get on to the Moselle without any delay."

After some discussion of details, General Eddy then ordered Reed to blow the bridges. The Corps Engineer was directed to dispatch trucks with demolitions at once, and the bridges were blown before dark. The enemy settled into a defensive position. The 35th Division was crossed at Troyes, and with elements of the 2d Cavalry left on the east bank, launched a strong attack in the morning.

The 3d Panzer Division was taken by surprise and had to withdraw quickly. The 15th Panzer Division likewise withdrew to the east. Our XII Corps advanced then without delay toward Châlons and Commercy. The switch of the attack from a frontal one to a flanking one saved at least two days in the advance, and an enormous member of casualties.

This probably was one of his quickest and best decisions Patton made during the entire war.

General Gay, Patton's Chief of Staff, remembered this incident when he commanded the First Cavalry Division in Korea and left a bridge intact across the Naktong River near Taegu. The North Koreans poured across this bridge in mass and were hit by artillery, mortar, and machine-gun fire. Two of their regiments were completely destroyed.

On the 24th of August the British Radio, BBC, announced that Patton's Third Army had taken Paris. Poetic justice. Patton believed it would be denied later, but no one would believe the refutation when it was made. However, Patton found out that when the French 2d Armored got into Paris they stated that they were still under the Third Army, although they were in the First Army at the time.

Patton's Third Army had French troops fighting side by side with the Americans, and Patton took great pride in their performance. The Fifth Army, fighting in Italy, was likewise augmented by the striking force of the valiant Brazilian Expeditionary Force which fought under the IV Corps of that Army. We can never forget the heroic assistance of our comrades-in-arms from Brazil, France and other allied countries. It was a war founded on international teamwork.

On one occasion in France, when particularly proud of the achievements of his subordinates, General Patton remarked, "Julius Caesar would have a tough time being a brigadier in this Army."

The fall of Paris did not halt the rapid advance of the Third Army.

Early in the fighting Patton had determined through his study of the roads that the best place to hit the Siegfried Line was through the Nancy Gap. He always felt that roads were of supreme importance to an army. To his delight he was sent in this direction. Now he was fighting over much of the ground he had first become acquainted with during World War I.

Supply was becoming a major problem. Patton's extreme speed had stretched the supply lines to the limit. Also SHAEF headquarters had decided that the major thrust was to come in the north, and Montgomery was given top priority in supply. When one of Patton's division commanders told him that he would have to stop as he was out of gas, Patton's reply was typical. He told his division commander to keep moving forward until his tanks were empty and then walk. Above all else, Patton was determined to destroy the enemy as quickly as possible, for he knew that every day of the war saw many American lives lost.

To supply an army during combat operations is a tremendous task. To supply General Patton's hard-striking, fast-moving forces was almost impossible, during the early combat operations on the Third Army.

A broad picture of the supply situation from the United States until the product reached the Third Army might well indicate the magnitude of the task undertaken by the American forces.

First, in the zone of interior, or United States, the products were manufactured, produced and shipped to ports of destination. This involved use of civilian personnel, and the Army service forces. At port, the United States Navy, or in some dire emergencies, the Army Air Forces, were responsible for the shipment of personnel and supplies to overseas ports of destination.

Next the services of supply in the European Theater of Operations, commanded by Lieutenant General J. C. H. Lee, were responsible for shipping the supplies from the port to the rear area of our armies in Europe. Geographically speaking, this is better known as the communications zone. As the Third Army moved forward, advance sections of the communications zone moved directly in rear of the army to keep it constantly supplied with personnel and equipment. From the rear army area, the combat forces of the Third United States Army were kept supplied by Army personnel of the various technical services. All of these technical services, which included engineers, ordnance, signal, medical, chemical, quartermaster and transportation, were banded under the G-4 of the Third Army, who was Brigadier General Walter J. Muller.

In order to expedite supplies across the communications zone in support of the rapid advance of the Third Army, the "Red Ball Express" was set up. This name was originated by the assistant G4 of the Third U.S. Army, Col. Redding F. (Speed) Perry, to designate the truck service he instituted to get supplies from the beach. It later became famous when it was expanded and developed by the Service of Supply (SOS) to move in supplies until rail service was established. Certain roads were reserved for this movement. Trucks would individually be loaded and drivers moved along the main supply route. At regular check points the drivers would be relieved by fresh personnel, and supplies continued on their way. Although at times supplies were short it can be said that the "Red

198

Ball Express" did much to continue the forward impetus of the Third Army.

Another interesting sidelight on supplies to the Third Army is given by this anecdote. At one time, General Patton's forward elements ran directly off the maps, so rapid had been their advance to the east. It has been said that General Patton sent a telegram to the engineer people of the communications zone, who were responsible for map supply, stating that he wanted ten tons of maps dropped by airplane at once.

A special situation not yet recorded developed when the Third Army began to get airlifts of gas, clothes and ammunition.

Patton's army having overrun large caches of cognac and champagne, each airplane on arrival was given liberal gifts of liquor and wine. The first plane in any flight to be unloaded received an additional prize. As airlifts became large, more of this hospitality spread and the news did not injure the tonnage delivered to the Third Army.

During these days of relentless pursuit in 1944, General Patton would often remark, "We may be tired, but think of the enemy—they're the ones doing the running."

General Bradley in *A Soldier's Story* pointed out that the Third Army's allotment of gasoline should have only taken it to the Meuse. Instead, the Army was led some 30 miles farther to the Moselle.

It is generally believed that the high command, while believing in Patton's great tactical ability, genuinely feared his "rashness." Hence one of Bradley's prime missions was to keep a restraining hand on him, sometimes by order, and sometimes by diversion of supplies, or troops, to other armies.

Patton refers to the "rock-soup" attack method in his September third diary entry.

We will get crossings at Nancy and Metz by the "rock-soup" method and I gave the orders today. This is the rock-soup method: once a tramp went to a house and asked for boiling water to make rock-soup. The lady was interested and gave him the latter, in which he placed two polished rocks he had in his hand. He then asked for some potatoes and carrots to put in the soup to flavor the water a little, and finally ended up by securing some meat. In other words, in order to attack, we have first to pretend to reconnoiter and then reinforce the reconnaissance and then finally attack. It is a very sad method of making war.

SHAEF decided, in early September, that Patton's troops could now be supplied along with Montgomery's. Patton had been planning for some time his crossing of the Moselle and was ready to put it into execution. However, the enemy had been given a chance to gather strength because of the slowing of Patton's advance during the gasoline shortage. The area from Nancy to Metz put up stubborn resistance.

Patton pushed, exhorted, and led his troops, and the Moselle was forced in several places. The fighting was intense. At times such as these, Patton knew his presence gave support to his men. He always took care to dress well, and presented a dashing figure. He also knew that he must be confident in order to inspire his junior officers; confident in his own plans and confident of his juniors' capabilities.

Patton then planned to send his XII Corps against the Siegfried Line. On September 6th, Third Army patrols entered Germany and penetrated the Siegfried Line in two places. Nancy was cleared as of September 15th, but Metz continued to resist strongly. On September 23rd, General Bradley informed Patton that he would have to assume the defensive. SHAEF had decided to concentrate offensive action in the north.

General Patton's old friend General Houdemon of the French Army wrote an article in *Éclair de l'Est*, Nancy, September 26, 1947, dealing with the operation across the Moselle to take the fortified hill directly behind Pont à Mousson. The following is the story in the form of translations of extracts from this article entitled "The Genius of Patton."

Three years of combat; three years of victory, where Patton successively appears as the victor of Avranches, Anjou, Normandy and the Palatinate! He appears as the wall of stone, like his model "Stonewall Jackson," hero of the War of Secession, at Bastogne and the bitter battle in Lorraine. His cavalry maneuvers executed with tanks; his violent spearheads followed by raids were the operations of which he was proudest.

I first knew him in 1913 at Saumur in the French Cavalry School, and I still see his proud and elegant figure accompanied by Mrs. Patton, brightening the threshold of my house—a tall, thin cavalryman, with a keen eye and firm hand, either to wield a sword or to guide a horse (my horse), riding the race course over the training obstacles at Saumur.

This comradeship, begun thirty-five years before in our enthusiastic youth when we were both passionate horsemen, was to bloom again during the difficult hours of September, 1944.

General Houdemon, who had escaped the Gestapo and returned to his home in Pont-à-Mousson, advised the Chief of Staff of the U.S. 80th Division on September 7, 1944 that to bomb the town would kill the French, and all the Germans would be safe in bomb shelters. He also showed how the hill could be taken by the use of two fords on the Moselle, one above and the other below Pont-à-Mousson.

The Americans were suspicious and planned to bomb Pont-à-Mousson. Finally General McBride of the 80th Division called General Patton on the phone on September 7, 1944 and said:

"A man came here who called himself a French general and said his name was Houdemon, and said he was your friend."

"Quite right," said Patton, "General Houdemon is my dearest French friend; follow his orders as if they were my own."

During the night he countermanded the attack ordered by McBride, and prepared the attack across the Moselle by way of the fords.

We saw each other once more, at my home, a month before his death. Then America lost her greatest general, the greatest guarantee of her future security; France lost her best American friend, Pont-à-Mousson her liberator and savior, and I my best friend of good and bad days.

On the morning of 13 September Patton sent to General Wade H. Haislip a message to wait at Attigneville until his arrival, although Haislip told him the CP of the XV Corps was at that time moving to Boulaincourt. Haislip waited until midafternoon when Patton arrived in a towering rage. He had been lost and had finally reached the new CP at Boulaincourt where he took everyone he met to pieces. He was redirected to the place outside Boulaincourt where Haislip was waiting for him. He lit into Haislip in no uncertain fashion for "running away from him," and his temper wasn't improved when he was told that the responsibility for keeping in communication was on Army and not on Corps. Haislip had fairly lost his temper by this time and added that if the Army signal units were worth a damn they could keep up with the movements of Corps Headquarters. Both were mad so finally Haislip said, "All right. Take your choice. Do you want me to sit back and wait for your lousy units to get in their communications, or do you want me forward where the fighting is? You can't have both." Instantly Patton calmed down and said, "You've got something there. Of course I want you forward." He then gave a perfect example of his *delightful* inconsistency by ending up with "but, dammit, don't you run away from me any more, either."

Patton had been fighting over the same ground he fought over in 1918. He refers to World War I in this September 16th diary entry.

I then drove to XX Corps via Toul, Essey and Pannes. I could recognize all the places where I was 26 years and 4 days ago. From what I noted today I must have walked a long distance on that 12th of September. Everything looked natural except a wall behind which I observed the enemy from Pannes in 1918. As I remembered it, it was a low rubble wall. As I found it today, it is a high, thin, cement wall. They must have built a new one.

On the 17th of September Bradley notified Patton that General Montgomery wanted all Americans to stop so that the 21st Army Group, under Monty, could make a "dagger thrust" at the heart of Germany. Patton asked Bradley not to call until after dark on the 19th, to which he agreed. Patton believed he could thus be so involved that they could not stop him.

On the 22nd of September Patton visited the 3d Cavalry Group. This group was commanded by Colonel Jimmy

Polk, whose father had been a roommate of Patton's at West Point.

Colonel Polk was a very young officer to be a regimental commander. He was given command of the 3d Cavalry in August of 1944. The Regimental Commander, Colonel Drury, had been seriously wounded and captured. Patton's staff recommended to him that Lieutenant Colonel Polk be given command of the regiment. Patton sent for Polk and said to him, "Jimmy, if you weren't so young I would give you command of the 3d Cavalry; but I have never heard of an officer under thirty years of age commanding a regiment."

Quick as a flash, Polk said, "I have, sir."

Patton asked, "Who?"

Polk replied, "George S. Patton, Jr., in World War I."

General Patton said, "Jimmy, you get it."

Patton was actually about thirty-two in France, during World War I, but Polk got away with it.

To the north of Metz the enemy had been cleared from the west bank of the Moselle. The Third Army held substantial bridgeheads across the Moselle to the south of Metz. This was the situation when the Third Army assumed the defensive.

Thus the Third Army ended its dash across France. "Touring France with an Army" is the way in which Patton referred to this period in his book *War As I Knew It*. Patton's reputation was rewon. Again he had come to the top after a new start.

General Patton never expressed in writing his concept of how the war should be carried to and through the Germans to the point where they would seek an armistice. However, he often expressed his ideas to individuals of his staff. When, as he so aptly put it, the lights were out and he was faced with nothing but Willy (his pet bulldog) and stark responsibility, he divided the war as he saw it into three distinct phases. Upon this concept he based, insofar as possible, his strategical employment of the Third Army, and his recommendations to higher headquarters.

Phase I: Perhaps the break-through from Avranches to the Moselle or to the Seine River was, in his mind, the period when by a multitude of rapid thrusts all simultaneously and in many directions, he would break through the German lines with such speed and savagery that they would be unable to concentrate their forces at any one given point, or on a definite line. This was to be the period of confusion, when the morale of the enemy would be disrupted to such an extent that they would be harassed by their own fears and by the many conflicting reports. It was the period which by the impetus of his armored thrusts at so many places at one time (armored thrusts amply supported by infantry and artillery), he would absolutely disrupt the orderly and deeply indoctrinated German General Staff procedure. He often said to his staff how much he hated the stabilized warfare of World War I, which through inactivity, and through indecisiveness, cost so many lives in the long run. He stated time and time again, "We will save hundreds of thousands of lives by the suddenness and violence of our attack."

He saw Phase II as a phase in which after disruption of the orderly procedure of the German mind had been accomplished and the morale of the German soldier badly shaken, we would defeat large enemy forces, would cross over into German territory proper, destroy and disrupt their lines of communication and shake the morale of the German public. At the same time he envisioned the employment of psychological warfare designed to make the German public seek the protection of the American armies.

He saw Phase III near the end of the war when by further psychological warfare, and by kind treatment to the German public, and to prisoners of war, we would woo the German nation to our side and would forever cement them to us as allies.

Later, as the war neared its end and immediately thereafter, he often said, "How un-American it is, or will be, for us to hit an opponent when he is down." As he so aptly stated, "That is something our good old mothers in America taught us never to do."

The Patton Poem "Dead Pals" indicates that many would prefer to be buried on the soil where they fell. Patton is buried in Luxembourg with the Allied soldiers who fought with him there.

DEAD PALS

Dickey, we've trained and fit and died,
Yes, drilled and drunk and bled
And shared our chuck and our bunks in life.
Why part us now we're dead?

Would I rot so nice away from you,
Who has been my pal for a year?
Will Gabriel's trumpet waken me,
If you ain't there to hear?

Will a parcel of bones in a wooden box
Remind my Ma of me?
Or isn't it better for her to think
Of the kid I used to be?

It's true some preacher will get much class
A tellin' what guys we've been,
So, the fact that we're not sleeping with pals,
Won't cut no ice for him.

They'll yell "Hurrah!"
And every spring they'll decorate our tomb,
But we'll be absent at the spot
We sought, and found, our doom.

The flags and flowers won't bother us,
Our free souls will be far—
Holdin' the line in Sunny France
Where we died to win the war.

Fact is, we need no flowers and flags
For each peasant will tell his son,
"Them graves on the hill is the graves of Yanks
Who died to lick the Hun."

And instead of comin' every spring
To squeeze a languid tear,
A friendly people's loving care
Will guard us all the year.

The Patton poem, "Through a Glass, Darkly" deals with
the reincarnation of a fighting man through the ages.

THROUGH A GLASS, DARKLY

Through the travail of the ages,
Midst the pomp and toil of war
Have I fought and strove and perished
Countless times upon this star.

In the forms of many peoples
In all panoplies of time
Have I seen the luring vision
Of the Victory Maid, sublime.

I have battled for fresh mammoth,
I have warred for pastures new,
I have listed to the whispers
When the race trek instinct grew.

I have known the call to battle
In each changeless changing shape
From the high souled voice of conscience
To the beastly lust for rape.

I have sinned and I have suffered,
Played the hero and the knave;
Fought for belly, shame or country
And for each have found a grave.

I cannot name my battles
For the visions are not clear,
Yet I see the twisted faces
And I feel the rending spear.

Perhaps I stabbed our Savior
In His sacred helpless side.
Yet I've called His name in blessing
When in after times I died.

In the dimness of the shadows
Where we hairy heathens warred,
I can taste in thought the life blood;
We used teeth before the sword.

While in later clearer vision
I can sense the coppery sweat,
Feel the pikes grow wet and slippery
When our Phalanx Cyrus met.

Hear the rattle on the harness
Where the Persian darts bounced clear,
See their chariots wheel in panic
From the Hoplites' leveled spear.

See the goal grow monthly longer,
Reaching for the walls of Tyre.
Hear the crash of tons of Granite,
Smell the quenchless eastern fire.

Still more clearly as a Roman,
Can I see the Legion close,
As our third rank moved in forward
And the short sword found our foes.

Once again I feel the anguish
Of that blistering treeless plain
When the Parthian showered death bolts,
And our discipline was vain.

I remember all the suffering
Of those arrows in my neck.
Yet I stabbed a grinning savage
As I died upon my back.

Once again I smell the heat sparks
When my flemish plate gave way
And the lance ripped through my entrails
As on Crécy's field I lay.

In the windless blinding stillness
Of the glittering tropic sea
I can see the bubbles rising
Where we set the captives free.

Midst the spume of half a tempest
I have heard the bulwarks go
When the crashing, point-blank round shot
Sent destruction to our foe.

I have fought with gun and cutlass
On the red and slippery deck
With all Hell aflame within me
And a rope around my neck.

And still later as a general
Have I galloped with Murat
When we laughed at death and numbers
Trusting in the Emperor's star.

Till at last our star had faded,
And we shouted to our doom
Where the sunken-road of Ohein
Closed us in its quivering gloom.

So but now with Tanks aclatter
Have I waddled on the foe
Belching death at twenty paces,
By the starshell's ghastly glow.

So as through a glass and darkly
The age long strife I see
Where I fought in many guises,
Many names—but always me.

And I see not in my blindness
What the objects were I wrought,
But as God rules o'er our bickerings
It was through His will I fought.

So for ever in the future,
Shall I battle as of yore,
Dying to be born a fighter,
But to die again once more.

11. Assuming the Defensive

AS pointed out on many occasions within these covers, defensive warfare was not at all in keeping with Patton's ideas of winning a war. He literally abhorred the thought of being on the defensive. He felt it was against the American way of doing things and in the long run lives were wasted because the war, to be won, eventually had to shift to aggressive action. His method of assuming the defensive, when necessitated by lack of supplies along the Moselle, was continually to probe into the enemy lines allegedly to "rectify the line." Patton felt that by employing such tactics his troops would retain their offensive spirit. Although these tactics were unauthorized, they were always undertaken with small units so that higher headquarters did not interfere.

The forts around Metz put up a stubborn resistance. There were about twenty and they were among the most heavily fortified in the world. They were all underground in the hills surrounding the city. The fighting was bitter and costly.

Besides the Germans, the Third Army was fighting another enemy: The weather. Although climatic conditions were a constant threat in the Pacific theater they were strictly seasonal in Europe. October and November comprised the rainy season in France. Equipment rusted and the mud was unbelievable. Trench foot became a constant danger to the men exposed to these conditions. In fact, at one point the sick equaled the battle casualty rate. Patton was very strict in his orders that the men receive a daily pair of dry socks. If too many cases of trench foot occurred in any unit he was ruthless with the commanding officer. He always felt strongly that his men must be made as comfortable as humanly possible. He continued his daily visits to the front to raise morale and to check first-hand into the condition of his men.

The territory around the Moselle which the Third Army occupied during these trying days sparked many memories of World War I in its commanding officer. Many places he visited were indeed familiar.

Patton received a wire from General Marshall asking him to contact Madame Jouatte at Gondrecourt. She had been Marshall's landlady during World War I. Patton's diary entry of September 26, 1944 shows his vivid memory for detail.

Colonel Campanole, Codman and I drove to Gondre-court only to find that the Jouatte family no longer live there. We got this information through the Mayor, who was a great friend of the family and who gave us their address.

We then drove via Neufchâteau to Chaumont and had lunch at the Hôtel de France where 27 years ago Generals Pershing, Harbold, Colonel de Chambraun and I lunched the day we selected Chaumont for Headquarters American Expeditionary Force.

After lunch we went to General Pershing's house in town and to the barracks where our offices used to be. The barracks had been badly bashed in by our air force, about 15 days before we retook Chaumont. We then drove to Langres and stopped on the way at Val des Ecoliers, where General Pershing lived during the latter part of the war. It had apparently been vandalized by someone. Langres looked very natural, but we had no time to stop and drove on to Bourg. The first man I saw in the street here was standing on the same manure pile which he undoubtedly stood on in 1918. I asked him if he had been there in the last war and he replied, "Yes, General Patton, you were then here as a Colonel." Then we had an Old Home Week. He offered to show me around the town, which I really didn't need, but nevertheless I permitted him to do this. I visited my old office, my billet, and the Château of Madame de Vaux and took pictures. On the way back to Headquarters we drove past the airfield from which Codman's squadron operated in the last war and we took pictures of him with the airfield as a background. A day full of memories.

For on this day in 1918 General Patton was severely wounded while leading a tank attack at Cheppy-en-Varennes.

On one occasion, while inspecting a unit during this defensive phase, he noted two machine guns so placed that they were only effective at extreme ranges. Yet the ground for which they were responsible was within 400 yards range. The mistake, made by the officer who was responsible for the employment, was that he stood up when he picked the positions, thus his eyes were five feet above the guns. For an officer to commit such a basic error was beyond Patton's comprehension.

During this period Eisenhower and Bradley visited Third Army Headquarters. Eisenhower, on asking for suggestions, was told the following points which continue to emphasize some of Patton's characteristics. First, someone should arbitrate the conflicting demands for supplies between the Twelfth Army Group, Communications Zone and the Air Corps. Secondly, he felt that the Communications Zone was too inflexible in its methods. Combat units took notice of this and felt they were being improperly supported. Thirdly, that the names of all officers down to include regimental commander be publicly released. Other names had already been released.

One of the regimental commanders of the 5th Division

persuaded the Assistant Division Commander that he could take Fort Driant, one of the most heavily defended forts protecting Metz, without too much difficulty. The Assistant Division Commander, in turn, influenced the Division Commander into believing the same thing. This chain reaction went from the Division Commander to the Corps Commander, XX Corps. They paid a visit to General Patton's headquarters, which at the time was near Étain. There at a conference, General Patton's Chief of Staff and his G-3 advised that they, pursuant to instructions from General Patton, had made a long and careful study including personal reconnaissance of the Metz area, and that they advised that neither Fort Driant nor the town of Metz itself could be taken by a frontal assault; that their plan envisaged a double envelopment of Metz using five divisions, one making a holding frontal attack, one infantry and one armored division to make a wide envelopment from the north and one infantry and one armored division from the south, in each case the armored division to be on the flank.

This is one of the few times that General Patton ever overruled such a study by his staff and at the time gave General Walker orders to proceed with the frontal attack on Fort Driant. Patton later called off this attack. To another general, the decision to call off the attack on Fort Driant might not have been so difficult as it was to a man such as Patton. In his book *War As I Knew It,* he includes this decision as one of the thirty-four instances when he felt he had earned his pay. He felt that an attack should never be called off. But as he pointed out in his book, in this case too many lives were being lost. When Metz was finally taken later, it was with comparatively small losses.

During October Patton was constantly asking permission to resume the offensive. His staff was hard at work perfecting the plans for an attack so that the Army would be ready to roll the instant the restraints were lifted. At last Patton was told that he could attack any time after November 5th when the weather was favorable.

Patton's staff had always envisaged a highly mobile situation. The plans of the staff were flexible, and based on mobility because the Third Army was an army of movement. The full implication of this can be grasped when it is considered that the forward echelon of the Headquarters of the Third Army moved on an average of once every three days, until it settled down in the Nancy Area in

October 1944. Patton was occasionally criticized for not having individuals on his staff of greater academic professional standing. Patton always replied to such criticism by stating that he preferred that his staff be loyal and flexible rather than of high academic skill.

Since the cessation of hostilities in World War II, and more especially during the Korean debacle, much has been written about the inability of tactical commanders to get the riflemen to fire his weapon. General Patton recognized this early in the war. He talked to front-line troops on the lessons of combat, offensive spirit and marching fire whenever he got the opportunity. He once wrote, during these days on the defensive, "I am sure that if I could get the American infantryman to shoot his rifle, we could win the war much more cheaply."

About this time, Patton had an amusing idea for the improvement of the uniform. His thought was that the Quartermaster Corps should issue uniforms to the soldiers without buttons, thus saving money. "The soldiers would buy buttons and have them sewed on at their own effort and expense and because of their own trouble be sure to use them."

As the day for the attack approached, Patton kept busy talking to the troops, attending church, checking last-minute details and keeping in touch with higher headquarters.

He spoke to all divisions in the XX Corps except the 4th and 6th Armored Divisions. Later he heard that they felt hurt because he didn't talk to them. He had not included them because he honestly believed that there was nothing new about war that he could tell them. Two days later he spoke to these two divisions and told them why he had not included them in his itinerary. He also told the 4th Armored that in their case he could quote from the Bible, "The first shall be last and the 4th shall be first." The same day he also presented colors to a new engineer battalion. At this occasion he stated, "When a unit gets its colors it gets the symbol of its immortal soul."

The day for the attack was pushed back to the 8th of November—rain or shine. On the 7th Patton knew of nothing more he could do to prepare for the attack except read the Bible and pray. His diary reference to the weather and the Lord is typical.

On November 7, 1942, there was a storm but it stopped at 1600. All day the 9th of July 1943 there was a storm but it cleared at dark. I know the Lord will help us again. Either He will give us good weather or the bad weather will hurt the Germans more than it does us. His Will Be Done.

When two of Patton's subordinates requested that the attack be postponed until the weather cleared he merely requested that they recommend the men they would like appointed as their successors.

As the Third Army is about to jump off, it would be well to take stock of what the months of defensive fighting had brought. The XV Corps had been removed from his Third Army by order on September 29, but the III Corps was assigned to the Army on October 10. However, this corps did not become operational until December 6. The XX and XII Corps were thus all the Third Army actually had on the fighting line, with about 220,000 troops between them.

General Patton's probing attacks had succeeded in establishing a strong line from which to attack. About 125 square miles of territory had been captured. To the north of Metz the Third Army was strong enough to cross the Moselle at any point.

Patton woke up at three o'clock on the morning of the attack. He felt nervous and got up and read Rommel's book *Infantry Attack*. He stated that it was most helpful as Rommel described all the rains he had in September, 1914, and also the fact that, in spite of the heavy rains, the Germans got along. He went back to sleep at 0345 and slept until the artillery preparation woke him. The rain had stopped, the stars were out and he thanked God for His goodness to him. Bradley and Eisenhower called Patton at 0745. Bradley was pleased that Third Army jumped off despite insufficient air support. Ike said, "I expect a lot of you; carry the ball all the way."

Patton's attack on November 8 was part of a planned Allied offensive all along the line. Montgomery was to continue to attack through the Low Countries to the north. The First and Ninth American Armies were to attack five days before Patton to the north of the Ardennes, while Patton attacked to the south of that wooded sector that was later to make such disturbing headlines, for the battle of the Ardennes is familiarly known to the Americans as the Battle of the Bulge. The Seventh Army was to attack south of the Third. The weather stopped the jump-off of the First and Ninth Armies, so Patton, with his determination to advance regardless of the elements, led the way.

The rains continued and the Moselle and the Seille rivers were flooding badly. The Seille expanded from 200 to 500 feet in width. With bridges washed out, Patton had to carry his troops and supplies across these rivers on rafts and small assault boats; a slow, tedious process.

Tanks bogged down in the mud when they left the roads, until Patton set his ordnance to work on the manufacture of "duck bills." These were metal extensions attacked on the outside of each joint of the tank tracks which improved tank flotation, permitting them to traverse mud and thus avoid the elaborate defenses the Germans had erected on the roads. Another addition to Third Army's tanks was an added plate of armor on the front that deflected the shells when the tanks did have to take to the roads and advance straight into a road block.

The XX Corps made the attack in the vicinity of Metz in a movement that enveloped that city. The 95th and 5th Infantry Divisions moved straight toward the heart of the city, one from the north, one from the south, while the 90th Infantry Division bypassed the city to the north to cut off reinforcement from Germany. The 10th Armored Division followed closely to take advantage of any situation which would allow a break-through, and later advanced to the Siegfried Line.

The XII Corps headed for the Siegfried Line, across the Seille River to the south of Metz. This consisted of the 80th, 35th and 26th Infantry Divisions, with the 4th and 6th Armored following for a break-through.

In spite of the adverse conditions, the advance was steady. By November 19 Patton could say that Metz was in his control although the last of its forts did not officially surrender until December 19.

Metz was no longer a danger to the advance of the Third U.S. Army. The planning for the attack on Metz was an interesting and historical operation. G-2 studied the forts and the terrain around Metz in preparing data for an attack plan. Historical analyses were made in the field in black-out tents, bringing history up to date with changes made in the area by the French and Germans. When an estimate was finally prepared, General Patton was briefed, and the broad plan of the recommended tactical approach, worked out by cooperation between the various staff members, was accepted. Patton was to be its first conqueror in 1400 years.

Though the final planning for the taking of Metz was made in the fall of 1944 it is interesting to hear from Colonel Koch, his G-2, that Patton was planning to take that city as early as February, 1944. Patton had been studying a Michelin road map, from which he liked to operate. As he said, the road map gave you "railroads, road nets and rivers, all that you have to know about terrain in general." He put his finger on Metz and said, "I want all your planning directed here. I do not intend to cross the Loire unless it is necessary to avoid a right-angled turn." Colonel Koch said that this was the only general directive for planning, and that thereafter the staff was planning all the time, and were never caught short.

After November 19, 1944 the main effort was no longer directed at Metz.

The two corps pushed on to the Siegfried Line. Small units were fighting inside Germany by November 21. By early December several Third Army divisions had reached, and were crossing, the Saar River.

The XV Corps under General Haislip which had made a remarkable record in forcing a mountainous barrier over roads and trails covered with ice and snow, was transferred from the Third Army in the latter part of November to the Seventh Army. Haislip had not seen Patton since the transfer but a few days after the capture of Strasbourg by the XV Corps, he was called to the phone and a distant voice said, "This is George Patton. I just want to congratulate you on a brilliant victory. It is the finest thing that has happened yet." Haislip said on putting down the telephone, "There was generous George always ready to go out of his way to give others credit."

The many sidelights during this period give revealing glimpses of Patton's methods of command and his tactics. Ammunition was short but Patton was not the sort of man to hoard his share. He felt it should be used to kill Germans as quickly as possible. If his shells ran out, he would then dig in. Replacements were especially short, and he was forced to turn some of the troops in nonfighting sections into infantrymen. It is interesting to note that when he was sending forward some captains as replacements, he first put them in under lieutenants, until they had proven their capability to command in battle. This is not authorized by Army regulations. Patton always felt that of all the qualities necessary to an officer, battlefield courage was the most important. Without this the highest intellect was useless in war.

During this period he repeatedly showed what seemed to some of his subordinates a fatalistic disregard for his own safety; a disregard that unquestionably strengthened and stiffened his whole army.

In discussing an attack on the Siegfried Line, Patton was asked by one of his staff, "General, what do you think of the Siegfried Line?" Patton said, "It is a monument to stupidity. When natural obstacles—oceans and mountains —can be so readily overcome, anything that man makes, man can overcome."

Patton lost the XV Corps by orders from the High Command and disagreed with the theory that each army should consist of approximately 12 divisions. He felt that he should have retained the XV Corps, because his Third Army had a wide front and needed many troops. The First and Ninth Armies were on narrow fronts and needed fewer divisions.

He further believed that it was a mistake to leave the VIII Corps static, and remarked to his staff that it might result in the Germans building up strength east of that corps. It was against this corps that Von Rundstedt broke through 21 days later and the Battle of the Bulge was on.

Mr. Averill Harriman, who was the Ambassador to Russia at that time, visited Third Army headquarters. Patton's diary notes reveal his (Harriman's) feelings toward the Russians at that time.

Harriman told me that Stalin had praised the Third Army in the highest terms of which he is capable when he said to Harriman in the presence of the Chief of Staff of the Red Army, "That the Red Army could not have conceived and certainly could not have executed, the advance of the Third Army across France." Harriman says that Stalin is a strong, ruthless revolutionist and therefore a very potential threat to future world conditions. He says that discipline in the Red Army is the most rigid and ruthless he has ever seen, and that

216

the officer caste is a new nobility. This is a strange result of communism.

The advances of the Third Army had been successful enough to call for a new set of plans; a break-through to the Rhine. Plans were being made for a tremendous three-day air blitz, executed by one thousand bombers a day to open the attack. As Patton had said before, he had the greatest respect for the air arm. He felt that the Americans were above all a mechanically minded people. Just as he felt an individual should exaggerate his basic qualities to achieve greatness, so he felt a nation should do. In the future he hoped to see much more use made of air and armor.

Patton was naturally full of enthusiasm for the proposed plans. He felt, and rightly so, that he was best equipped for break-through operations. This time destiny had another role for him to play. The news of the German counterattack through the Ardennes postponed the Third Army's dash for the Rhine. Patton's sixth sense had warned him of the possibility of a German attack in this sector, and he had already considered it in his plans.

The Third Army was set to attack due east to the Rhine. The future command post was to be near St. Avold. Communications were for all intents and purposes already in, and the date for the attack set. The Third Army G-2 had completed the necessary estimates and studies of the Siegfried Line to be encountered. In addition, G-2 followed the over-all pattern of covering not only the Third Army's front but also the enemy situation some 150 miles to the north and south of its flanks (coinciding with the limits of the Third Army's tactical air reconnaissance, which provided not only visual reconnaissance from the air, but air photographs as well). Then, too, that distance represented a maximum day's march, by motor, of enemy troops that might appear in front of Third Army. Enemy action on large scale against either the First Army on the north, or the Seventh Army to the south, might well affect Third Army's operations.

Through the disappearance of enemy armor from Third Army and other fronts, and intelligence gained through normal channels over a considerable period of time, it became apparent that an armored force was being reconstituted in the Padern area to the north. In Third Army, certain enemy armored divisions were considered as "favorites" over a period of time. Their movements, appearance, or relief from combat with Third Army were used as a gauge in forecasting events to come.

On December 9 at one of the informal conferences, Koch briefed General Patton on the potentialities of an attack and the German capabilities to execute it. Deduced from the location of the massing of enemy tanks, it was estimated that such an attack, if launched, would be north of Third Army's zone of advance. It was estimated that Third Army, if the attack was large enough, might well be indirectly affected. It could at least be "spoiling" in nature, i.e., it could upset plans and affect Third Army offensive. Such capabilities were definitely established. The "when" of the execution of this capability was considered only in terms of "spoiling" Third Army's offensive before it was launched, or while under way. As a result of this briefing, and as a precautionary step, General Patton directed that plans be laid to meet such an attack, if and when it should take place.

On the morning of December 16, 1944 at the staff meeting held at 0700 in the Office of the Chief of Staff, the G-2, Koch, reported to the Commanding General that the German forces, which had been concentrating to the north in the vicinity of Trier for the past week or more, had gone on radio silence.

General Patton asked him what that meant.

He replied, "I do not know what it means when the Germans go on radio silence. When we place one of our units on radio silence, it means they are going to move; therefore, in this case I believe the Germans are going to launch an attack, probably at Luxembourg."

As the Saar campaign closes, let us see what the six weeks of offensive fighting had accomplished. The Third Army had advanced approximately 50 miles and closed on the Siegfried Line along most of their front. In one place, between Saarlautern and Saarbrucken, a 30-mile wedge had been driven through the Siegfried Line onto the soil of Germany.

In the north, the offensive of the First and Ninth Armies had been stalemated in their drive for the control of the Roer River dams. The Seventh Army, to the south of Patton, had succeeded in reaching the Rhine and then turned along its banks to join with Patton's southern flank.

Although always forthright during operations then in progress, Patton played down the enemy capabilities when discussing them with his major commanders: "No use scaring hell out of them."

Patton's recognition of fear as a great destroyer is disclosed in one of his poems.

FEAR

I am that dreadful, blighting thing,
Like ratholes to the flood.
Like rust that gnaws the faultless blade
Like microbes to the blood.

I know no mercy and no truth,
The young I blight, the old I slay.
Regret stalks darkly in my wake,
And Ignominy dogs my way.

Sometimes, in virtuous garb I rove,
With facile talk of easier way;
Seducing where I dare not rape
Young manhood, from its honor's sway.

Again, in awesome guise I rush,
Stupendous, through the ranks of war,
Turning to water, with my gaze,
Hearts that, before, no foe could awe.

The maiden who has strayed from right,
To me must pay the mead of shame.
The patriot who betrays his trust,
To me must own his tarnished name.

I spare no class, nor cult, nor creed,
My course is endless through the year.
I bow all heads and break all hearts,
All owe me homage—I am FEAR.

12.   The Battle of the Bulge

THE task given to Patton when the Germans launched their attack in the Battle of the Bulge was a monumental one. He had to move most of his army, poised for a planned attack of their own, 125 miles to the north, and without stopping to rest, hurl them against the enemy's southern flank. At the same time he had to be sure that he did not so materially weaken his former lines as to lose the ground gained in the past six weeks. The XX Corps was left in the Saarlautern wedge with three divisions and a cavalry group. They not only held, but improved, their position, although the Germans intensified their attacks in that area also. This is certainly proof that General Patton could direct defensive warfare, even if he did not believe in it. It also strengthens the old adage that a good offense is the best defense.

The speed with which Patton moved his two Corps, the III and the XII, north to help stem the German offensive in the Bulge is testimony to his leadership. Only men who were devoted to their commander could have performed such a feat. The weather was at its worst during the move, with snow and ice clogging the roads. It is characteristic of Patton that he gave full credit to his staff officers and men for his success. This is undoubtedly one reason why they were so willing to do the almost impossible for him. It was always his policy that a general should attribute success to his men, while any failure should always be assumed by himself.

The plans for this movement north to help the First Army were made after 48 hours of continuous study so that when General Patton was called to a conference at Verdun on December 19, he was in a position to tell General Eisenhower that the Third Army could attack on December 22. General Eisenhower, realizing that this meant pulling out an army in battle, turning it on a 90 degree angle, and launching it into a new battle, allegedly said, "Don't be fatuous." General Patton never told him that he had complete plans for such a movement in his pocket. The Patton Third Army team had again shown its flexibility. He had been quick to capitalize on the brilliant staff work of his G-2, one of the most astute intelligence officers the war produced. It is probably an understatement to say that the Battle of the Bulge was materially influenced by Patton's instant readiness to move to the assistance of the First Army, and the incredible speed of that movement.

Before the meeting with Eisenhower on the 19th, Patton had arranged with his staff exactly what would be done. Thus, he could tell Eisenhower, when asked how long it would take him to engage the German flank, that he was already on the way.

Three roads to the north were designated one-way roads and by midnight Patton's troops were roaring northward. Patton, in utter disregard of standard black-out regulations, told his troops to drive with all headlights blazing and with throttles open wide, for time was of the essence and without headlights the pace of night driving is slowed. Thus was staged one of the most phenomenal troop movements of the war. By December 22 the Third Army was fighting the enemy in the Bulge.

The Germans had gathered a large force of 23 divisions for their offensive. They rapidly opened a hole 80 miles wide and 50 miles deep through the thinly held VIII Corps line. They isolated the city of Bastogne, which was still held by the 101st Airborne Division and elements of other divisions. The VIII Corps was turned over to Patton for the battle. Its headquarters was moved to Neufchâteau. Under Patton's instructions, it attacked the German salient at its nose, toward St. Hubert. The XII Corps, which had been located on the extreme south during Patton's offensive, was instructed to attack on the east toward Echternach and Diekirch and Wiltz. The III Corps moved from Metz to attack in the middle, with the primary objective of liberating Bastogne.

The first news of the German attack, which earned the title the Battle of the Bulge, was naturally a great disappointment to General Patton. At first he wanted to continue with his own offensive. This was before he learned of the strength of the German offensive. Even after he learned of their strength, he thought that the most effective way to stop their drive forward was to attack them. This is an example of his belief that an enemy who is being attacked in sufficient strength will not have time to attack you. He always believed in the offensive. This cannot be emphasized too many times in any picture of Patton, the man or the general.

On December 20, Lieutenant Colonel Albin F. Irzyk, commanding the 8th Tank Battalion, was ordered by Brigadier General Holmes E. Dager, Combat Commander B, 4th Armored Division, to send a task force to Bastogne.

On the road to Bastogne, the task force came upon two battalions of friendly artillery in position along the road, but the guns were not manned. These two battalions had received counterattacks early that same morning, and had been decimated, leaving their equipment intact. The task force commander, Captain Ezell, made contact with the 101st Airborne Infantry Division in Bastogne and was given the situation, and the plan in which he was to be used. The task force saw no enemy on this expedition into Bastogne. Before the plan was executed, however, Task Force Ezell was relieved of its mission at 1200 by the higher command, and ordered to leave Bastogne and return to a designated assembly area. On the return no enemy troops were encountered.

Evidently Bastogne was not, as yet, completely surrounded on December 20, thus accounting for the fact that Task Force Ezell had no enemy action. It went through a gap in the enemy positions, and egressed through the same opening; one of the most remarkable incidents of the war considering the bitterness of the battle which immediately developed. From this time on, Bastogne was besieged from all sides and in desperate straits. It was not until December 26 that the Americans were able to slug a corridor through the enemy to effect relief of our surrounded troops.

Patton's staff officers were under great stress at this time. This, if ever, was the time for Napoleonic utterances. At the staff meeting when the Third Army was becoming engaged in the Bulge, Patton rose from his seat in front of the situation map after the briefing of the operations officer, glared into the anxious faces of his subordinates and said, "This will get the bastards out of their holes so we can kill all of 'em—now go to work." This broke the terrific tension at that moment.

There was a five-day break in the weather, beginning on December 23, which allowed air supply to Bastogne and assistance to the group troops who were engaged in attacking the Germans. The day before, Patton's prayer for clear weather, written on December 11 to be issued just before the offensive on the Siegfried Line, had been distributed on cards to Third Army troops. Patton was sure the Lord would understand the change in direction of the attack, and when clear weather came he was sure he had a Chaplain with powerful influence in Heaven.

PRAYER

Almighty and most merciful Father, we humbly beseech Thee, of Thy great goodness, to restrain these immoderate rains with which we have had to contend. Grant us fair weather for Battle. Graciously hearken to us as soldiers who call upon Thee that armed with Thy power, we may advance from victory to victory, and crush the oppression and wickedness of our enemies, and establish Thy justice among men and nations. Amen.

On the reverse side of the card were Christmas greetings to each member of the Third Army team.

HEADQUARTERS
THIRD UNITED STATES ARMY

To each officer in the Third United States Army, I wish a Merry Christmas. I have full confidence in your courage, devotion to duty, and skill in battle. We march in our might to complete victory. May God's blessing rest upon each of you on this Christmas Day.

s/G. S. PATTON, JR.
Lieutenant General
Commanding, Third United States Army

The fighting was bitter and advances were slow. To Patton, always looking for the sudden break-through, this was discouraging. Eisenhower, in his book *Crusade in Europe,* relates that Patton called him several times to express his regret that the advance was not more rapid. Eisenhower, however, was satisfied with the fact that he was advancing at all, for he knew how difficult the conditions were.

Brigadier General Anthony McAuliffe was in dire straits in Bastogne and the Germans had asked him to surrender. It was here that General McAuliffe in reply to the demand for surrender made the historic reply, "Nuts," which will always be remembered with pride by all Americans.

On Christmas Day Bradley and Patton were talking after dinner at Bradley's mess. Patton continually believed in attacking whereas Montgomery desired to regroup and fall back. Patton's diary entry points up his disgust at such thoughts.

After supper Brad and I had a talk. Monty says that the 1st Army cannot attack for three months and that the only attack that can be made is by me, but that I am too weak; hence we should fall back to the Saar-Vosges Line or even to the Moselle to gain more divisions. I feel that this is disgusting and might remove the valor of our army and the confidence of our people. It will have tremendous political implications and probably condemn to death, or slavery, all the inhabitants of Alsace and Lorraine, if we abandon them to the Germans. If ordered to fall back, I think I will ask to be relieved.

About Christmas day in 1944 in the Battle of the Bulge, Maj. Gen. Willard S. (Stew) Paul, who then commanded the 26th Division, was at his command post directing the attack. The 26th was faced by elements of nine German divisions who were desperately trying to keep that division from cutting the main German supply road into Bastogne. Paul was under great pressure to get his division going forward and progress was very slow. At the command post appeared Patton, apparently in a vile humor. Paul was sure he was going to be relieved. Patton sensed the situation and walking up to Paul, who was a man of small physique, threw his arm around his shoulder and said, "How's my little fighting sonofabitch." Paul said later that Patton could never have asked anything of him after that that he would not have done cheerfully, even to trying the known impossible.

Christmas passed with no letup in the fighting. The day after Christmas brought good news. Elements of the 4th Armored Division met elements of the 101st Airborne Division in the woods outside Bastogne. It was here where the experience of the battle-hardened troops of the 4th Armored Division paid dividends. Lieutenant Colonel Creighton Abrams, commander of the 27th Tank Battalion, made the decision to move in and around Assenois, a scant two kilometers from the front lines of the beleagured garrison in Bastogne. Despite the fact that there was barely an hour of daylight left, tank ammunition was low, and the 37th Tank Battalion was badly under strength, the sight of the disorganized enemy troops as seen from a hill caused Colonel Abrams to attack. Many tank battles had instilled in him the sixth sense of battle, for battle judgment is a complex of many factors, and he moreover took counsel of his own aggressive spirit. He also noted that our C-47s were absorbing a great deal of enemy flac as they were flying supplies to the 101st Airborne. He stated, "If they can take that flac we can try and get in there now." Several C-47s were shot down. When Captain William A. Dwight, S-3 of the 37th, had fought through to the surrounded troops under Brigadier General Anthony McAuliffe, both dismounted from their vehicles, shook hands, and the link-up was established. Within the next few hours the narrow path was widened, mines cleared, and before midnight the ambulances and trucks of supplies were rolling into Bastogne. A hundred trucks were pushed in to bring out the wounded —the first coming through the gap without tank escort. They traveled under the briefest of orders: "Get the hell in —and get the hell out."

The liberating of Bastogne forced the Germans to concentrate their strength in that area, for it was imperative to their success that they secure that city. On the XII Corps front, the situation remained relatively static. Patton's troops were closing on the Sauer River between Echternach and Diekirch. The VIII Corps was stopping further German advances in the west.

Patton again realized to attack would save lives and it is so noted by his diary entries on December 26.

Why in hell the SHAEF thinkers hold the 11th Armored Division, 17th Airborne and 87th Infantry Divisions at Reims is beyond me. They should be attacking.

The German has shot his wad. Prisoners have had no food for from three to five days. We should attack. Last night during an air raid, 100 German prisoners rushed the guards and were killed. So far we have taken about 5,000 prisoners and killed more.

Patton felt that if he could get three more divisions he could win the war.

General Patton sent a letter to his wife on December 29

summing up the events in the Battle of the Bulge to that date.

HEADQUARTERS
THIRD UNITED STATES ARMY

Office of the Commanding General

APO 403

29 December, 1944

DEAR BEATRICE:

I am dictating this to give you a little insight into what is actually going on, because I do not have time to write very often, but at the moment am waiting for a counterattack and am not at all near where it will take place.

On the 19th it was decided to send me up here to stop the Germans. At that time all the divisions—five of them —which started my original attack were in action between Saarlautern and Sarreguemines. I started telephoning to Hap Gay, being myself in Thionville, and that night Hugh[1] moved out. The next morning the 80th followed. The 26th was already out—which is not in consonance with my original statement—and was at Metz refilling. I alerted them to move.

The next day the staff of the Third Army, which consisting of myself and Sergeant Mims, visited two corps and five division commanders; reshuffled two divisions; and telephoned for the engineers, tank destroyers, extra tank battalions, etc.

As a result of this, we made a coordinated attack, jumping off at 6:30 on the morning of the 22nd. We could have jumped off on the morning of the 21st, but the attack would have been a little ragged.

The most outstanding achievement was that of the 35th Division—if you put in such a solution at Leavenworth, you would go to the doghouse or St. Elizabeth's. On the morning of the 24th, the 35th was attacking at Sarreguemines. It stopped the attack, entrucked and arrived at Metz on midnight of the same day. On Christmas day it filled up with 3,000 replacements. On the morning

---
[1] Major General Hugh Gaffey.

226

of the 26th, it entrucked again, drove to Arlon, and had one regiment fighting by dark. The remainder of the division attacked in the morning; and the attack has been very successful.

The break-through into Bastogne was effected by the Reserve Combat Command of Hugh's outfit under Colonel Blanchard, who, you remember, was in the Second at Benning.

We had been smashing at the place for three days. About 2:30 on the 26th, Hugh called up and said that if I would authorize the gamble, he could break through the enemy with a sort of tank charge and get in with this one outfit. I told him to go ahead. As a result of this, we made contact with the 101st Airborne Division and other members of the garrison, and have since evacuated the wounded. Also, a large number of prisoners were taken, and we have moved in a number of other divisions, which secrecy prevents my mentioning.

We are now hoping that the Boche will attack us this afternoon with three divisions—his divisions are much depleted—because we intend to attack him in the morning, and it would be very nice to go in after him when he starts to retreat.

This is a sort of thumbnail sketch of what is going on, and I am enclosing several extra copies which you might send to Nita, General Harbold, and General Summerall, and General Henry.

With warm personal regards, I am

Devotedly yours,

GSP, Jr.

Mrs. G. S. Patton, Jr.
Green Meadows
South Hamilton, Massachusetts
U.S.A.

The attack planned for December 30 toward St. Vith was continued over the protests of Patton's subordinates, as had occurred in the past. Whatever the reason for his success on these occasions, it was events such as these which have placed Patton's name on the list of our country's great generals.

German counterattacks were numerous during this period, as they desperately tried to regain control of the situation. Often the battle would seesaw back and forth over a small area for hours. However, the Third Army troops repulsed the attacks and scored advances, even if these could occasionally only be measured in yards.

A shortage of replacements harassed General Patton during this period, and continued through January. He put as many of his Army and Corps troops in the battle lines as possible, and rarely had any reserves. He was operating under the same principle he had during the Saar offensive. In that case he was dealing with a shortage of ammunition. He believed in attacking with all he had, for he felt that only by doing so could he win. This was a calculated risk he felt forced to take, and was successful in both cases.

It is interesting to note in a diary entry of January 4 Patton's statement, "We can still lose this war." This is the only time during the entire war in Europe that he made such a statement. The next sentence in the diary is, "However, the Germans are colder and hungrier than we are." At all other times he was confident of eventual victory. He typically often set his sights on an impossible objective. For example, he had planned to reach Houffalize on the 30th. Actually this town was not taken until mid-January. By aiming for a distant objective, however, he probably managed to make the amazing progress that he did.

By January 8 there were some encouraging reports that the Germans were withdrawing tanks. This was a characteristic tactic of the Germans when they were planning to abandon an area. Heavy attacks were continued by the German infantry, however. Planning was under way for an attack all along the Third Army's line on the 9th. This involved some very clever tactics in pushing the 90th Division through the 26th in an attack on Wiltz. The artillery fire supporting the attack was used in a very ingenious way, which was entirely Patton's idea. For example, as the 90th Division artillery guns moved into position, they immediately would register in their pieces. Then the 26th Division, who were being relieved, would cease firing. In addition a deception group would maintain the radio net in the old area by sending canned messages.

Patton's plan, as prepared in detail by his staff, was to make an attack straight north following the ridge line from Diekirch to Bitburg. The attack was to be made by the XII Corps consisting of four divisions and to be made in a column of divisions; in other words, a power play. The corps was to be reinforced by other divisions as soon as necessary.

This ridge line later became famous and known by many different names: Purple Heart Trail, Honeymoon Trail, etc.

Patton was not given permission to use this plan. On December 23 or 24, he had previously broached this subject to the Army Group Commander, recommending that the American VIII Corps, General Middleton, fall back toward Meuse, thus allowing the German Army to further extend itself so they could be hit on the flank.

If the attack had been made on Bitburg as planned, and if it had succeeded, it would have placed a very powerful American corps behind the greater part of Von Rundstedt's troops, cutting them off from their supplies and from possible retreat across the Rhine.

Patton pushed his immediate subordinates relentlessly in order to maintain the initiative in the continuation of the attack. How he handled two corps commanders is revealed in his diary.

January 6, 1945

I had to use the whip on both Middleton and Millikin today. They are too cautious. I know that their men are tired, but so are the Germans.

We have to push people beyond their endurance in order to bring this war to its end, because we are forced to fight it with inadequate means. Only three small counterattacks today—all repulsed. I fear this indicates the enemy is getting away.

Patton attended a luncheon at General Bradley's headquarters for Paul McNutt and the Manpower Board. Patton made the statement that the manpower situation had been badly handled by the Board and that it, including Mr. McNutt, was to blame for the critical shortage of replacements. A Professor Lowell from Harvard remarked to Patton that apparently he (Patton) did not give a damn what people thought of him. Patton's reply was that it depended upon who the people were, but that in any case he did not give very much of a damn.

The general attack of all the corps went off on the 9th as planned, again over the protests of some of Patton's junior officers.

There were many rumors, during this period, of planned enemy counterattacks. An especially strong build-up of German forces was reported opposite the XX Corps in the

Saar area. Patton was very irritated by orders from SHEAF that he place certain divisions to repel the rumored attacks. He always felt strongly that command should not extend too far down the line. Never should divisions be directed by anyone higher than their own Army commander, who was on the scene and had the clearest picture of the situation. He continually was analyzing the possibility of enemy offensive action. As always, his solution was to attack himself, in the area of expected counterattack, before the enemy had time to move.

The Germans were now beginning to pull out more rapidly, and by the 11th Patton felt that the operation was over, except for driving a defeated enemy back behind the Siegfried Line. On the 16th the Third Army contacted the First Army, which was moving down from the north, near Houffalize, and the German salient had been chopped off.

This historic sealing off of the Bastogne Bulge was effected by the two units dearest to Patton's heart, for his own 2d Armored Division from the First Army junctioned at this point with Patton's Third Army. This division, here again commanded by Maj. Gen. Ernest Harmon, after having achieved its signal victory in the Celles pocket, drove through the northern shoulder of the Bastogne Bulge.

By the 11th of January Patton believed that the Bastogne operation was ended. He felt that from then on it was simply a question of driving a defeated enemy. He also felt that it was the biggest and best operation the Third Army had accomplished, including the Battle of France. His one strong desire was that the troops get credit for their great work.

He also believed that the attack should continue regardless of location. If we failed to attack he felt the Germans would capitalize and stage their own attack. He believed that the troops now realized that they were on the winning side and so notes it in his diary.

January 13, 1945

There is a distinct difference in the mental attitude of the officers and men today, and that prior to today. Today they all feel that they are on the winning side, pursuing a beaten enemy; while yesterday or the day before, they were dubious as to whether we could stop the German attack. It is an interesting psychological situation. Now that all feel the enemy is licked, they are sure of

230

themselves. Until today I was the only one sure of victory. The fighting today has been bitter, but it is just what one would expect as it is to the north and northeast of Bastogne where the enemy must hold in order to extricate what he has left east of the town. We will get them.

The last days of January were occupied in driving the remaining Germans east of the Siegfried Line. The troops were given a chance to rest after their hard days of fighting and morale was high. From the Russians came the cheering news that their offensive had opened on January 18.

Plans were being formulated for a future offensive, which Patton naturally was eager to get under way. While the troops of the Third Army were busy chasing the Germans from the Bulge, Patton was conscious of getting them into the most favorable positions for the future drive into Germany. Bradley, Hodges, and Patton were in agreement on their plans for the attack, but the Twelfth Army Group again was involved in a tug of war with the British as to who should attack and receive priority on supplies and men. Patton was set to continue forward without a halt. The British did not plan to attack until February 8. It was natural that Patton should abhor any delay.

Getting the divisions into position for the offensive involved much fast movement. At this time the roads were like sheets of glass. Again the Third Army showed its ability to maneuver rapidly in spite of adverse conditions.

As Patton hated Nazis, so they hated him. They took the trouble to drop leaflets on a Third Army prison camp for captured Germans at the medieval walled city of Toul, behind the Third Army front, in which they urged the prisoners to escape, and warned them they were in the hands of America's leading gangster and Public Enemy Number One. This was General Patton, who was unjustly accused in these leaflets, among other things, of mistreating his prisoners.

The Battle of the Bulge was over at last. It had been the bloodiest campaign in the Third Army's career. The toll taken of the enemy was much higher, however. Every bit of ground that the Germans had taken had been recovered, and in the XX Corps zone in the Saar some advances had been made. Patton's defensive action in this location had again involved offensive action which had been successful.

Patton had demonstrated his capacity for leadership

231

throughout the campaign. His men performed many unbelievable feats of heroism that helped to turn the tide against the enemy and Patton was more than willing to emphasize this repeatedly with praise and decorations.

The move from the Saar up to the Bulge was phenomenally fast. In spite of the shortage of replacements, the Third Army had beaten the enemy by cutting the staffs of the army and corps to the bone and using everyone possible in the fighting. Patton's attitude toward reserves was very characteristic of him. To him, reserves were to be used. In this respect he differed greatly from a man such as Montgomery. Montgomery's method of fighting was to let the enemy wear himself out with attacks, and then to decimate him with a fresh offensive by his reserve units. The initial withdrawal that this method entailed was impossible for a man of Patton's temperament.

It is interesting to note that the Germans had assembled more troops for this break-through attempt than Patton had used for his operation at Avranches.

After pulling unprecedented maneuvers against the enemy, such as having two corps use one road (Avranches) or crossing troops in movement (Battle of the Bulge), General Patton would say, "I'd hate to go to Leavenworth after the war. One would certainly get a 'U' for our successful operations. The Leavenworth instructors will be in a tough spot, their tactical principles will be subject to too many exceptions, historically."

The instructors cannot call on the master to explain.

Valor, about which Patton wrote the following poem, was to him one of the greatest human virtues.

VALOR

When all hearts are opened,
And all the secrets known,
When guile and lies are banished,
And subterfuge is gone.

When God rolls up the curtain,
And hidden truths appear,
When the ghastly light of Judgement day,
Brings past and present near . . .

Then shall we know what once we knew,
Before wealth dimmed our sight,
That of all sins, the blackest is
The pride which will not fight.

The meek and pious have a place,
And necessary are,
But valor pales their puny rays,
As does the sun a star.

What race of men since time began,
Has ever yet remained,
Who trusted not its own right hand,
Or from brave deeds refrained?

Yet, spite the fact for ages known,
And by all lands displayed,
We still have those who prate of peace,
And say that war is dead.

Yes vandals rise who seek to snatch
The laurels from the brave,
And dare defame heroic dead,
Now filling hero graves.

They speak of those who love,
Like Christ's, exceeds the lust of life,
And murderers slain to no avail,
A useless sacrifice.

With infamy without a name,
They mock our fighting youth,
And dare decry great hearts who die,
Battling for right and truth.

Woe to the land which, heeding them,
Lets avarice gain the day,
And trusting gold its right to hold,
Lets manly might decay.

Let us, while willing yet for peace,
Still keep our valor high,
So when our time of battle comes,
We shall not fear to die.

Make love of live and ease be less,
Make love of country more.
So shall our patriotism be
More than an empty roar.

For death is nothing, comfort less,
Valor is all in all;
Base nations who depart from it,
Shall sure and justly fall.

13.   The Capture of Coblenz and the Palatinate Campaign

AS the Third Army renewed its offensive, the plans for attack were settled upon when orders from higher command on February 1 changed them. SHEAF's strategy called for the First and Third Armies to hold defensively while the British and Canadians assumed the offensive in the north. Patton was furious. In Patton's opinion every division should be attacking. He felt that the Germans did not have the resources to stop such an attack. He stated, "Personally, I think that this is a foolish and ignoble way for the Americans to end the war." Many of the commanders were quite gloomy and agreed with Patton that the American armies should continue the attack instead of going on the defensive while Montgomery prepared to move. Patton planned to continue his attack with the XII Corps. As he feared he might be ordered to stop, he did not inform his superiors of his plan.

He spent some uncomfortable moments with Eisenhower and Bradley at a meeting at Bastogne. He carefully avoided mentioning the impending attack by one of his corps. Patton stated he felt as Nelson must have felt when, the night before the attack on Calvi, in Corsica, he discovered the enemy were twice as strong as believed and carefully refrained from telling his superior. Patton avoided talking about this attack for the same reason. He hoped that, with the Germans moving to meet the British attack, he might still reach the Rhine first.

Patton's parady of "O Little Town of Bethlehem" in his

diary shows his peculiar sense of humor. The town of Houffalize was practically blown off the map. Patton said that he had never seen anything like it in this war.

O little town of Houffalize, how still we see thee lie; above thy steep and battered streets the aeroplanes sail by. Yet in thy dark streets shineth not any Goddamned light; the hopes and fears of all thy years were blown to hell last night.

Patton received a letter from Abbé Charles Balland, curé of Bouxières-sous-Froidmont, dated February 2, 1945, which shows the type of army which had been developed by Patton.

MON GENERAL:

I esteem it a duty to make known to you and to bring to your attention the fine conduct of the officers, non-commissioned officers, and enlisted men of your Army during the repatriation of the inhabitants of the village of Bouxières-sous-Froidmont last December. Their names are set forth in the attached list.

All of them acted with an energy and obligingness, a tact and a devotion which profoundly touched us and which are worthy of the highest praise.

After the return of the inhabitants, the officers, non-commissioned officers, and men desired to take part with them at the first Mass in the Church of Bouxières. This touching gesture, the crowning touch of their fine conduct, will always remain for me a beautiful testimonial to American friendship.

If I dared, I would ask you, mon Général, to express to these officers, noncommissioned officers and men, our profound gratitude and the assurance that we will always keep them in our memory.

Deign to receive, mon Général, my most ardent wishes for the success of your Army, and accept the homage of my profoundly respectful sentiments with which I have the honor to remain,

Your servant,
ABBE CHARLES BALLAND
Curé de Bouxières-sous-Froidmont

Patton's opinion of soldiers who inflicted wounds upon

themselves in order to avoid further combat duty was not any different than most commanders'. However, he was a bit more vehement than others in his condemnation of men who would take such methods to shirk their duties. His diary comments emphasize those points.

I visited the hospitals and found an extremely small number of wounded, but came on three self-inflicted wound cases . . . two shot through the left foot and one through the left hand. I told the Chief of Staff to get out an order that all who receive self-inflicted wounds will be tried on two counts before leaving the Army area; first, for self-inflicted wounds; second, for negligence. On the latter count they can get six months. They should get life, the yellow dogs. It is very difficult to prove self-inflicted wound cases, but the negligence charge can give them six months so that they will not get off for nothing. In my opinion there is nothing lower than a man who, in order to save his own self, maims himself and leaves to his more heroic comrades an extra duty to perform. Went to church.

Beatrice Patton believed that her husband had control over his subconscious mind, and that he could set it going to complete his conscious thoughts. Many people are in accord with this belief that the subconscious can be trained. She felt certain that he had this faculty. His diary entry for February 6, 1945 bears out this thought.

I woke up at 3:00 o'clock this morning, and it suddenly occurred to me that if we get a break-through in either the VIII or XII Corps, or in both, we have a situation which will permit launching two or possibly three armored divisions, and we have the opportunity of re-enacting the Brest Peninsula show. Whether ideas like this are the result of inspiration or insomnia, I don't know, but nearly every tactical idea I have had popped into my head like Minerva and not as historians attempt to describe generals who work things out on paper in a laborious manner. If we do launch three divisions, we will have practically nothing to hold the line defensively; however, it is my considered opinion that if we launch three divisions, there will be no line left to hold. In any case, I will take a chance. The Lord will provide.

Anything that held up the advance of the Third Army irritated Patton. He invariably showed his displeasure. He would become moody, hot-tempered, and react sometimes like a spoiled child. If it was climatic conditions deterring him, he would improvise any method whatsoever to combat the elements. If it was higher headquarters he would argue with the commanders; "Personally, I fight every order that I do not like, which makes me unpopular but successful." He truly felt that he was a man of destiny; his calling to be a great military leader was as great as any young man's calling to the ministry. His diary entry of February 10, 1945 bears out some of these thoughts.

> Yesterday I called Bradley to protest an order taking three more engineer battalions from me. He said he would do what he could, but it was necessary for us to obey orders and pull all our forces to the north.
> He also asked me how soon I can go on the defensive. I said I was the oldest leader both in age and in combat experience in the Army and that if I had to go on the defensive, I would ask to be relieved. He said I owed it to the troops to stay. I said that there was a lot owing to me too. I was very mad.
> Spent a most useless morning seeing people.

On February 13 it was reported that General Patton swam the Sauer River at the head of his troops. This was not true. He had actually crossed the river on a partly submerged assault bridge, on foot. Thus, a soldier, excited by the battle, could conceivably have believed him to be swimming. Crossing that assault bridge was in itself a dangerous operation, for the smoke restricted visibility to less than a foot, and there were no guardrails on the bridge. Patton reported that he was glad to be across.

Often the General went up to the front among his men, and although he did not do anything as dramatic or foolhardy as swimming the Sauer, was often under fire. Beatrice Patton said that his swimming of the Sauer River was first told by some men who came home to address workers engaged in war production. When Patton heard the story, he wired General Marshall asking if he should deny it, and was told to say nothing. In a letter to his wife, he explains the misconception as follows:

I crossed over on a partially submerged assault bridge without life lines, and as I had to jump several bodies without being able to see where my feet were going to land, it was quite a feat. To a scared soldier seeing me through a heavy smoke screen, I might have looked as though I was swimming.

Beatrice Patton described the telephone call she received from a reporter about the "swim."

About 11:15 a reporter called her on the phone and asked, "Mrs. Patton, what do you know about this story of General Patton swimming the Sauer River under fire?"

"I haven't heard it."

"What is your reaction?"

"I haven't heard it. What is it?"

The reporter then told the story, and Mrs. Patton said: "Has this story been confirmed by the War Department?" To which the reporter replied, "No—we don't bother with that—we just want to get *your* reaction."

Mrs. Patton replied, "My reaction is call the War Department and see what the story is."

"But we want *your* reaction."

Mrs. Patton remained silent.

"By the way, Mrs. Patton, can the General swim?"

Mrs. Patton then hung up. At about 1:30 A.M. the phone rang again and the same voice said, "Mrs. Patton, I'm on my way to your house. Please meet me at the door in three quarters of an hour with a picture of the General in a swim suit."

Mrs. Patton said, "Has it ever occurred to you that if General Patton did swim the river he didn't do it in a swim suit?"

"My God," said the reporter, "I never thought of that."

On February 16 Major General Harmon, who was taking command of the XXII Corps and leaving the 2d Armored Division, which he had commanded, sent a letter to General Patton quoted in part as follows:

MY DEAR GENERAL:

I am enclosing my farewell message to the officers and men of the Second Armored which will be of interest to you, as I know your long-standing affection and regard for the old "Hell on Wheels."

The Second Armored to me is a living example of the

truth of the statement that if an organization gets off to a good start, it has a good chance of always remaining a great unit. The Second Armored got a great start from you and General C. L. Scott who gave it the initial foundation of sound tactical doctrine and a great esprit de corps and willingness to take the offensive. I have tried my best to continue this tradition and I feel that the Division has already done a great service to the Country, and will undoubtedly continue to do so.

Sincerely yours,
E. N. HARMON
Major General, U.S. Army
Commanding

Returning from a short leave, his first in approximately thirty months, Patton was informed that the XX Corps was in position to exploit a break-through if they could obtain an armored division. Patton immediately wangled the 10th Armored for this operation. As they began to advance Patton decided that he could and would take Trier and thus clean out the Saar-Moselle triangle. This is a perfect example of the way in which Patton believed in exploiting a situation. Before he could this, however, he had to receive an okay from above. After much discussion he received permission to continue his attack on Trier, and Bradley stated that he would keep away from the telephone so as not to receive contrary orders.

As the 10th Armored advanced on Trier from the south, Patton sent part of the XII Corps toward it from the north, thus closing the city in a vise. The city was entered on March 1st. Patton's tactical ability had caught the Germans off base. But Patton had to plead with higher headquarters to continue his attack on Trier. He stated that he believed it was the first time in the history of war that a commander had to fight and plead with his superiors to continue the attack. He also gave advice to future commanders when he said, "It may be of interest to future generals to realize that one makes plans to fit circumstances and does not try to create circumstances to fit plans. That way danger lies."

On February 27, 1945 Patton wrote a letter to his wife in which he said:

. . . I am constantly amazed at the human animal.

Hardly have we cleared a village till the people come back and start doing the things they have done for generations. To them the war is over. I guess that is a race instinct. They have been destroyed so many times.

About this time, Patton received a message from headquarters asking him to be less jocular in his reports since they would become part of recorded history, and ending with orders to bypass Trier as it would take four divisions to capture the city. But when the message arrived, Trier had already fallen. General Patton replied: *Have taken Trier with two divisions. Do you want me to give it back?*

While the XX Corps was occupied with capturing Trier, the "defensive" action of the XII Corps had resulted in advances to the Kyll River line. On February 26 the 4th Armored Division had broken loose and proceeded to capture bridges over the Prum and Nims Rivers and advanced to high ground overlooking the Kyll. In this area Patton decided to make a major try for a break-through to the Rhine. The Germans had reinforced the Saar area, expecting the attack to continue in that locale. There was also a strong German force, known as the Mettlach salient, south of Saarburg. But Patton was never one to worry about his flanks, when there was an opportunity to advance.

Bridgeheads were secured over the Kyll by both the VIII and XII Corps and on March 5 the 4th Armored broke out. It was accompanied by one motorized regiment of the 5th Infantry Division. In three days General Gaffey had reached the Rhine, covering 55 miles. Bradley referred to this sweep in his book *A Soldier's Story* as "the most insolent armored blitz of the western war."

Next the 11th Armored of the VIII Corps broke loose and drove a second spearhead to the Rhine, paralleling the advance of the 4th further north. The rest of the troops mopped up the area.

In the meantime Patton was at work on his next operation. This was to be another swift turn, this time to the south across the Moselle to clear out the Palatinate, advance along the Rhine, and come on the rear of the German forces opposing the American Seventh Army.

The following excerpt is from a letter by Patton to his wife:

. . .The German General, Graf von Rothkeich, Commander of the 53 Corps whom we caught, said 60% of the army was opposed to the December attack (the Battle of the Bulge) but that Hitler ordered it. It was a costly mistake for them. He says that they have no men and no munitions, but just fight because they are soldiers; great people, but fools.

The Third Army now held the area bounded by the Moselle River on the south and the Rhine on the east as far north as Andernach. The Eifel, supposedly slow going for an army, and not good tank country, had been overrun in 12 days. The Eifel is a hilly, wooded section, with many gorges. This supposedly would give the advantage to the defenders, but Patton did not give the enemy time to dig in. His audacity had again been a great success.

A very large number of prisoners was taken in this operation, including two generals with their staffs. Hitler had ordered his army to stand and fight instead of retreating behind the Rhine, and thus it looked as though there would not be many left to fight east of the Rhine.

There should be something said in tribute to Patton's staff, whose planning was the foundation of the battle successes of the Third Army. On numerous occasions, General Patton would want to discuss plans with Bradley or Eisenhower the next morning. Some of these plans would merely be ideas given to the staff as late as five o'clock the day before his meeting. The completed plans were always ready for him by 7:00 A.M. Graphic aids would be furnished by Patton's staff in which all dispositions were shown by a series of overlays, which folded upon one another. These were easy to understand and greatly appreciated by all. Patton often remarked on these graphic aids and their excellent contribution to quick comprehension of the plans.

Patton's whirlwind dash through the Eifel had left an army of Germans on their southern flank in the area known as the Palatinate. This enemy force was opposing the Seventh Army's attempt to cross the Siegfried Line. Patton laid his plans for a sudden turn to the south to trap this force in accordance with the idea that had sprung into his head on February 6. The break-through to the south was to be executed by the XII Corps, which would cross the Moselle, pass through the Hunsruck and head for Mainz and Worms on the Rhine. The Hunsruck is a wooded mass of hills, with few roads. Its rugged terrain had kept out assaulting armies throughout modern times. However, the Third Army had just been successful in the Eifel, where the going was also rough, and not favorable for tanks, so Patton was confident of his ability to perform this second difficult operation.

The 11th Armored was added to the XII Corps for its advance. The infantry divisions of the VIII Corps took over the mopping up of the enemy north of the Moselle, and were then to capture Coblenz. After Coblenz was taken, the VIII Corps was to follow the XII Corps south, clearing everything from the west bank of the Rhine. As the two corps were hitting the rear of the German Army group, the XX Corps, still along the Saar, was to attack the enemy head on in an eastern drive.

Patton was spurred forward by his wish to reach the Rhine in the vicinity of Mainz before the Seventh Army, for the SHAEF plans called for the Seventh Army to cross the Rhine at this point. Patton was always competing with someone for the honors of first place.

The 4th Armored again spearheaded the attack, and broke through the Hunsruck to the Nahe River in two days. The XX Corps also made good advances. To Patton's delight, Eisenhower gave him the 12th Armored Division for use with the XX Corps. At the same time Eisenhower told Patton that the Third Army should be more boastful of their exploits. This must have amused Patton and his staff greatly, for they had never been exactly shy about their previous deeds. Patton's diary entry of March 17 confirms Eisenhower's belief in the Third Army.

At a briefing this morning Ike stated that we of the Third Army were such veterans that we did not appreciate our own greatness and should be more cocky and boastful, because otherwise people would not realize how good the American soldiers are. He stated specifically that the newspapers reported the fighting in front of the 4th Armored Division very weak, but did not mention the fact that it was weak on account of the phenomenal speed with which the 4th Armored had advanced. He was also extremely complimentary and stated that not only was I a good general but also a lucky general, and that Napoleon preferred luck to greatness. I told him this was the first time he had ever complimented me in the two and a half years we have served together. We then flew to headquarters of the Seventh Army at Luneville, where we were met by General Patch and General Devers. Patch and Devers were extremely nice.

The 4th Armored ran into quite a German counterattack on the 18th. Patton's forces shrugged this off, for Patton had reinforced his spearhead sufficiently. His battle wisdom like a sixth sense seemed to warn him of impending danger points in his lines. The intelligence reports had not foreseen this attack.

Patton's desire to cross the Rhine was intensified by his fear that he might lose troops to the British and Canadian armies in the north for their river crossing. He pushed his four armored divisions forward more rapidly, with the infantry on their heels. By March 21 the Palatinate had been overrun and the Third Army had joined with the Seventh Army coming up from the southwest. The German First and Seventh Armies were decimated.

On March 18, 1945 Patton wrote to his wife, in part:

I am dictating this letter so as to get it off faster than otherwise and sending it by the hands of Nick Campanole, who is going home due to kidney stones, and who will hand it to you.

The present operation of the Third Army, which started when we drove to the Rhine and is now headed towards Mayen and Worms, is probably the best operation we have ever put on. We now have 14 divisions, 4 armored and 10 infantry, which is quite a bunch of divisions.

Yesterday, Troy Middleton took Coblenz with practically no resistance, and the whole east bank of the Rhine in the vicinity of Coblenz was waving white flags.

In the vicinity of Bad Münster, the 4th Armored Division was run into by the infantry of the 2d Panzer who were apparently attempting to escape. They were driven back, but it delayed the advance. Further to the south, Morris is not going fast enough and is headed on St. Wendel.

Ike came the day before yesterday and spent the night,

and was extremely complimentary not only to me personally but also to the assembled staff officers.

It seems to me perfectly possible that this fight may be the fight to end all wars, as I cannot see how the Germans can resist. The Third Army has now destroyed the German Seventh Army twice and is at the moment working on the First German Army. A great deal of what will happen depends on how fast we can move, and the situation is so fluid, both at my level and also on the upper brackets, that Ike suggested that I should not change my CP as I had intended to.

Ike was quite apologetic about the 4-star business, but has, however, good reasons—that is, you must maintain the hierarchy of command or else relieve them, and he had no reason for relieving them. He said that George had promised that I would be number one Army Commander on the list. At the moment I am having so much fun fighting that I don't care what the rank is.

The story of launching the Palatinate Campaign is a good example of how circumstances controlled planned action. On March 9, Patton was called to Bradley's headquarters for a conference and a decoration ceremony. He spent the night of 9 to 10 March at that headquarters. Previously his staff had planned the Palatinate Campaign, that is to cross the Moselle, move south between the Moselle and Rhine Rivers and in back of the infamous Siegfried Line. The attack was to be launched with two corps abreast, the XII Corps on the north, the XX Corps on the south with the preponderance of strength in the XX Corps, while at the same time the VIII Corps was to take Coblenz and hold that shoulder. By SHAEF orders, the 80th Division was in General Reserve and not available to the Third Army.

At about 10 o'clock on the night of March 9, the Commanding General of the XII Corps, Major General Eddy, telephoned the Third Army Chief of Staff and told him that the 2d Cavalry under Colonel Charles H. Reed had secured a bridge intact across the Moselle River and asked what he should do. The Chief of Staff told him to exploit this success at once and secure a firm bridgehead, that the Chief of Staff would call Patton, who was at Bradley's headquarters, and see if the Third Army could get authority to launch the planned Palatinate Campaign in view of the fact that we already had a bridge over the Moselle.

Gay then called the XX Corps and relayed the above information to them. Next, he called Patton at Bradley's headquarters in Liége. Eisenhower was present at that headquarters. The situation was explained to Patton, and his Chief of Staff could hear him over the telephone talking to Bradley and Eisenhower, both of whom agreed that the Third Army should exploit the capture of the bridge. Patton was asked to find out if this would include authority to launch the Palatinate attack and would it include the release of the 80th Division to the Third Army. Eisenhower replied in the affirmative. Thus orders were given to the Third Army to launch the attack.

Some three or four hours later, General Eddy called the Chief of Staff, Third Army, again on the telephone and told him that his previous statement as to the capture of the bridge across the Moselle was all a mistake. He was told that the telephone was out of connection and he could not be heard and that the Palatinate Campaign would be launched as planned. Thus, the most successful campaign of the Third Army had its beginning.

Patton's reduction of the Palatinate in ten days was considered by many, especially the Germans, to have been his greatest campaign. During it he had made full use of the mobility of his armor, and its ability to open a path for the following infantry. Patton himself was proudest of this campaign.

Many Germans prisoners who were taken in this campaign stated, to those interrogating them, that they considered it no disgrace to be captured by Patton and his Third Army.

As General Patton had predicted over a year before, the last great battles of the war were fought west of the Rhine. Heavy casualties were inflicted on the enemy. During this campaign almost all of the German Seventh and First Armes were annihilated. The enemy was not able to recover from these heavy tolls, although the war did not end for two months.

"The Moon and the Dead" is one of the more peaceful Patton poems.

THE MOON AND THE DEAD

The road of the battle languished,
The hate from the guns was still,
While the moon rose up from a smoke cloud,
And looked at the dead on the hill.

Pale was her face with anguish,
Wet were her eyes with tears,
As she gazed on the twisted Corpses,
Cut off in their earliest years.

Some were bit by the bullet;
Some were kissed by the steel;
Some were crushed by the cannon,
But all were still, how still!

The smoke wreaths hung in the hollows,
The blood stink rose in the air;
And the moon looked down in pity,
At the poor dead lying there.

Light of their childhood's wonder,
Moon of their puppy love,
Goal of their first ambition,
She watched them from above.

Yet not with regret she mourned them,
Fair slain on the field of strife,
Fools only lament the hero,
Who gives for faith his life.

She sighed for the lives extinguished,
She wept for the loves that grieve,
But she glowed with pride on seeing,
That manhood still doth live.

The moon sailed on contented,
Above the heaps of slain.
For she saw that manhood liveth,
And honor breathes again.

14. Forcing the Rhine and Across Germany to the Mulde

PATTON ordered his first assault crossing of the Rhine to be made by the XII Corps the night of March 22. Speed was all-important, for the enemy was disrupted by his two dashing campaigns through the Eifel and the Palatinate. If the enemy was given time to regroup, the war would be prolonged, with more American lives lost. Patton was always conscious of this fact, and much of his effort to hurry ahead was his determination to spare lives.

With no artillery preparation or warning the 8th Infantry Division literally sneaked across the historic Rhine, to the surprise of the Germans. Patton's delight in this operation, and his personal satisfaction that he had beaten the Seventh Army across remind one of the small boy racing down the hill on his bicycle shouting, "Look, Ma, no hands!"

During the next few days all the units of the XII Corps were passed over the Rhine at the Oppenheim bridgehead. On the 24th of March the VIII Corps also made an assault crossing at Boppard, and the next day one at St. Goar.

At Oppenheim Patton took advantage of both the ground on the take-off side and the current. At Boppard and St. Goar he figured that the landing would be so difficult that the places would not be defended. He was right; they were not defended.

On March 23, 1945 Patton wrote a letter to his wife which shows his humane side.

. . . The displaced persons are a problem. They are streaming back utterly forlorn. I saw one woman with a perambulator full of her wordly goods sitting by it on a hill crying, an old man with a wheelbarrow and three little children wringing his hands, a woman and five children and a tin cup crying. In hundreds of villages there is not a living thing, not even a chicken. Most often houses are heaps of stone. They brought it on themselves, but these poor peasants are not responsible.

Am I getting soft? I did most of it.

When General Patton left his headquarters on the 26th of March, he had with him a prepared plan to send a combat command on a mission to Hammelburg for the purpose of recapturing some 900 American prisoners who were known to be in that stockade. Unfortunately, the Corps and Division Commanders talked him into sending a small force instead of a strong combat command.

This is the second time during the war, the first being at the time of the initial attack on Metz in November, 1944, that he allowed high-ranking subordinates to influence his decision to the extent of sending a boy to do a man's job.

Characteristically of him and all outstanding commanders, he makes no mention of this fact in his diary, thus assuming full responsibility and blaming no one.

Two hundred and ninety-three officers and men with 50 vehicles, including 19 tanks, were sent on this expedition. Patton hoped the expedition would not only rescue the Americans but lead the Germans to believe the Third Army intended to move east and not north. The operation was a risky one, behind enemy lines, and unfortunately most of the men who had gone on the expedition were killed or captured. This was one of the few times that Patton's audacity boomeranged and he was severely criticized for undertaking the raid. Later he admitted that Hammelburg was his one error of the war, in that he should have sent a combat command to make the rescue. He always felt keenly the loss of these men.

Patton received much adverse publicity at the time for this incident, hence the diary entries are included for accuracy.

March 26, 1945

I flew to the Headquarters of the XII Corps and directed General Eddy to send an expedition to the east about 60 miles for the purpose of recapturing some 900 American prisoners alleged to be in a stockade.

Both Eddy and the Commanding General of the 4th Armored were reluctant to do this because they said if I failed, I would be severely criticized. However, I do not believe that fear of criticism should prevent my getting back American prisoners, our men might be murdered.

March 27, 1945

I was quite nervous all morning over the "task force" I sent to rescue the prisoners, as we could get no information concerning them. I do not believe there is anything in that part of Germany heavy enough to hurt them, but for some reason I was nervous—probably I had indigestion.

March 28, 1945

There is still no news of the task force to Hammelburg.

March 30, 1945

. . .The German radio announced today that the American troops that had been sent on a special mission to Hammelburg had been captured or destroyed. We have no confirmation of this statement, but, on the other hand, we have not been able to locate them either from the air, due to bad flying weather, or by radio. It is therefore probable that they are lost.

The Third Army was advancing rapidly. Patton had reshuffled his troops and the order of advance was as follows: The XX Corps had moved onto the northern flank, and advanced to Kassel in one of the fastest movements of the Third Army, covering 100 miles in three days; the XII Corps was on the southern flank heading east in a general line with Wurzburg; the VIII Corps was in the middle and to the rear to mop up the enemy bypassed by the others.

General Eisenhower wrote to General Patton, on March 26, a letter of encouragement and congratulations to the Third Army. It reads:

DEAR GENERAL PATTON:

I have frequently had occasion to state, publicly, my appreciation of the great accomplishments of this Allied force during the past nine months. The purpose of this note is to express to you personally my deep appreciation of the splendid way in which you have conducted Third Army operations, from the moment it entered battle last August 1. You have made your Army a fighting force that is not excelled in effectiveness by any other of equal size in the world, and I am very proud of the fact that you, as one of the fighting commanders who has been with me from the beginning of the African campaign, have performed so brilliantly throughout.

We are now fairly started on that phase of the campaign which I hope will be the final one. I know that Third Army will be in at the finish in the same decisive way that it has performed in all the preliminary battles.

With warm personal regards,

As ever,
s/ DWIGHT EISENHOWER

At this time the Third Army's XX Corps was ordered to halt until the First and Ninth Armies came up on a line with it. Patton then moved his VIII Corps into the front zone and it moved east toward the Mulde River. On April 5th the XII Corps' line of advance was shifted slightly to the south toward Beyreuth. Third Army was given a stopping line running generally Rochlitz-Wilkau-Plauen-Hof-Beyreuth. By April 15th the corps were drawn up on this line.

Diary entries on the 4th of April shed more light on the Hammelburg affair.

April 4, 1945

In the afternoon, two lieutenants who came from the prison camp north of Hammelburg, which I tried to rescue, walked in and gave me the following account:

On Tuesday, March 27, at 2:00 P.M., they heard small arms fire in the vicinity of Hammelburg. At 4:10 P.M. the German general commanding the camp, which contained not 900, but 1200 American officers, came in and surrendered to Colonel Goode. At 7:30 P.M., tanks broke into the camp.

The prisoners were informed that, owing to the lack of transportation, only 250 could be transported, but the rest were advised to accompany the column as best they could. It would have been impossible for me to send enough transportation to remove 900, much less 1200, men. Of course, it was hard on those who had to walk, but at least we gave them a chance for their white alley.

The two men I talked to decided to walk south of the road which the column probably took going back. They said that all during Wednesday they heard firing, and then they turned north and heard nothing more until they reached our lines in the 2d Cavalry, exactly a week after escaping. They stated that they had been captured when the 106th Division was overrun in the Bastogne Bulge and had been in the camp three months, during which they had each lost thirty pounds. They said that the normal bill of fare consisted of one cup of ersatz coffee without milk or sugar for breakfast, a gruel of potatoes and water for lunch, and a similar gruel of potatoes, or carrots, or beets for dinner. They also stated that the guards were very unnecessarily rough and that during their stay in camp two officers had been shot for violating very minor regulations. In one case the officer was at the latrine when the alert signal for an air raid went on. When this happened, all men were supposed to be in the barracks in two minutes after the signal. This man was running to the barracks, but when the two minutes were up, he was shot and killed. After this event, orders were issued that during air alerts, which often lasted several hours, prisoners could go individually to the latrine because many of them had diarrhea, owing to their diet. The second officer went to the latrine and was shot on the way because the Lieutenant in charge of the guard had forgotten to tell the sentinels that the men had authority to go.

During the evening General Patch called up and said that three oher officers who had escaped had reported to his Army and stated that Johnny Waters had been with the tanks and had been badly wounded and re-captured. Apparently the wound is serious, but not dangerous, as it is in the leg.

I believe that the Seventh Army will probably relieve the camp today or tomorrow.

I felt very gloomy over the fact that I may have caused Waters' death, but I believe that I did the right thing, and I certainly could never have lived with myself had I known that I was within 40 miles of 900 Americans and not made an attempt to rescue them.

These two young men also stated that the group of prisoners in which Waters belonged had marched from a point in Northern Poland, leaving on the 19th of January, at which time they numbered about 1,000, and had arrived in the present camp on March 5, having marched on foot 325 miles. That during the march they had lost about 40% of their number. What had become of these men, they did not know.

The prisoner of war camp at Hammelburg was divided into two compounds. One compound was occupied by the Americans; the other compound on the lower level was occupied by the Yugoslav officers. The Yugoslavs wear a uniform very similar in color to the German uniform. When the American tanks appeared over the hill and saw the Yugoslav officers, they mistook them for Germans and fired into their compound. This action set several of the barracks on fire. The senior Yugoslav officer than came to the German camp commander, General Von Goeckel, and requested that Americans be sent out to the attacking American forces and request that their fire be lifted. The German general called on Colonel Goode, senior American officer, and requested that this be accomplished.

Three American officers, including Waters, volunteered to go on this mission with Captain Fuchs, the German interpreter. These officers left the camp by the main gate to go through the town outside of the compound and approached the American forces around their left flank. They marched in a column of twos, carrying an American flag and a white sheet tied to a pole. About 700 or 800 yards from the main entrance of the camp as they were getting into the country, they approached a barnyard fenced in by a plank fence. They noticed an individual soldier at one corner of the barn. He resembled an American paratrooper. Waters called to him inquirng whether he was American or German. This attracted his attention.

He was a German paratrooper, not an American. He moved over to the gate of the fence, about 15 yards from the Americans, took one look at the group, put his sniper rifle through the fence and without aiming, fired one round. This round struck Waters in the front and came out the rear. The German paratrooper then proceeded to back Captain Fuchs up to the side of an adjacent building, screaming and yelling at him, trying to find out just what was going on at that time. Eventually their argument was settled and Captain Fuchs, assisted by a German soldier and a blanket, and the other American officers, carried Waters back to the German hospital in the little town outside the American compound.

At the conclusion of World War II many of our top commanders retired from the service. Many of them entered other fields of endeavor to keep occupied. It is believed that it can be stated unequivocally that all of them had developed the ability to withstand the strains of combat under undue hardships and terrific pressure. Patton realized early that the boredom of a peaceful life would indeed bother him. He wrote to his wife on April 12, . . . *I love war and responsibility and excitement. Peace is going to be Hell on me. I will probably be a great nuisance.*

Several days later Patton was invited by General Plank of the Communications Zone to be present at the opening of the Rhine Bridge at Mainz. He was requested to cut the ribbon across the bridge and was handed a pair of scissors for the purpose. He made the statement that he was no tailor and asked for a bayonet, with which he cut the ribbon.

The next six days were devoted to preparations for a new line of attack to the southeast along the border of Czechoslovakia. The XII Corps was turned in this direction on the 17th and by the 21st had reached Weiden.

There was much shifting of divisions and corps for the new offensive. This involved long-distance moves in which the Third Army had become most proficient.

Patton received his fourth star. Upon acquiring it he stated that while he was glad to be a full general, he would have appreciated it more had he been in the initial group.

At the time confirmation for this four-star rank was up before the United States Senate one of the senators remarked, "If you have a thoroughbred race horse that bites the stable boy and kicks hell out of his stall, you would be silly not to give him the best treatment possible if he wins a race for you every Saturday."

This campaign had in many places been a road march, although tough resistance was met at several places such as Kassel. The Third Army had overrun the district of Saxe, Coburg, and Gotha, had crossed the Mulde River above Chemnitz, and were beyond Nuremburg to the south. Germany was split in two. Tremendous numbers of Germans were surrendering. Over 280,000 prisoners were taken during this short campaign.

Patton had showed his complete understanding of the use of each branch of the Army. At some points his armor led the way, while the infantry mopped up behind. At others the infantry reduced a strong point, thus opening a hole for the armor to use; the appropriate arm at the proper place.

In its last campaign of the war the Third Army struck to

the southeast with three corps: the XII Corps continued its advance in that direction, heading for Linz in Austria along the north bank of the Danube; the XX Corps was shifted to a point below Neumarkt and crossed the Danube at Regensberg, then headed for Linz along the Danube's southern bank. On the right flank was placed the III Corps, transferred from the First Army. This corps headed south over the Danube on a line with Salzburg and was to break up the so-called German Redoubt in the mountains of Bavaria.

These last days of the war saw a wholesale route of the enemy. Only Nazi fanaticism continued the war. The Redoubt turned into a myth. At some points there was stubborn resistance. One fanatical attack against the III Corps was executed by sixteen- to eighteen-year-old Nazi boys.

On April 26 the 65th Infantry Division of the XX Corps made an assault crossing of the Danube. Resistance here increased, but as soon as the bridgehead was firmly established the resistance melted. On April 27, the III Corps also crossed the Danube River further west against stubborn resistance.

My May 1 the XX Corps had cleared Landau on the Isar River. The III Corps was also crossing this river into Redoubt area. The XII Corps had entered Austria to the north of the Danube and met some strong counterattacks.

The VIII Corps had been ordered relieved from the Third Army command and Patton, as was customary, gave General Middleton full and generous credit for his contribution to the successes of the Army. Patton wrote the following letter to him.

MY DEAR GENERAL MIDDLETON:

Again the exigencies of war have separated the VIII Corps and the Third Army. We are all most regretful.

None of us will ever forget the stark valor with which you and your Corps contested every foot of ground during Von Rundstedt's attack. Your decision to hold BASTOGNE was a stroke of genius.

Subsequently, the relentless advance of the VIII Corps to the KYLL River, thence to the RHINE, your capture of COBLENZ and subsequent assault crossings of the RHINE at its most difficult sector, resulting in your victorious and rapid advance to the MULDE River, are events which will live in history and quicken the pulse of every soldier.

Please accept for yourself and transmit to the officers and men of your command my sincere thanks and admiration for the outstanding successes achieved.

May all good fortune attend you.

Very sincerely
G. S. PATTON, JR.
Lieut. General, U.S. Army,
Commanding

Patton had been accused by many of being inconsiderate and wasteful as to the supply situation. In some instances this might be true. There are many stories to the contrary, however. One of these occurred near the end of the war. The 16th Armored Division was assigned to the Third Army and he hoped to get it into battle. However, he asked that it be swapped with another armored division because he felt that the distance it had to travel did not justify the expense of the gasoline required to move it. This division did later get into action with the Third Army.

The III Corps was stopped in the Redoubt area and the XX Corps were also given stopping points at which they were to await the arrival of the Russians. As always General Patton resented any orders to halt. However, he was cheered by the opportunity of launching an offensive into Czechoslovakia, to Pilsen, with the V Corps descending from the north and the XII Corps turned northeast to attack from the south. This was the last offensive of the war and Patton was very pleased that his army executed it. This was a fitting finale for a general whose watchword was "Attack!"

At midnight, May 8, the war in Europe was over.

Patton felt that the orders not to go into Prague were a great mistake, for he believed that by going into the capital of Czechoslovakia we would have an important position in that country, and thwart the plans for domination by the Russians. He was quick to realize the political importance of our placating the Russians. Patton ranked this failure to permit the Third Army to take Prague as the second greatest mistake in the Third Army operations. The other, as before stated, he believed to be the failure to plan the closing of the Falaise Gap, about the middle of August, 1944, which, in his opinion, permitted the German Seventh Army to escape.

It seemed to Patton, at the time, that a nation as great as ours should move to where it desired to stop and tell the Russians of our intentions. He also was deeply concerned as to the possible harm which might be inflicted on an alleged 100,000 White Russians that wanted to surrender to the Third Army. He realized that they would probably face death if they were turned over to the Russians.

Some of the captured German generals had high praise for Patton's ruthless energy, his battlefield intuition, and his discernment of the points where Germany was weak. Among those to make comments was Field Marshal Karl Gerd von Rundstedt, Commander-in-Chief of all the German armies in France and in the Battle of the Bulge. He talked to Patrick Mitchell, correspondent in Germany for the *Stars and Stripes* after the surrender. The quality of the American generals was under discussion. Spitting out the unfamiliar words with great emphasis, the defeated Nazi Marshal made his unbiased announcement: "Patton, he is your best!" [1]

In reference to all the Allied Commanders, Rundstedt said: "Montgomery and Patton are the two best that I met." [2]

On May 9, 1945 Patton wrote to his wife:

. . . all the Germans are trying to surrender to us so that the Russians will not get them. It is really a serious problem. There are hundreds of thousands of them all without food.

I have been working on my victory order.

The order he mentioned follows:

[1] From the book by Alden Hatch, *George Patton, General in Spurs*, page 176.
[2] Liddell Hart, *The German Generals Talk*, page 257.

APO 403

9 May 1945

GENERAL ORDERS
NUMBER 98
SOLDIERS OF THE THIRD ARMY, PAST AND PRESENT

During the 281 days of incessant and victorious combat, your penetrations have advanced further in less time than any other army in history. You have fought your way across 24 major rivers and innumerable lesser streams. You have liberated or conquered more than 82,000 square miles of territory, including 1500 towns and cities, and some 12,000 inhabited places. Prior to the termination of active hostilities, you have captured in battle 956,000 enemy soldiers and killed or wounded at least 500,000 others. France, Belgium, Luxembourg, Germany, Austria and Czechoslovakia bear witness to your exploits.

All men and women of the six corps and thirty-nine divisions that have at different times been members of this Army have done their duty. Each deserves credit. The enduring valor of the combat troops has been paralleled and made possible by the often unpublicized activities of the supply, administrative, and medical services of this Army and of the Communications Zone troops supporting it. Nor should we forget our comrades of the other armies and of the Air Force, particularly of the XX Tactical Air Command, by whose side or under whose wings we have had the honor to fight.

In proudly contemplating our achievements, let us never forget our heroic dead whose graves mark the course of our victorious advances, nor our wounded whose sacrifices aided so much to our success.

I should be both ungrateful and wanting in candor if I failed to acknowledge the debt we owe to our Chiefs of Staff, Generals Gaffey and Gay, and to the officers and men of the General and Special Staff Sections of Army Headquarters. Without their loyalty, intelligence and unremitting labors, success would have been impossible.

The termination of fighting in Europe does not remove the opportunities for other outstanding and equally difficult achievements in the days which are to come. In some ways the immediate future will demand of you more fortitude than has the past because, without the inspiration of combat, you must maintain—by your dress, deportment and efficiency—not only the prestige of the Third Army but also the honor of the United States. I have complete confidence that you will not fail.

During the course of this war I have received promotions and decorations far above and beyond my individual merit. You won them; I as your representative wear them. The one honor which is mine and mine alone is that of having commanded such an incomparable group of Americans, the record of whose fortitude, audacity, and valor will endure as long as history lasts.

G. S. PATTON, JR.
General

In addition to the remarks of the captured German generals, noted before, the opinion of Field Marshal Albert Kesselring may be quoted: "Among American commanders, General Patton was certainly outstanding. His speed and drive were recognized and appreciated by us. He showed great initiative in his operations and did not fear for his flanks."

General Patton has been pictured as harsh and ruthless, but many enlisted men knew another side of him. The following is quoted from a letter sent to the author by Sergeant Herman A. Jakubiec formerly of the 2d Armored Division, now living in Dunkirk, New York, in reply to a request to him to write how enlisted men felt about Patton.

He was kind and friendly. He was a true army man, a disciplinarian though not too harsh or rigorous. He was held in high esteem and regard by all men whom he commanded, led or fought with. His associations, contacts, and close union with the fighting men and personnel of the army cannot be excelled. He possessed a high feeling and profound reverence toward all enlisted men.

General Patton, to me, and to every enlisted man that served under his command, goes in the book of my memory as the Greatest General of World War II. Patton was always respected by his men for his courage, training and especially his respect for the enlisted man.

I remember the speeches the General gave and how every man would whistle and clap his hands when the General finished speaking. One incident that happened and stands out to me as how the men respected General Patton is this: General Patton was leaving the *2d Armored* to take command of a newly formed *1st Armored* Corps. The whole division assembled and thought we would hear one of Patton's fiery speeches. Instead Patton stood up—raised his hand and said, "Good-by." He took out his handkerchief and wiped his eyes and sat down. General Devers was there from Fort Knox. He was the speaker who informed us that Patton was leaving for a new assignment and would join us sometime later. This he did when we invaded Africa.

This story is very true and by that little token of wiping his eyes, every man and officer respected General Patton for his thoughts were of the men he was leaving. Many times this same story was repeated by men who served under him. Another famous saying he used during his speeches was: "Make every man respect the *Deuce* —the 2d Armored."

Though Patton was a ruthless officer in combat, his feelings for his men and bereaved families of those killed in conflict disclosed a side of him that the press rarely ever glimpsed. A portrait of this man would not be complete without emphasizing this aspect of the great battlefield commander.

On analyzing his campaigns it becomes clear that the reason Patton has become such a legend and a popular hero to our generation is because he represented an American way of doing things. The way he fought, every man believes to be typical of the best of the American qualities. He was quick to seize an opportunity and to exploit it to the fullest; he rode over opposition; he was never fettered by convention. He aimed to get the enemy off balance and to keep him off balance. During his life he gained the admiration of the public, the worship of those who fought with him; but he has gained in stature since World War II. The Patton legend is part of the American heritage. His personality will always be remembered, including his faults, and we shall draw strength from him when our country is in peril.

"A Soldier's Burial" by Patton is considered one of his most beautiful poems.

A SOLDIER'S BURIAL [3]

Not midst the chanting of the Requiem Hymn,
Nor with the solemn ritual of prayer,
Neath misty shadows from the oriel glass,
And dreamy perfume of the incensed air
Was he interred;

But in the subtle stillness after fight,
And the half light between the night and the day,
We dragged his body all besmeared with mud,
And dropped it, clod-like, back into the clay.

Yet who shall say that he was not content,
Or missed the prayers, or drone of chanting choir,
He who had heard all day the Battle Hymn
Sung on all sides by thousand throats of fire.

What painted glass can lovelier shadows cast
Than those the evening skies shall ever shed,
While, mingled with their light, Red Battle's Sun
Completes in magic colors o'er our dead
The flag for which they died.

15. After Victory—Prediction of Things to Come—The Russian Menace

THE war was over. The U.S. Third Army was in contact with the Russians. It is customary for allied armies who are fighting together to decorate each other. The usual method is for one army to tell the army of their allies that they have a certain number and a certain type of decorations to be awarded. The recipient army then selects those who are to receive the decorations.

Patton planned such a ceremony to decorate the Russians in his sector. The 65th U.S. Infantry Division furnished the guard of honor. He stated that he didn't want to be under any "obli-goddamn-gations" to the Russians.

After the ceremony was concluded there was a lunch held at the Division Officers' Club which consisted mostly of whiskey. The Russians tried to drink American whiskey without water with very bad results. Patton said afterward, "I unquestionably drank the Russian Commander under the table and walked out under my own steam." As they were to return the call two days hence, Patton and his officers prepared themselves by drinking mineral oil because they were certain the Russians would try to get them drunk. On the 14th day of May Patton was to receive a Russian award. His diary entry best recounts the events of this meeting.

May 14, 1945

The same group of officers that participated in the festivities on the 12th went to the Headquarters of the 4th Russian Guards Army where we were received by Marshal Tolbukhim, Commander of the 3d Ukranian Front. He apparently is the next highest ranking Marshal to Stalin, and in order to present me with the Medal, the order of Kutuzov (first Degree) he had to be present. He was a very inferior man and sweated profusely at all times.

They certainly put on a tremendous show. The whole road, which I should think was 15 miles from the bridge where we met them till we reached the château formerly belonging to the Emperor Francis Joseph of Austria, had actually been swept. There were soldiers about every hundred yards along the road, standing at present arms, and also extremely buxom female MP's.

When we got to the château, they had soldiers with a sort of shoeblackening arrangement to clean our boots. They had a great many women retainers who did everything except wipe your face. They did go to the extent of spraying your head with perfume.

No Russian could sit down or get up without asking the Marshal's permission.

After lunch they had a very splendid show which unquestionably had been flown in from Moscow. They did their best to get us drunk but we had taken the precaution of drinking two ounces of mineral oil before starting on the expedition. We were also very careful what we drank. The medal given me is No. 58, which indicates that it is quite highly considered.

I have never seen in any Army at any time, including the German Imperial Army of 1912, as severe discipline as exists in the Russian Army. The officers, with few exceptions, give the appearance of recently civilized Mongolian bandits. The men passed in review with a very good imitation of the goose step. They give me the impression of something that is to be feared in future world political reorganization.

The dining room, which formerly belonged to Emperor Francis Joseph of Austria, was beautiful. All the appointments were exquisite. As General Patton's group entered the room, all was of the most severe formality.

General Patton's Chief of Staff had decided that he would not take a drink because he wished to make certain that the party broke up in time for the trip to the airstrip, which was not lighted, prior to dark. The party lasted for hours and included caviar, roast beef, roast chicken, and many other delicacies. As the food was passed, the Russians made no use whatsoever of the cutlery. Instead they used their hands. There were numerous speeches, and music which was beautiful and stirring. Undoubtedly, the musicians had been brought in from Moscow, although the Chief of Staff of the Fourth Guards Army stated they were just local musicians brought in from the border.

Finally it was time for the party to end if General Patton's group were to reach the airfield in Germany before dark. Marshal Tolbukhim stood up and entwined arms with General Patton, stating that this was the last toast and glasses should be drained to the bottom. The Marshal and General Patton drained their glasses, upon completion of which the Marshal fell limp in his chair. General Patton, tall and straight, and without a quiver, marched out of the room. He did not even deign to look back or toward Marshal Tolbukhim. It was a great show of utter disdain for the Russian capacity. When the American party reached the plane, Patton said, "I didn't think I could ever do it."

There were several of these affairs held by the Russians and the Americans. All this fraternization between the Russians and the Third Army disgusted Patton. On return from one of the parties given by the Russians for his officers, he remarked to one of the staff that here was an utter lack of comprehension by the Americans of the ruthless long-range plans for conquest that he sensed were surely in the minds of their Russian hosts. He felt so strongly concerning the naïve conduct of his officers that he said, "Father, forgive them; for they know not what they do." [1]

The Russians have created a class of peers, the officer class. In no army is there such great disparity between the pay of the officers and their privileges and the pay and privileges of the enlisted men. A Russian general's pay is one hundred times more than the pay of a Russian private.

It is remarkable that Communism has bred this class of aristocrats. At the start of the Russian-Finnish war before World War II, there was much fraternizing between the Russian officers and their enlisted men. The Finnish war was a proving ground for these ideas. Then, officers and men were "comrades" and called each other such. War has never been successfully fought on such a basis, and the Russian-Finnish war proved again that this was an impossible approach to the grim business of battle. When the pendulum swung in the Russian army, it carried policy to the other extreme.

Elimination of distinction between officers and men has been tried at various periods by various nations. The present U.S. Army now comes as close to the ideal as has been achieved to date. The officers in the U.S. Army are held to strict accountability for the comfort and welfare of those under their command, which come before their own comfort and safety, yet there is no lack of respect for the uniform towards those in command, and discipline is held to a comparatively high standard.

About May 16 Patton received word to report to General Eisenhower at Rheims to take charge of the situation that was being engendered by the belligerent actions of Tito of Yugoslavia.

General Marshall had notified Eisenhower that the prestige of the Patton name and the Third Army might quiet the situation. For this reason the sector fronting Tito's troops was assigned to Patton. At this time the question was not Tito but whether or not he was the pawn of the Russians.

---

[1] Luke: 23rd Chapter, 34th Verse.

For an insight into Patton's beliefs at this time much of the diary is quoted.

May 18, 1945

The question at issue is not so much Tito but as to whether or not he is the pawn of the Russians and, if so, whether he is being used as a red herring to pull us to the South so that the Russians may resume an offensive in Central Germany; or whether the Russians are actually backing Tito with the idea of getting a port, or ports, on the northern end of the Adriatic. The situation should clarify itself within a few days. If it does not, considerable complication will arise on redeployment.

In my opinion, the American Army as it now exists, could beat the Russians with the greatest of ease, because while the Russians have good infantry, they are lacking in artillery, air, tanks and in the knowledge of the use of the combined arms; whereas we excel in all three of these.

I believe that by taking a strong attitude, the Russians will back down. So far we have yielded too much to their Mongolian nature.

On May 20, 1945 Patton wrote to his wife:

The desire to fight is evaporating and these soldiers will not be much good unless they get in soon.

I doubt if I go to China unless something happens to Doug.[2]

I wrote George C.[3] that I would be willing to go in command of a division. Well, the future will show. So far I have done my job as I saw it and never planned or schemed and it has worked out pretty well.

I hope that Tito does not keep me from coming home on the seventh of June. If he does I am going to give him a special licking.

Some time after this event, there was a joint review of troops in Berlin. Patton and several high-ranking Russians were the reviewing officers. Afterward one of the Russian generals through an interpreter, asked Patton to have a drink with him. Patton told the interpreter to tell the Rus-

[2] General Douglas MacArthur.
[3] General George C. Marshall.

264

sian son-of-a-bitch that the way the Russians were acting, he considered they were enemies, and that he did not care to drink with him; he would rather cut his throat.

The interpreter said that he would not tell the Russian general this, but Patton insisted. The Russian broke out in a broad smile and his message was that he felt the same way toward Patton—and why couldn't they have a drink? On this basis they had a drink.

Patton flew on a planned good-will trip to the United States. He was ill with a "strep" throat at the time, but went notwithstanding, arriving at Bedford Airport, on June 7. His cadet son, George, was allowed to leave West Point to meet him. This was the last time he saw his father. Both his daughters came to Boston to see him.

He told his children that he would never see them again. They said the war was over and there was no occasion for such a gloomy prediction. He maintained that nevertheless this was true, because it had been revealed to him. He never saw them again. Could this have been his subconscious working again?

On June 30, 1945 Bradley made an efficiency report on Patton from which the following is an extract:

> Colorful, courageous, energetic, pleasing personality, impetuous. Possesses high degree of leadership, bold in operations, has a fine sense of both enemy and own capabilities. An outstanding combat leader. . . . of the ten general officers of this grade known to me, I would list him Number One as a combat commander. Renders willing and generous support to the plans of his superiors, regardless of his personal views in the matter.[4]

Upon completion of this trip he returned to Europe in early July. He was met at the airport by a good-will guard of honor and escorted to the Headquarters of the Third U.S. Army.

Patton wrote to his wife on July 21, 1945 as follows:

> Berlin gave me the blues. We have destroyed what could have been a good race and we are about to replace them with the Mongolian savages and all Europe with Communism.

---

[4] Quoted from *Atlantic Monthly*, November, 1947. Copyright, 1947, by Atlantic Monthly Co.

The son of Adjutant Cléry—the Adjutant Cléry of Saumur days, who taught George Patton the sword in 1912 and 1913—wrote the following letter in August, 1945 to Patton:

Paris, August 3, 1945
5 Rue Laugier (XVIIᵉ)

MY GENERAL:

As the eldest son of your Maître d'Armes at Saumur (1913) I have hesitated to address you until I could be sure that you are the same Captain Patton who used to spoil me as a child. General Des Cilleuls has lately assured me that you are the very man my mother and I have long held in veneration. Permit me now to say that for years the name Patton has meant America to our family. The memory of your kindness to us at the time of our father's death is ever living; and our admiration for you has been reinforced by your superb campaign which has freed us from the Boche.

I am a career officer who was marked by our Vichy army as working for the allies and tracked by the Gestapo; I have done my full duty to my country and can now wear my officer's uniform with pride; and I have been awarded several decorations by General De Gaulle.

Permit me, my General, to salute in you not only the splendid memory of my childhood, but the magnificent General whom, as a fellow officer, I admire for your high military value.

Please accept the assurance of my deep gratitude and admiration.

CAPITAINE CLÉRY

A letter to Mrs. Patton dated August 6, 1945 said:

I am most upset about universal service. If we do not have it we are sunk and soon too.

Patton, during the succeeding weeks, was busy attending to peacetime duties connected with the Army of Occupation and in bidding farewell to those who had fought with him in his Third Army.

His analysis of the Russians, their mentality and their aims, was not obscured by any nostalgic regard for an ally.

A high churchman came to see me and stayed to lunch. He is a very bright man, speaks perfect English, and hates the Russians with a reason. He told me some of their methods. For example, in order to make one of his subordinates sign a false certificate with respect to two priests, they did nothing to the subordinate but brought a young girl into his cell and began to methodically beat her to death in order to cause him to write. The girl urged him not to, but naturally he could not stand the sight of this brutality and signed. In order to make the best of the thing, the Russians had had a sound recorder put in the room, making a record of the girl's screams, which they then played outside the room of any other men they intended to work on at a future time. He stated that several Polish Bishops had been shot because they refused to become members of the Greek Church, but that this took place only in Eastern Poland.

Another form of securing testimony is to hang a man by his wrists, but with bandages around them so as not to cut in and make marks—then to make two incisions in the lower abdomen and allow a portion of the intestines to hang out. After the man has taken all he can without dying he is cut down, sewed up, and restored to health with the promise that if he does not do, or write, whatever he is told to, the operation would be repeated. In almost every case the fear of the second torture induces the man to behave as they desire.

According to this religious leader, more than two million Poles have been taken to Russia for slave labor. In every case, when they do this they split families. Furthermore, they always lie as to what part of Siberia the Poles were sent. He states that if they tell you they have gone to Northern Siberia, the place to look for them is in Southern Siberia.

When I was in Cairo, General Anders, Commanding the 2d Polish Corps and who had been a General Staff Officer of a Russian Division under the Emperor in World I, told me that he was certain the Russians had deliberately murdered quite a few thousand Polish officers.[6] He was himself kept in jail for about two years. He

---

[5] Diary entry.
[6] This is probably the first news of the Katyn Forest slaughter.

told me that if he ever marched his Corps of two divisions in between the Russians and the Germans, he would attack in both directions.

The contemplation of a peacetime existence did not bring personal pleasure to Patton. This can be compared to his statement at the start of the Third Army operations in France in July, 1944, when he said he would swap places with no one in the world.

August 10, 1945 [7]

Another war has ended, and with it my usefulness to the world. It is for me personally a very sad thought. Now all that is left to do is to sit around and await the arrival of the undertaker and posthumous immortality. Fortunately, I also have to occupy myself with the de-Nazification and government of Bavaria, and the recruiting of the industries of the German people so that they can be more self-supporting.

Patton inspected the 820 mm. cannon that Hitler's bad judgment had caused to be built. On the way from the airstrip to the location of the cannon, Patton, riding in his own jeep, passed through many German villages. Somehow the villagers had learned of his impending visit and without exception greeted him with cheers and by throwing flowers from the windows, all shouting, "He is our savior. He has saved us from the Russian mob." Even then they seemed to sense the future.

Patton did not believe that the atomic bomb would eliminate the necessity of trained armies. It was just another weapon to him. This particular point is being discussed, both pro and con, in our country today by not only our military leaders but key civilians as well. His diary entry of the 18th of August elucidates this situation. Also portions of a letter written to his wife on this same date are worthy of perusal.

August 18, 1945

The use of the atomic bomb against Japan was most unfortunate because it now gives a lot of vocal but ill-informed people—mostly fascists, communists and

[7] Diary entry.

s.o.b's assorted—an opportunity to state that the army, navy and air forces are no longer necessary, as this bomb will either prevent war or destroy the human race. Actually, the bomb is no more revolutionary than the first throwing-stick or javelin, or the first cannon or the first submarine. It is simply, as I have often written, a new instrument added to the orchestra of death, which is war.

And to his wife:

The atomic bomb was most unfortunate. It gives pacifists, politicians and fools a chance to say, "All we need is a bomb, no Army."

Patton had publicly made the statement that the Russians were to be feared. At this time it was an unpopular thing to say.

On September 11, 1945 he wrote to his wife:

On the seventh there was an Inter-Allied review to celebrate V-J Day. U.S., England, France and Russia each had 1000 men and 50 vehicles in the parade. Marshal Zhukov was senior, I was next. He was in full dress uniform much like comic opera and covered with medals. He is short, rather fat, and has a prehensile chin like an ape but good blue eyes. He was in the cavalry. Our troops looked the best, the Russians next. The Russians had a lot of heavy tanks of which they were very proud. The Marshal asked me how I liked them. I said I did not, and we had quite an argument. Apparently I was the first person ever to disagree with him.

Patton noted the disturbing situation created by the Russians in Poland in a diary entry.

September 15, 1945

I have just read a report by Commandant Philippe de Forceville, Senior French Liaison Officer with the Third United States Army, describing the situation in the Krakow district of southern Poland. According to him, the present government of Poland is a Quisling government run by the Russians. I know by my own knowledge that the present President of Poland spent twenty years in Moscow and hardly knows the Polish language. The

Church is very much afraid that the Russians will force them to join the Russian Orthodox Church. In fact, certain Bishops in the eastern part of Poland were told to join the Russian Orthodox Church and when they refused were put in jail. The Polish Army seems to be numerous and well armed with armor, guns and trucks. However, all officers above the grade of captain are Russians whereas the junior officers, captains and lieutenants, are looking forward to the day when they can rise against the Russians.

The Russians have changed to their six-foot gauge the railway running from Lemberg to Krakow. I have also heard they have done the same thing to the railways running in western Germany, but have no proof of it as yet.

The wealthy landowners have all been expelled from their properties and a great many have been sent to Siberia, as is the case with the intellectuals.

It seems to be quite a hell of a mess.

It was about this time that a Russian private had come over into the territory occupied by the Americans to enjoy the freedom and conviviality that was enjoyed in our zone, which was unknown in the Russian Army. He was drunk and brought into Third Army Headquarters. A Russian officer at that headquarters was brought into the room where the American MP that had picked up the Russian private was holding him. An American officer through an interpreter was trying to get the story from the MP and the Russian. The Russian officer asked what the private was charged with. It seems that he had been shooting civilians, had set fire to some buildings, and had raped several women.

The Russian officer said, "You don't like this man do you?" The answer was a diplomatic no, we don't. The Russian officer thereupon pulled out a rusty pistol and shot the culprit through the temple, saying, "We don't like him either."

General Patton's farsighted analysis of our approaching difficulties with Russia back in 1945, when so few people saw the danger, was most remarkable. His wide study of world and military affairs and his analysis of conditions, unaffected by contemporary mush and sentiment, allowed him to see quite clearly where we were heading.

One of his colonels had been called to Bad Tolz from his

position on the Czech border for an interview relative to conditions there, since they were near the Russians. After finishing the meeting with some officers of Patton's staff, he was talking to someone in the Chief of Staff's office when General Patton sent for him and asked him to sit down and talk over his impressions about the Russian troops in Czechoslovakia. They had discussed that and other matters for about five or ten minutes when Colonel Harkins came in and said: "General, the acting European Theater Commander is on the phone and wants to talk to you." He arose to go out, but General Patton said: "No, stick around. You may enjoy some of this—I want to talk to you further."

After some preliminary remarks, the acting Theater Commander apparently told General Patton that he would have to disarm completely and get busy on disbanding the several intact German units still in his area, one of these being the 11th Panzer Division that had never been disbanded or confined. The acting Theater Commander said that the Russians resented their not being all in tight prison camps.

General Patton replied: "Hell—why do you care what those goddamn Russians think? We are going to have to fight them sooner or later; within the next generation, I am sure, maybe a whole lot sooner. Why not do it now while our Army is intact and the damn Russians can have their hind end kicked back into Russia in three months? We can do it ourselves easily with the help of the German troops we have, if we just arm them and take them with us; they hate the bastards."

Apparently, the other end of the line felt as if it had been hit with a hammer, but after a minute this came on the line: "Shut up, Georgie, you fool, this line may be tapped and you will be starting a war with those Russians with your talking!"

General Patton replied: "I would like to get it started some way; that is the best thing we can do now. *You* don't have to get mixed up in it at all if you are so damn soft about it and scared of your rank—just let me handle it down here. In ten days I can have enough incidents happen to have us at war with the sons-of-bitches and make it look like their fault. So much so that we will be completely justified in attacking them and running them out."

After that there was some screaming on the other end of the line and a hang-up followed. General Patton laughed and said: "I really believe that we are going to fight them and if this country doesn't do it now, it will be taking them on years later when the Russians are ready for it and we will have an awful time whipping them. We will need these Germans, and I don't think we ought to mistreat people whom we will need so badly."

Patton noted the hostility of the American public to the use of Germans who had any connection with the Nazi government. He felt that many who had some dealings with the Nazis were forced by circumstances to give lip service to Hitler and that unless some of these people were used the population would suffer hardships.

This was the start of a bitter campaign against his administration of Bavaria that resulted in his eventual relief from his beloved Third Army and his assignment to the Fifteenth Army.

He had been told to report to General Eisenhower concerning his statements about his administration of Bavaria.

Patton believed that Germany should be strengthened as a bulwark against the Russians. His beliefs when seen almost a decade later were indeed accurate. In 1945 they were inacceptable to many of the American public, though some of the more farsighted agreed.

What can be said of his statements is that they were audacious, 100 per cent true, and very undiplomatic from the point of view of the leaders in political control at the time.

The Third Army was transferred to Lieutenant General Lucian Truscott. Patton was relieved because his statements concerning the administration of conquered Germany and about the Russians did not meet with the approval of those who made the policy in government. It was then thought by those in authority that if we made strong efforts to be friends with the Russians all would be well and this view, no doubt, was being urged by the pro-Russians in the government.

Patton wrote to his wife on October 5, 1945:

My head is bloody but unbowed. All that I regret is that I have again worried you.

I have been helping Lucian to get the hang of the show and he feels rather depressed. I don't blame him.

I was terribly hurt for a few days but I am normal again.

The speech of General Patton to the officers and men of the Third Army on the occasion of his departure follows:

"General Truscott, Officers and Men:

"All good things must come to an end. The best thing that has ever come to me thus far is the honor and privilege of having commanded the Third Army.

"The great successes we have achieved together have been due primarily to the fighting heart of America but without the coordinating and supply activities of the General and Special Staffs, even American valor would have been impotent.

"You officers and men here represent the fighting, the administrative, and the supply elements of this Army. Please accept my heartfelt congratulations on your valor and devotion to duty, and my fervent gratitude for your unwavering loyalty.

"When I said that all good things must come to an end, I was referring to myself and not to you because you will find in General Truscott every characteristic which will inspire in you the same loyalty and devotion which you have so generously afforded me.

"A man of General Truscott's achievements needs no introduction. His deeds speak for themselves. I know that you will not fail him.

"Good-by and God bless you."

Patton felt quite strongly that the Potsdam conference was leading us to another war and discusses it quite profusely in his diary.

October 13, 1945

As I stated before, I cannot imagine a situation in which if the Devil and Mars had conspired together to produce a new war, they would have found a more happy set of circumstances. Poland is under Russian domination, so is Austria, so is Hungary, so will be Czechoslovakia and so is Yugoslavia—and we sit happily by and think everybody loves us. Already the atomic bomb has been countered and the war will go on, and yet idiots have the temerity to criticize people like General Marshall on the subject of war.

After referring to the Russians, it is of interest to note that whereas our troops in Czechoslovakia have been reduced to two very weak divisions, the Russians have not only not reduced their forces, which initially were around

350,000, but probably have brought in another 200,000 from Bohemia. All these troops are living off the country. Some of them have built semi-permanent winter quarters in the forest and others are evacuating Czechs and living in their houses—that is, where they cannot find Sudetan Germans to drive out. There is certainly no evidence of their leaving Czechoslovakia. Practically no supplies from Russia come to their armies with the result that they quite rapidly eat up a country. Within the last two weeks they made a dicker by force, or guile, to have the Czechs provide them with cattle and other commodities from the American occupied portion of the country, and they started to send Russian troops over to collect. General Harmon very correctly told the Czech government they could sell what they wanted to but they would have to collect it themselves and not let the Russians cross the line. An interesting phenomenon is that on the American side of the line there are ample flocks and herds of cattle, sheep, chickens and geese. On the Russian side animal life practically does not exist.

In a letter written to his cadet son on October 22, 1945 Patton discusses strategy and history.

MY DEAR GEORGE:

I am glad you are living up to the best traditions of the family in Military History. I stood first in it. Don't let Economics get you down because on your maternal grandfather's side you should be good at it.

What you admire about saying what you think is undoubtedly connected with the necessity for being self-confident which I am always preaching to you. Napoleon did not fall through lack of excessive self-confidence but through an error of judgment induced by dishonest advisors and probably as a direct act of God because, had he gone on to his final objective, we would have had a world of peace—strange as it may seem. At least, we would have had the Pax Romana which, as I remember, lasted some hundreds of years.

Jena and Auerstadt were excellent fights. There is a big book which you may someday read called the *Étude de Jena* which includes all the orders and letters written or issued by Napoleon for those two battles. Of course,

Auerstadt was not fought at his instigation but by accident.

What you mention about his putting more trust in battalion squares and numerical superiority than in strategy is the price every conqueror has to pay because, the more he conquers, the fewer good soldiers has he left. Therefore, his means must become simpler and his losses heavier.

I rather believe that as to size Friedland was bigger than the other two fights you mention because, as I remember it, the total French Army at Jena/Auerstadt was 100,000.

I did not know until you told me that Napoleon crossed near Oppenheim. I had picked this when I was still in England as the place to cross the Rhine because the terrain on my side dominated that on the other side as the former was far enough away from the Frankfurt hills to prevent direct fire on the bridges and because, above everything else, there was a barge harbor there from which we could launch boats unseen.

You are pretty near the end of your course now and, if possible, I am going to arrange to get you and your mother over and, after securing an open car, drive from Avranches to Bad Tolz—provided I can get past the fifteen cities en route of which I am citoyen d'honneur. I doubt if any digestion can drink fifteen cities under on a second tour.

In October Patton wrote a letter to his wife that expressed his thoughts on the Western Task Force landings in French Morocco on November 8, 1942. He believed that this landing was the most dangerous operation of all his campaigns. The letter reads in part as follows:

Three years ago today almost to the hour, the *Augusta* sailed out of Hampton Roads. I shall never cease regretting that I did not have the intelligence to have you stay over and see the show. Of all the operations in which I have participated, or of which I have read, that was surely the most dangerous. Only the direct interposition of God on the morning of November 8 made it possible.

Patton had a meeting with General Giraud, at which

time Patton explained that a great migration from the east was taking place. The diary tells of this meeting.

October 19, 1945

Yesterday General Giraud, of the French Army, who had been talking to General Eisenhower, asked if he might come to luncheon. I was, as always, delighted to see him. His purpose in coming was to thank me for having rescued his wife, daughter-in-law and some other relatives from a German detention camp near Weimar. He jokingly stated he and I were the two best Generals and worst politicians which our respective countries possess. I certainly am glad to have him class me with himself as a soldier because I think he is a good one.

Giraud also stated that he felt that America was being bluffed by Molotov and that the Russians, being Asiatics, could not and did not want to understand us.

At lunch today we were discussing the origin of the Breton, and I was explaining that he was probably the second race to occupy France and was pushed west by the Gaul, who was later pushed west by someone else. It suddenly occurred to me that the same thing is happening now and that the reason our finite minds do not appreciate that another great migration from the east is taking place is that we are not historically conscious.

I heard last night from a reliable source that when that eminent Tartar, Marshal Zhukov, arranged to fly to the United States, he refused to do so unless either General Eisenhower or his son John accompanied him on the plane—by way I suppose, of hostage. I think this a very good insight on the mentality of the Russian, who, being totally dishonest himself, cannot believe that anyone else is honest.

After this visit Patton was invited to Paris to receive some French decorations. While there he was entertained royally. He visited the *Folies Bergères* and the management told Patton to come there and rest whenever he could. He remarked to an officer of his staff, "I cannot imagine any less restful place—packed as it is with a crowd of practically naked women."

An amusing sidelight occurred about this time. Colonel Redding F. (Speed) Perry was assistant G-4 for Patton all across Europe. His imagination and drive contributed greatly to the successes of the Third Army. Supplies flowed to the fighting troops until the higher command cut off the fuel supply. This item could not be substituted. Although highly educated and a Latin and Greek scholar, Perry assumed a country-boy attitude toward life. One story circulating Army headquarters involving Speed happened while he was on leave in Paris. While standing in the foyer of the *Folies Bergères,* Perry was approached by a pretty little French girl who made the customary proposition. Colonel Perry looked her right in the eye and replied with a smile, "Sorry, baby, you are just one war too late."

In his diary for November 17, Patton stated that he believed that the American familiarity and skill in handling machines should be capitalized in wartime to save manpower. He also points up the aims and actions of the Russians in the diary.

November 17, 1945

Today I have been working on my thoughts as to how to reduce the human expense of war by a judicious increase in mechanization. Americans, as a race, are adept in the use of machines, and also in the construction of machines. The people whom they will have to fight will be the Russians who are not adept in the use of machines nor in their construction; but who have a large manpower which they are willing to expend recklessly. It therefore behooves us to devise military formations which will exploit our natural aptitude for machines and at the same time save our somewhat limited and very valuable manpower.

It seems highly possible that the Russians have spheres of influence in Korea, Manchuria and Mongolia. Now, while in many of the states such as Czechoslovakia and Austria, alleged democratic forms of government exist, they are actually under the thumb of the Russians and it is quite certain that the Russians will not permit any large scale economic relations between the Bolshevik-ruled countries and the rest of the world because if they did, too many foreigners would be able to look behind the curtain and see what actually goes on in these Communist countries, because if the Communist people and the rest of the world found out how Communism is run, the leaders would have to either retreat or retire, and retreat for a Communist leader means death.

One result of the Bolshevik conquest of half of Western Europe is that they have reduced the scale of living in those countries to the Russian scale, which is very low, and furthermore, have prohibited the United States and England from selling to about a third of their former markets. In view of the fact that the world financial arrangements were based on sales to and between all members of the world nations, the removal of a third of these nations is bound to upset the political economy of England and America, and therefore throw large numbers of men out of work and consequently make them readily acceptable victims of the virus of Communism.

The Americans quickly disbanded the most powerful fighting force the world has ever seen and the Russians rushed in to fill the vacuum, subjugating by infiltration and by conquest many adjacent lands lying along their borders. Thus an Asiatic despotism was imposed on these helpless people and Russia proceeded to govern them as she has her own country; employing all the intrigues and ruthless methods that have gone out of fashion in the free world many centuries ago; ruling by torture and the phony "confession trials" followed by the firing squad, or exile to Siberia. Government by murder since World War II has been established over many blameless people, whose only crime was to have been born in the wrong place and at the wrong time.

About the end of November, his old competitors of the 1912 Olympics, through the Swedish-American Society, asked Patton to visit them in Sweden. It was strictly a pleasure trip. The friends he had made thirty-three years before were anxious to do him honor, and to renew the ties formed by competition when they were all in the prime of youth. He took Sergeant George Meeks with him as he did on all his trips after the war. The Swedish Army made special efforts to give them both a hospitable welcome and a good time.

During this trip he engaged in pistol competition with his Swedish opponents of the 1912 Olympic days. Surprisingly, Patton shot better in 1945 than he had in 1912. This trip did a great deal toward cementing the relationship between Sweden and the United States.

About this time, he wrote one of his most characteristic poems, "The God of Battles," which some consider his best.

From pride and foolish confidence,
From every weakening creed,
From the dread fear of fearing,
Protect us, Lord, and lead.

Great God who, through the ages,
Has braced the bloodstained hand,
As Saturn, Jove or Woden
Has led our warrior band.

Again we seek Thy council,
But not in cringing guise,
We whine not for Thy mercy,
To slay: God make us wise.

For slaves who shun the issue
Who do not ask Thy aid,
To Thee we trust our spirits,
Our bodies, unafraid.

From doubt and fearsome bodings
Still Thou our spirits guard,
Make strong our souls to conquer.
Give us the victory, Lord.

16.   A Leader Passes

ALREADY advised of his forthcoming return to the United
States to assume command again of his Third Army, on
December 9th General Patton went pheasant hunting with
his Chief of Staff, Hap Gay. The two were riding in the
back seat of a staff sedan on the Frankfurt-Mannheim-
Speyer Road, in the vicinity of Neckar Stadt, en route to
the Mannheim-Speyer locality where pheasants were plenti-
ful. An army truck coming from the opposite direction
turned to the left into a side road in front of the staff car.
The vehicles collided, although both drivers swerved, as

much as possible, to avoid a head-on collision. The staff car, though damaged, was driven away from the scene of the accident under its own power.

While looking to the left, apparently, General Patton's head struck the back of the front seat, as recounted by General Gay: "General Patton, who was sitting on the right-hand side of the back seat, apparently was thrown forward and then backward, because at my next recollection of the accident (I was unhurt except for slight bruises), I was sitting in the back seat on the left side, half faced to the right with my right arm around General Patton's shoulders. His head was turned to the left and I was practically supporting him on my right shoulder in a semiupright position. He was bleeding profusely from wounds of the forehead and scalp. He was conscious. He said to me, 'Are you hurt?' I said, 'No, no, not a bit.' He then said, 'I think I am paralyzed. I am having trouble in breathing. Work my fingers for me.' I worked his fingers several times and then he said, 'Go ahead and work my fingers.' I told him that I didn't wish to do so as it might be inadvisable to move him."

General Patton was immediately taken to the 130 Station Hospital in Heidelberg. There his condition was considered critical; his partial paralysis probably caused by spinal injuries in his neck.

Beatrice Patton flew over to Germany as soon as the word was received. She went straight to the hospital. He said, "This may be the last time we see each other." She told him to get well and not speak of anything else.

Twelve days after the accident, the morning of December 21, although hope for his recovery had increased for some days, he, too, sensed his new condition. To his wife he whispered, "It's too dark—I mean too late." That afternoon he fell asleep. General George Smith Patton, Junior, was dead.

Eulogies filled the papers throughout the nation. Official statements of Government executives, states' governors, mayors of large cities paid official tribute to his passing. Here was a national loss which would place the name of Patton in the annals of American military history alongside other great leaders. His was a name that would be associated forever with the employment of armor and Blitzkrieg, mastered by one who had outblitzed Hitler at his best.

It was more than a national loss; it was personal. Radio announcement of his death was accompanied by expressions of regret by many people, some of whom, though actually unknown to Patton, felt they knew him personally.

Steward's Mate George Robinson, U.S.N., a Negro mess steward who left school after the fourth grade, wrote a tribute to Patton. Technical Sergeant Paul P. Wilhelm, 355th Engineers, composed a poem, "Taps for General Patton." Miss S. L. Snowderr of Scarsdale, New York, contributed a poem, "A Leader Joins His Men." These were but a few of the many tributes received by the family.

In charge of the funeral was Lieutenant General Geoffrey Keyes, who then commanded the Third Army and who had been Patton's deputy in the Moroccan and Sicilian campaigns. He had the inner walls of the Kronberg castle of the V.I.P. house (house of Very Important Persons), an old estate of German royalty near Frankfurt, where the body lay in state, lined with evergreens. It resembled a forest lit with candles, fragrant and beautiful. Thousands passed through in tribute.

Church services were held at Providenzhirche on December 24. A chorus of 200 soldiers sang "The Strife is O'er," the hymn General Patton had always wanted sung at his funeral. Was this sheer coincidence? His wife never learned.

The pallbearers were old friends and army comrades. Rank was immaterial. Some were generals; some enlisted. His faithful Negro orderly, Master Sergeant George Meeks, was one. As the cortege went through the streets of Heidelberg to the railroad station, thousands of Germans looked on and all stood with bare heads. Was this custom, or in reverence to an American general who had so materially hastened their unshackling? It was an enemy-occupied country.

The special train taking the body to Luxembourg for burial was divided into two sections; Beatrice Patton accompanied the body in the first. The route passed through French-occupied Germany and, although not on a fixed time schedule, six times between 4 P.M. and midnight, the train commander ordered the train stopped en route because of a "reception waiting outside." From the windows could be seen the lines of waiting troops; some with bands, some with bugles, some with muffled drums, all with flags and flowers. Those on the train had no previous notice of these planned but unannounced tributes, nor could the troops waiting at the stations have had any idea of the time of the train's arrival. They had been standing in formation for hours in dismal weather, waiting in a downpour, to do honor to the memory of an American general.

At each stop, Mrs. Patton, accompanied by General Keyes, left the train and walked the length of the ranks and spoke to the troops. They were mostly boys in their teens, and by appearance many of them were too young to have fought in the war. As a final tribute, the baggage car with its flag-drapped coffin in the center was lined with their flowers, in December, in a devastated land.

In the central square of Luxembourg City stands a marker like hundreds of others marking every kilometer of the march of the U.S. Third Army from the beaches of Normandy to the German border. From this marker in the square, the Boulevard General Patton runs to the American military cemetery of Hamm. As one drives through the gate, the chapel is at the right and the cemetery fans out over a grassy, rounded slope at the left.

It was there, on Christmas Eve, 1945, that General Patton joined his soldiers in a pouring rain with the ground a sea of mud. A five-star French General, walking with the aid of two canes, helped Mrs. Patton out of the car. "Your husband saved my life." He was, he explained, General Patton's old friend of earlier Saumur days, long given up for dead—General Jean Houdemon. Others, then, pressed forward; official representatives of various governments, many Belgians, French, and Luxembourgeois, who came themselves, representing themselves, individually to honor the soldier.

A caisson moved forward with its flag-covered coffin, followed by the traditional saddled funeral horse with its reversed, empty, but spurred, riding boots. The tolling of the bells of all the churches in Luxembourg was plainly audible. Under a tent as the coffin was lowered, Sergeant Meeks, with reverence and quiet ceremony, took the folded flag from the soldier escort and passed it to the waiting arms of Mrs. Patton.

During the graveside ceremony, an unseen plane could be heard circling overhead in the downpour. It departed in the direction of Metz, and when Mrs. Patton reached the airport, that evening, General "Johnnie" Walker, an old family friend, was there to meet her. He had flown from the United States to attend the funeral. Because of weather delays, they had arrived too late to land, so to pay his own and his Government's last respects, the best they could do was circle the cemetery.

The cemetery at Hamm, now a beautiful, green, grassy, rounded slope, meticulously attended, is truly American. It is comprised almost entirely of men who fought in the battle of the Ardennes, popularly called the Battle of the Bulge; the names on the crosses are Italian, Polish, French, Belgian, English, preponderantly members of the U.S. Third Army—"Patton's Army," then and now.

Although the American government keeps a caretaker at the cemetery, the people of Luxembourg themselves have assumed a loving care, decorating the many graves, not only on holidays, and fair weather, but also in rain and snow. Two families have claimed the care of General Patton's grave—the Grand Duchess Charlotte and her husband, Prince Felix (once attached to the Third Army), and one named Mousty, a restaurateur at Esch-sur-Alzette, a one-time member of the underground. Luxembourg is truly a democratic country. To this day the train passing through the nearby woods still slows down and whistles twice in salute.

So there, forever, General Patton lies beside the flagpole at the head of his men, the one he had told in life that although he had received acclaim and recognition to which others were entitled, it was his privilege, and his alone, to command.

There was an American Legion Post in Washington called the Tank Corps Post. This Post changed its original name to the George S. Patton, Jr., Tank Corps Post in 1946, and in the spring of that year sponsored a memorial service at the Washington Cathedral.

The Washington Cathedral was packed to overflowing. In the audience were Secretary of War Stimson, General Eisenhower, and many of those who had soldiered with Patton as officers and men. Some of those who attended that morning, January 20, 1946, had come from other cities. Some from abroad were there to do homage. Beatrice Patton asked that I, as an old friend, give the memorial address which follows:

"We, of George S. Patton, Jr.'s Post of the American Legion, are here today to lay our modest sheaf of green bay and yellow broom upon the tomb of the man who was our comrade and friend through many years.

"We think of our friend, the man. When we were a small group just out of the first war, in straitened circumstances, he supplied us with our national and post colors. By his presence whenever possible, by his words, and by his very existence, he encouraged us to organize twenty-seven years ago and to carry on throughout the intervening years—including another and vaster war.

"Nothing could be more appropriate than that his body should lie in the soil which twice he helped to rescue from the descendants of Attila. His militant spirit now is in that American Valhalla from which we hope it will emerge, from time to time, to aid our people in the serious years ahead. A generous fate has decreed that an American should bequeath us the spirit and tradition of Patton. Generations yet to come will be enriched and strengthened by that heritage.

"We think of our friend, the soldier. His was a full life dangerously lived. Pictures come before my eyes of many scenes. I see him riding the outside of a tank into battle at Saint Mihiel in World War I. He lies next to me on a cot in an evacuation hospital in a roofless church near the Argonne forest, on the first day of the Argonne battle.

"World War I is over and some of his officers, who had served and fought splendidly under him in that war, have to pass examinations in mathematics, which they have never studied, to retain their commissions. George Patton, generous to a fault, and the most loyal to those under him of any man I have ever known, hires the best coach available to tutor them. They all pass and keep their commissions.

"Between the wars he maintained leadership in his chosen profession, and used polo and fox hunting as an outlet for his unbounded energy. Many of us who are fond of the horse have shared hours of sport in the field behind a red fox with George Patton, on frosty days in Maryland and Virginia, when hounds ran a true line.

"World War II is here.

"There are days of tank training under him at Fort Benning where his beloved 2d Armored Division was born and trained.

"He has often said: 'An outfit which you have had for three months is you. Never forget that.' The superbly disciplined and valorous 2d Armored Division is a monument

284

to Patton, the soldier, who never asked anyone to do what he would not do himself.

"There come to mind:

"The feverish days in Chesapeake Bay training for the African landing.

"The landing and engagement at first light at Mehedya Plage; Patton takes Casablanca.

"The ceremony for the dead at Mehedya, Africa, and the American flag flying in the blinding African sunlight is reflected from the gleaming new white crosses, so that each cross wears a dazzling halo.

"Patton turns the Germans at El Guettar in Tunisia.

"The Sicilian campaign; his roaring armored columns sweep from the pass high above Palermo into the city, lying white against the turquoise of the Mediterranean.

"England; the glorious Third Army is born; his advancing columns sweep through Normandy, France, Germany; the Hun is again conquered.

"We think of our friend, the symbol of America. We are gathered together today to do him homage; great American, great soldier, great sportsman, great friend who life has ushered in a new day in the affairs of man.

" 'Awake! for Morning in the Bowl of Night
　Has thrown the Stone that puts the Stars to Flight': [1]

"George Patton, your old comrades-in-arms and friends, both living and dead, salute you. A thousand years of unborn Americans will look down on what you have done and find it good."

Since the start of this book, Mrs. Patton has died. She too had planned to live dangerously, and did. She went in the way she would like to have gone, while riding to hounds in the hunting field.

A personal friend of hers, Maj. Gen. Charles D. Herron, wrote a letter to the Editor of the *Washington Post* on October 6, 1953, praising Beatrice Ayer Patton for her distinguished success as a wife, a mother, and a friend. *In her great qualities of heart and head, and even in courage,* he wrote, *she was not overshadowed by her distinguished husband, General George Patton, the foremost battle leader of his rank in the Second World War. . . . By nature timid, she*

---

[1] *The Rubaiyat,* Omar Khayyam.

*first steeled herself to the risks of the hunting field and then
learned to be thrilled by them because she thought that in
so far as could be done, she could go with her husband, not
only in his work, but in his play.*

Years later, it is a bright sunny Easter morning in that
cemetery at Hamm in Luxembourg. The graves are green
and peaceful in the golden light of the spring sunshine. The
rows of white crosses stand out against the background of
the colorful new grass. Three figures gather in front of Patton's grave. They come from different walks of life and
from different countries. Pilgrims all, they did not plan to
meet there. One is a United States soldier of World War II;
one is an ambassador of a European country; one is a Luxembourg peasant woman from the countryside nearby; all
English-speaking: "I have always planned to come here to
see this grave," said the soldier. "We GI's that served with
him thought he was the greatest general ever in our Army.
Mary and I saved for this trip abroad this spring, but she
died. I came anyhow."

"We could use some of his straightforward thinking now
in these confusing times," said the Ambassador. "Sometimes I think that if we could speak out what was truly on
our minds, without the roundabout approach to all questions that people in our calling must use, it would be easier
to adjust the problems of the world. The General was a
man of action. His formula for deeds rather than endless
talk may be the best way to solve our difficulties. Talk with
the Russians has no meaning. We are coming to realize
that. We must rely on action. If he had lived we would have
sensed that sooner."

"You both admire General Patton," said the Luxembourg peasant woman, "for reasons different than mine. To
Luxembourg he was a savior. We call him 'The Liberator.'
We were a conquered people. We are proud. For us our little nation is a religion. We lost our religion under the occupation. I lost our only son in the Ardennes—you Americans call it the Bulge. Patton gave us back our country. We
will never forget the day his armor rolled into our city. It
was if a load had been lifted from our souls. I repeat, to us
in Luxembourg, he is the savior. The city square now bears
his name on a marker for the Third Army. They say that
many towns in France and Belgium have a 'Place Patton.'
I do not know."

"Yes," said the soldier, "you are right. Not only are there many 'Places Patton' in Europe, but in Africa as well—in Rabat, Morocco—I know."

"They tell me," said the woman, "that many people visit this grave every day. Look at the many fresh flowers. We feel honored that he was left in the land where he fought. He would have wanted to rest here with his fallen soldiers. To us he is a symbol of freedom."

The ambassador turned to leave. "Some of his spirit remains with us. I will never forget this beautiful Easter morning and this quiet place. With renewed faith I go back to the frustrations of my work."